The Uncommon Investor III

By the same author
The Canadian Small Business Survival Guide
The Contrarian Investor's 13
The M.B.A.-Hobo Poems

Plays by the same author
Curator's Park
Dark Ages Romance written with Guy Petzall
The Death of Parent God
The Gray Zone a translation of Jaromir Novak's work
Les Toilettes
Pseudopod Rejects written with Guy Petzall

The Uncommon Investor III
How to Earn Superior Returns in the Stock Market Despite Everything

Benj Gallander

INSOMNIAC PRESS

Copyright © 2008 by Benj Gallander

All rights reserved. No part of this publication may be reproduced, stored in a retrieval system or transmitted, in any form or by any means, without the prior written permission of the publisher or, in case of photocopying or other reprographic copying, a license from Access Copyright, 1 Yonge Street, Suite 1900, Toronto, Ontario, Canada, M5E 1E5.

Library and Archives Canada Cataloguing in Publication

Gallander, Benjamin, 1957-
    Uncommon investor III / Benj Gallander.

Includes index.
ISBN 978-1-897178-62-1

    1. Stocks. 2. Investments. I. Title.

HG4521.G353 2008   332.63'22   C2008-904289-1

The publisher gratefully acknowledges the support of the Department of Canadian Heritage through the Book Publishing Industry Development Program.

Printed and bound in Canada

Insomniac Press
192 Spadina Avenue, Suite 403
Toronto, Ontario, Canada, M5T 2C2
www.insomniacpress.com

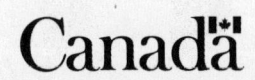

Canada

To my two favourite guys in the world…

Caellum
&
Cristophe

Acknowledgements

There are a number of people to whom I am deeply grateful for their help in this work. Ben Stadelmann, who is not only my business partner in *Contra* and a fellow co-founder of the SummerWorks Theatre Festival but also gave me the honour of being best man at his wedding; Todd Vercoe of Open Mind Productions, who helped with both the original design of *Contra* and made numerous suggestions for this book, including some key baseball analogies, and has enhanced my creativity multi-dimensionally; Guy Petzall, who was also involved in the original *Contra* design and took the time to write two plays with me before treating me to the ultimate eclipse experience; Michael Speyer, who not only offered his advice on this project but also shared a paper route with me a lifetime or two ago, which provided some of the very, very early seed money for *Contra;* Joe Sellars, who offered suggestions on every chapter of this work; Lori Beauchamp, who helped particularly with character development; Yeing-Moi Yeung, who helped edit; Shelley Zane, who was a firm backer throughout this writing process; Kate Harding, who did the brass tacks final edit to round the work into final form; and Mike O'Connor, my publisher and friend, who was willing to take a risk on this unconventional book.

Thanks.

Table of Contents

Foreword by Ben Stadelmann — 11
Preface — 13
Preface to the Second Edition — 15

The Cast — 17

The Warm-Up: The Pre-Game Show
World Series: Game Seven — 18
What's a Contrarian, Anyhow? — 21
Contrarian Psychology — 22
History, Baby, History — 23
The Bandwagon Plays—From Tulips to Real Estate — 23
Supply, Demand, Reality — 24

Inning 1: Rookie Hopes and Prayers
The Magic of Compound Interest — 29
The Rule of 72 — 30
Setting Financial Goals — 31
Investment Bases — 31
The Risk/Reward Ratio — 32
Eggs and Your Stage of Life — 33
Diversification — 36
Alternative Investments — 37
Paying Down Debts — 38
Interest Rates and Inflation — 40
The Advantage of Investing Early — 40
Hardcore Discipline — 42
Box Score Inning 1 — 45
Averaging Down — 47

Inning 2: The High-Contract Players

Mutual Funds Defined	51
Types of Funds	51
Advantages of Mutual Funds	54
Disadvantages of Mutual Funds	56
Box Score Inning 2	60

Inning 3: Hope and Bravado

Politics, Testosterone, and Miniskirts	65
The Efficient Market Theory	65
Pedantry	66
The Random Walk theory	67
Averaging Up, Up, Up	68
Dollar Cost Averaging	69
Short Selling	70
The Leveraged Margin Dance	71
Luck	72
Box Score Inning 3	73
Fear, Greed, Loathing	78
Health and Welfare	79

Inning 4: The Long-Term Contract

Traders Versus Investors	82
Beneficial Laziness	83
Technical and Fundamental Analysis	84
Chartists and Market Timing	85
Head and Shoulders Formation	85
Trading Volume	86
Top-Down, Bottom-Up, and Sectoral Investing	87
Growth Investing	87
The Full Service Versus Discounter Conundrum	88
Full-Service Brokers—Advantages	90
Full-Service Brokers—Disadvantages	91
Opening an Account	93
Box Score Inning 4	94
Stock Dividends	95

Inning 5: The Draft Pick, The Veteran, The Hanger-On

Gurus and Has-Beens	97
Joan's Skeletons	98
Cycles	99
Box Score Inning 5	107
Penny Stocks	108
Corporate Stock Repurchases	109
Kissing-Off Losers	110

Inning 6: Scouting

Refining the Search	113
The Bargain Bin	114
Reading Stock Tables	114
Corporate Contact	119
The Stock Watch List	121
The Internet and Other Sources	122
Insider Trading	125
Numbers—Oooh, Scary	126
The Income Statement	127
The Balance Sheet	130
Ratio Analysis and Other Critical Numbers	132
Box Score Inning 6	141

Inning 7: The Pitch

The Buy Decision	146
The Bid	146
Playing Percentages	147
Order Ratios	149
Order Quantities	149
Box Score Inning 7	151

Inning 8: The Set-Up Man

The Hold	156
Ongoing Research	158
Box Score Inning 8	159
The Fool's Game of Stop Losses	161
Takeovers	162

Inning 9: The Closer
Hunting the Sell Target   164
Staging the Sell   165
Sell Signals   166
Box Score Inning 9   169

Inning 10: Any Buddy's Game
Taxing Planning   174
Tax Deferral   174
Capital Gains   175
The Importance of Dividends   175
IRAs and RRSPs   176
Tax Loss Selling   177
Income Splitting   177
Box Score Inning 10   179
Giving Something Back   182

The Post-Game Show: Calculating Returns
Annualized Returns   185
Currency Translation   188
Incisive Investing   189
Final Box Score   191
Ethics   194
The Evolving System   196

Glossary   198
Appendix I: The *Contra* Philosophies   201
Appendix II: Financial Returns   202
Appendix III: The *Contra* Commentaries   203
Appendix IV: Recent Purchases   235
Appendix V: Bibliography and Further Readings 241
Index   245

Foreword

"It was the best of times, it was the worst of times...." Dickens' famous opening line is an appropriate theme as we consider the state of stock market investing at the close of the twentieth century. We have enjoyed the benefits of one of the most spectacular bull markets in history; for the first time, citizens have more money in stocks than in real estate; the percentage of the population that holds stocks is at an all-time high.

If you believe in endless prosperity, sparkling new technological eras, and wonderful parties that go on forever, then this book is probably not for you. And if, like the majority of folks, you believe that safety is achieved by sticking to "defensive" blue chips, then you are probably not concerned that the bluest of blue chips, General Electric, was trading at $396 in September 1929 and less than $9 three years later.

Perhaps you are the type of person who finds the mutual fund explosion to be a daunting example of lemmings jumping over a cliff. Or if your doubts are not as dramatic, you might simply opine that things tend to even out in the long run, in which case the Dow's sixteen-year run, averaging 18 percent returns, will look like a very tough act to follow. And if, despite this negative outlook, you still want to be in stocks and outsmart the "pros" at their own game, then you are an uncommon investor indeed.

This book will show you how to implement the oldest trick in the book: "Buy low, sell high." It is a methodology that can work in any kind of market because you are "commuting against the traffic"; there are always a large number of stocks that do not follow the track of the general market, and many can be found trading today at prices no higher than they were ten years ago. So does the contrarian ignore trends? No way! Observation of the long-term ebb and flow of a corporation's fortunes is our bread and butter. The "contra" part comes from the choice of timing within the trend.

Of course, many corporations that are down and nearly out deserve their position. Our capitalist system has little mercy for the last buggy whip manufacturer. The *Contra* methodology explains how to differentiate between firms that are temporarily becalmed and those that are hard against the reef and ready to be scavenged.

Where is the best of times to be found in this gloom? Today, individual investors have access to the full band of information about the companies they buy. What was once the exclusive domain of brokers at prestigious houses is now available to anyone with access to the Internet. Some wonder if this very mechanism of efficient information dispersal actually means that it is harder than ever to "beat the market." In theoretical terms, perhaps it should boost the old "efficient market" hypothesis, but in practical terms, there is plenty of evidence that the herd mentality remains alive and well. Sir Isaac Newton, who lost a bundle in the South Sea Bubble mania, lamented, "I can calculate the motions of heavenly bodies, but not the madness of people."

A fact of human nature is that the majority of people, "experts" included, will always interpret information in a way that keeps a close eye on the rear-view mirror and leans heavily on the opinions of colleagues for validation. Peter Lynch had it right when he observed: "Over the past three decades, the stock market has come to be dominated by a herd of professional investors. Contrary to popular belief, this makes it easier for the amateur investor. You can beat the market by ignoring the herd."

Certainly, there is an uncommon thrill when your own financial results outperform the norm. It's fun when the percentage gain on your modest portfolio mops the floor with some multi-billion dollar mutual fund wunderkid. Does this sound too much like macho posturing in the guise of competitive zeal? Perhaps. One thing is for sure, though: seizing the reins of your own financial destiny is an empowering experience in itself.

Our actions when we invest, our evaluation of risk, and the way we assess potential benefits are not so different from the way we approach the myriad life choices we have to make as individuals. There is a lot more to life than money, but financial success can provide the freedom, and especially the confidence, to make the rest of our lives all the more rewarding.

—Ben Stadelmann,
Co-Editor, *Contra the Heard* investment letter

Preface

The Uncommon Investor is, simply put, about how to make money. It was written for those of you who are interested in making personal investment decisions by better understanding stock market methodologies. Other types of investment options will be covered, but the primary focus will be on the market.

This book has been designed to be accessible to investment novices, but also provides information which should be useful to the seasoned stock veteran. Key concepts and basic strategies for successful investing are outlined in earlier parts of the book, while more complex investment topics are discussed later.

As the title suggests, this guide outlines a contrarian approach to stock market investing. To further enhance your understanding of this methodology, the book also contains articles and portfolio coverage from *Contra the Heard* investment letter. *Contra the Heard* is a quarterly investment publication co-written by Ben Stadelmann and me. In addition to receiving the newsletters, our subscribers are promptly informed of stock purchases, sales, and takeover situations that affect *Contra*'s portfolio by e-mail or, for the few dinosaur subscribers remaining, fax. However, we do not provide investment advice. The appendix section of this book includes excerpts from the investment letter: selected *Contra* commentaries, "Our Philosophies," and financial returns.

There are a few reasons why baseball figures into *The Uncommon Investor*. First, when, as a child, I was asked what I wanted to be when I grew up, my enthusiastic response was always: "A baseball player." Although I play the game regularly, the closest I've gotten to the major leagues was the eleventh row behind home plate when Joe Carter hit the winning home run in the World Series against the Phillies. Plus, I had the opportunity to keep box scores for one of the major newspaper syndicates and watch a few games from the press box. Second, as baseball is the most statistically based of sports, it has a tremendous amount in common with the stock market. Thus, the game offers an entertaining, apt metaphor for the book.

The guide is presented in a scripted format. My rationale behind writing the book in this style was simply to create a more enjoyable read. I have chosen a diverse cast of characters from various stages of life. Joan, an investment advisor who specializes in a contrarian approach to the stock market, has turned an evening watching the World Series into a financial seminar for her friends and their families. This alternative to the typical "how to" framework allows me to draw on my playwriting experience, and gives the two hemispheres of my brain a chance to frolic with each other, while explaining my investment strategy in a creative, accessible manner.

"Can Lefty come out and play?" Righty asked.

Mama Brain nodded her agreement before saying,

"Sure, but make sure he's home for dinner."

—Benj Gallander,
Co-Editor, *Contra the Heard* investment letter

Preface to the Second Edition

It has been ten years since the publication of *The Uncommon Investor*. A lot of things have certainly happened since then.

Back then, many suggested that we were beginning "A New Paradigm" and Internet and high-tech stocks were having their heyday in the sun. Unfortunately for the bulk of investors and the economy, the era was short-lived and many wished that the revolution had rested on the dark side of the moon, far away from where they might have made investments that tanked in this world.

Oil rose and dived and rose again, the latter time accompanied by commodities that had remained in a funk since the Bre-X fraud. China, India, Russia, and a number of other countries found their economic legs and began to push the old lions Germany, Japan, and the United States.

Derivatives and hedge funds became a standard order of the day and major lenders theoretically doled out risk, before it came back to bite them in the ass in the subprime and real estate meltdown crises. Interest rates were again rolled down to help avoid a global economic crisis, this time without the legendary Alan Greenspan to chief the rescue team.

I could go on and on.

Meanwhile, as all this went on, at the *Contra the Heard* investment letter (www.contratheheard.com), we continued on our normally merry path. We also were beaten down handily to the tune of 17.4 percent in 2000, which looked better than many of our colleagues and markets in general. But while many continued to flounder, our returns for the next three years were never worse than 47.3 percent, with two years in their sixties. Alas, as is virtually always the case, there was then a regression to the *Contra* mean, and in 2007, we lost money once again. Besides the damage to the ego and pocketbook, I can no longer use one of my favourite jokes when on the speaking circuit. Citing the losses in 1990 and 2000, I would say something like, "From now on we'll have to avoid years ending in zero." Darn, what will I utter now?

Fortunately, our results remain among the best in North America, with the fifteen-year annualized return ringing in at 21.8 percent.

Over the past ten years, both Ben Stadelmann and I feel that we have gotten smarter when investing. Hopefully the next ten years will show that. We better do well before Alzheimer's sets in.

There have been some changes to this edition of the book. Most are fairly nuanced, as the story remains entertaining, I believe, and the *Contra* investing system has only been tweaked. However, there is a new section tracing where the companies in the portfolio at that time are today. Since I wrote about these enterprises during the period from 1995 to 1998, they have changed over the past ten years. Some are no longer around. Others have prospered. It is fascinating to see how they have done in a longer term, offering additional insight into both the evolution of companies and the logistics of the buy-and-hold philosophy.

If you have any questions or thoughts after reading this book, or it intrigues you enough that buying *The Contrarian Investor's 13* becomes of interest, feel free to contact me at: gall@pathcom.com or (416) 410-4431.

Thanks for reading this book. I sincerely hope you enjoy it and that it aids you with your investment decisions.

—Benj Gallander
Co-Editor, *Contra the Heard* investment letter

The Cast
(IN ORDER OF APPEARANCE)

Peter Fairmount
lawyer, early forties

Tina McCleary
former nurse, Peter's wife

Phillip McCleary
retired widower, late seventies, Tina's father

Liam
second grader, son of Peter and Tina

Raj Dehal
thirtysomething, owns new trendy restaurant/catering business

Steve Bellwoods
mid-twenties, actor/server, Raj's life partner

Joan Beliveau
investment advisor, friend of Peter and Raj since university, single

Bucky
forgotten major league ball player turned announcer

Tom
professional radio announcer turned television personality

The Warm-Up
The Pre-Game Show

I like that chap. I like the way he looks you straight in the face and disobeys you.

—Aldous Huxley

World Series: Game Seven

Peter was racing around the house like the proverbial chicken with its head cut off. "Tina, have you seen my slippers?" he yelled.

"They're where you left them," she replied.

He tried unsuccessfully to conceal his exasperation. "I don't know where I left them!"

Shaking her head, she called back, "Did you check the bedroom closet, honey?"

Peter flew up the steps of their chockablock suburban home, like a south polarity drawn north. Flinging open the closet doors, he looked down. Immediate relief crossed his face. "Found them!" he yelled. After slipping them on, he wandered downstairs, wondering where his keys might be, and almost ran into his father-in-law, Phillip.

"When did you get here?" Peter asked, startled.

"About the time your game of hide-and-seek started."

"Daddy, how come you're always losing your slippers?" Liam asked, standing about waist-high to his grandfather. His brow furrowed as he eyed Peter with disbelief.

"Not always, Liam. Sometimes they just seem to disappear."

"How come they always hide in the same closet, but you can never find them?"

His father didn't have a ready answer to that question. "So, Phillip, who do you think will win the game?" Phillip sat down, claiming the easy chair with the ottoman. He was of average height, with bushy eyebrows and a surprisingly thick mat of grey hair for someone approaching his eightieth birthday.

Peter was a bit miffed at having his favourite spot taken, but tried to hide it as he sat in one corner of the sofa with Liam beside him. After comfortably settling in, he called, "Honey, need any help?"

Tina's voice came from the kitchen, where she was preparing guacamole dip, "Can you grab the door? Raj and Steve just pulled up."

"I'll get it, Mom," said Liam, jumping from the sofa and racing for the door.

He flung it open just as Raj was about to ring the bell.

"You're a fast one," Raj said.

"Hi, Uncle Stevie," Liam said excitedly, flinging himself into Steve's muscular outstretched arms. "Hi, Raj," he said upon landing.

"My, haven't you grown again," said Raj. "You're a little beanstalk."

"Uncle Stevie, who do you think will win the game?"

"The Mets all the way," he responded, noticing that Liam's shoes had left two big dirt marks on his blue jeans. They wandered in to hugs and "How are you?"s.

"Love your tank top, Raj." Tina teased. "Orange is your colour. Any construction workers mistake you for a safety cone?"

"Oooh, what fun," cooed Raj. "Then my sweetie could come and rescue me from the big bad construction workers."

"Not while the game's on," Steve responded. He settled into the middle red chair and grabbed a huge handful of cheesies, which he began devouring with Liam's help.

"Great hair, Tina. Did you go to that stylist I recommended?" As Tina nodded, Raj continued, "Isn't he the best? Don't tell anyone about him unless you really like them. All my friends are going to him now. It's impossible to get an appointment. Where goes the two-four?"

"Bring it in the kitchen. You can help me get a few things together." They took a few paces to the left, where Raj placed the case of beer on the counter. Peter was chuckling as he said, "I don't get it, Steve. You guys don't drink beer. Tina and I don't drink beer. What's with the case?"

"It's the World Series," said Steve, stroking his newly bleached hair. His perfect smile flashed as he added, "You've got to have beer at the World Series."

"And we brought this new yummy dip from the restaurant, Tina," said Raj.

"It's to die for."

"Great," said Tina. "I made that guacamole dip you raved about last year."

"Right," Raj said pensively. "It was you who gave me that recipe! Oh well. You can never have enough guacamole dip, I always say."

The doorbell rang. Phillip said, "Liam, are you getting it or should I?"

With a full orange mouth of cheesies, Liam said, "You go, Grandpa. I'll keep Uncle Stevie company."

Phillip ambled to the door and opened it to Peter and Raj's old friend. "Joan! Good to see you." They hugged warmly.

"Great to see you, Mr. McCleary. It's been a few months, hasn't it?"

"At least," he agreed. "Can I help you with one of those?"

"Sure can." They each grabbed an attaché case. "Do you carry those things everywhere?" Phillip grunted.

"Sometimes I think so. Tools of my trade, unfortunately."

"You work those biceps, girl," Raj called from the kitchen, with a laugh. Joan peered around the corner into the kitchen. "Yours look like they're being worked, Raj. Nice top. Does it glow in the dark?"

"Maybe," said Raj devilishly, walking out to greet her. "A little something I picked up for the World Series. My 'Go, Blue Jays, Go!' top."

Steve interrupted, "Hey, you guys got a new TV. When did you get it?"

"Peter picked it up this afternoon," Tina responded. "After watching the first six games with distorted waving men moving spasmodically on the screen, we decided the time had definitely arrived for an upgrade. There was a big sale on at Tee Vee Life. Peter couldn't resist."

"It's one of those Ultra HDTVs getting all the press," Peter said proudly. "I'm positive that we're the first on the block to get one. Mertz down the street was shopping at the store today, too, but I got in the checkout line before him and raced home. There's no way he beat me back."

"Such good colour," said Raj, containing his laughter. Peter's overly competitive nature was always good for a chuckle or two.

"Hey, isn't that Isiah doing the colour commentary?" Steve cried. "How did that guy get on national television for the seventh game of the World Series? He was a basketball player!"

"He looks good, is very eloquent, and is quite credible in a superficial way. He would have made a good lawyer," Peter stated.

"It's ludicrous! Here's a guy who had the opportunity to build Toronto's NBA franchise from scratch, and when things went sour, he deserted his team. C'mon! I don't want to listen to a guy like that. He sucks!" Steve threw his hands in the air, disgusted.

"Don't worry about it, sweetie," Raj said. "He's just doing the pre- and post-game shows and maybe a few obscure interviews here or there."

"That guy really irks me," Steve said in a huff. "Wouldn't mind earning what he does, though," Peter threw in. "What does he get anyway? A million or two just to talk. Not a bad pay day for an ex-jock." "And that's U.S. dollars," Tina interjected. "Too bad your take home isn't in American money, Peter."

"But that wouldn't make you love me more, would it, honey?"

Tina smiled. "Not like it would have in the old days when the American dollar was worth 50 percent more."

"How many years have you two been together?" Steve asked.

Tina feigned a moan. "Twelve years, if you can believe it. He was a geek with a nerdy smile posing as a struggling law student when we met. Little did this woman know she'd fall in love and put him through four years of university while pulling the night shift at the hospital! It was the biggest surprise of my life. Though, overall, I guess Peter turned out to be an okay bargain."

"Okay? Just okay?" Peter said with a hint of a boyish whimper. He reflexively pushed his few remaining tufts of hair in a futile effort to hide his expanding bald spot.

"We've made it this far on love, and no one in the house has gone hungry," said Tina.

"Yet," chided Steve.

"Maybe a straight trade is in order. Peter for Steve?" Raj suggested. "How would you like to support a struggling actor for a while, Tina?"

"Don't think so," Tina returned. "Besides, I can't imagine Steve would quite meet my, you know, needs."

"Or wants and desires," Peter said proudly. "I told you guys I was good for something around here."

"Sometimes," Tina teased.

"Ouch!" squealed Peter.

"Children, please," said Phillip, returning from the kitchen after grabbing himself a beer. "As the patriarch of this extended family, I suggest we focus on the matters at hand: baseball and investing. Joan's only here for nine innings."

What's a Contrarian, Anyhow?

"Thank you, Mr. McCleary. But if the fridge is even semi-full, you know I'll stick around." Joan looked like anything but a professional investment advisor. She was wearing blue jeans, an old cotton sweater, and high-top sneakers. Having been best friends with Peter since university days, Joan didn't need a business suit to make the McCleary clan, along with Raj and Steve, willing listeners. "Why don't we start with Isaiah? His buy-in-at-the-bottom-and-sell-out-as-things-turn-sour approach has worked well for him, even if that isn't appreciated by everyone here. In stock circles, especially if he could sell when things looked brightest just before they turned, he'd be called a 'contrarian'."

"I don't get it," said Phillip.

Joan explained, "A contrarian is like the fish who swims against the school—the sheep who separates herself from the flock."

"Sounds like my hubby before he went straight. As a lawyer that is," Tina joked.

"Remember when Peter was called 'The Radical One'?" asked Joan. "I seem to recall a certain newspaper picture taken in front of the university community centre, when a certain somebody was being hauled away by the police. Peter, wasn't that when you reached your height of sexual popularity?"

"Funny what handcuffs will do to improve a guy's reputation," laughed Peter. "So, Joan, a contrarian is someone who bucks against the trend. And this has proven to be an effective system for investing?"

"Yes on both counts," Joan replied. "But many roads lead to Rome. My method is a very effective one, but it's not the be-all and end-all of investing strategies. Still, although I downplay it, over the past ten years, my average annualized return has been 16.2 percent. In the last fifteen years, it works out to 21.8 percent. Both were better by more than 5 percent prior to 2007, which was a negative year and the USD dropping in value hurt the Canadian results."

"That beats the heck out of anyone I've known and my clock's been ticking a long time," Phillip said. "So, what are the nuts and bolts of this contrarian system?"

Contrarian Psychology

"That will be explained during the next nine innings, Mr. McCleary. However, there's one thing that should be understood from the get-go. Adopting a contrarian philosophy is psychologically one of the most difficult investing methods. This is because almost everyone will disagree with your thinking—like having the Bleacher Bums at Wrigley Field constantly taunting you."

"I know what that's like," said Steve. "Often I choose to forge a character in a different direction than other actors."

"That's the idea," agreed Joan. "But it's one thing to utter a line and exit stage left, and another to invest for your financial future and perhaps that of your family as well."

History, Baby, History

Steve nodded while Joan continued, "Let's preamble with a few examples. Most of you remember when the price of gold skyrocketed to over $800 an ounce back in the early eighties."

"I don't, Auntie Joan," Liam interrupted.

"Liam, that's before you were even a twinkle in your parents' eyes. Many forecasters predicted the gold price would skyrocket to over a $1,000 from what a few years before had been $35. On the other hand, financial pundits who suggested that the price would tumble were labelled as buffoons and laughed off the investment scene. Now those buffoons have been deemed prescient and the gold bugs, once in the vast majority, were hibernating until recently. But those contrarians of the day faced a barrage of opposing evidence, which would weaken even the hardiest constitution."

"I bought gold at $750 an ounce on that late seventies move," said Phillip with a sad shake of his head. "Another foolish decision."

"At least you admit your errors, Mr. McCleary. Many people don't learn from their mistakes."

The Bandwagon Plays—From Tulips to Real Estate

Joan continued, "History is littered with the carcasses of investors who piled on to a bandwagon looking for gains. For example, take the tulip mania. Has anyone heard of it?"

Phillip grinned before he spoke, "That was even before my time, but in Holland during the seventeenth century, the price of tulips went through the roof. Everyone had to have a tulip and some special rare ones assumed outrageous values. Call options on tulips became popular, where a person could pay, say, 20 percent of the cost, and only plunk down the rest if delivery was taken. Naturally, that would only be done if the price went up. The market was bedlam."

"Exactly," Joan said. "People literally 'invested' their life savings in bulbs, hoping to make fast gains by speculation. Some individuals did make fortunes, but an enormous number of people were deflowered, so to speak."

Raj moaned. "That was an absolutely awful pun. Worse than the dialogue in plays Steve's been in."

"Why, thank you," Joan laughed, evidently quite pleased with herself. "This is one of my favourite manias because I love flowers so much. But, more important, it shows how people will buy virtually anything if lots of other people are in on it and a large financial payoff seems to be in the cards. Individual thought is thrown out the window and the supposedly freethinking human animal assumes a position in the lemming brigade."

"Trends happen in the restaurant industry, too," Raj stated. "Sub joints were everywhere, and then there was Tex-Mex. Now raw fish seems to be peering from restaurant windows at every corner. Strange how people's tastes change."

"Precisely," said Joan. "Other examples include the South Sea Bubble, oil prices skyrocketing in the seventies...."

"Pokemon cards!" shrieked Liam.

"That's right, Liam," Joan confirmed. "It's funny to see grown-ups fighting over toys like little kids. Another frenzy was the real estate boom of the late eighties and the corresponding bust in the early nineties, and history is currently repeating itself in the States."

"I bought some houses to rent on spec when everything was going crazy and prices were going to the moon, Alice." Phillip thrust his arm in the air like Jackie Gleason before shaking his head despondently. "Unfortunately, they didn't. Should have known that a neighbourhood completely devoid of trees, yet full of street names like Maple Boulevard, Elm Crescent, and Fern Avenue, would lead to another bath for me."

"But you learned from your mistake, Dad, and told us to wait until the real estate market cooled before buying. Our house was a bargain and now our mortgage is locked in under 5 percent."

"Everyone makes mistakes," Joan counselled. "Still, many people hop on the bandwagon again and again and it costs them dearly, but to be a contrarian and go against the pack is not easy. Lesson number one: **Avoid crowd psychology**."

Supply, Demand, Reality

"I'm not quite clear. How does this lesson apply to the stock market?" Steve wondered.

Joan paused for a moment to gather her thoughts. "When demand increases relative to supply, prices tend to go up. Likewise, when supply increases relative to demand, prices tend to go down. Sometimes, the demand goes crazy and prices skyrocket for irrational reasons. After all, a tulip bulb is nothing but a tulip bulb."

"Is that the answer to my question?" Steve still looked very confused.

"Steven, the market is virtually a clone of these situations. Instead of tulips or gold or real estate, or left-handed pitchers—who are always in very short supply—the commodity is stocks. Some become popular and they are bid up to astronomical values in a craze. Other stocks are dumped far below their intrinsic worth because an industry has some momentary problems or isn't sexy enough."

"Stocks as sexy?" queried Raj. "Like Thai food is sexy?"

"For the moment," warned Joan.

"Stocks sure were sexy in the twenties," said Phillip. "When I was a young whippersnapper around 1935, my dad would talk about the money he lost in the Crash of '29. That was the mania of manias. Lots of human suffering after that. If my ears had been bigger, Black Monday in '87 might not have burned me so badly."

"Let's not forget Black Friday," added Joan.

"Black Friday? Don't recall that," said Phillip.

"Phillip's right, Joan. It was Black Monday," Peter said confidently.

"No, Peter, it wasn't. In 1869, heavy speculation was tied to the gold market. When the price plummeted, speculators liquidated, leading to margin calls where people had to pony up more money to cover their losses. These events caused the stock market to collapse. Sound familiar? The point is, these things happen regularly creating opportunities for contrarians."

"So a contrarian always goes against the crowd?" Phillip asked.

"Not always, Mr. McCleary, but it's a common misinterpretation of the term. **A contrarian chooses when to go against the crowd.** There is a major difference."

"A friend of mine often tried to do the 'different' thing," said Peter. "He went on a buying binge in August of 1987 when stock prices dropped, certain that they were bargains. Then came the October debacle, where they plummeted. Scared him from the market for life. Another colleague kept waiting for the bottom, and by the time he 'found' it, the market had already rebounded 25 percent."

"I don't want to miss a major opportunity," said Steve. "When that big train comes around the corner, you have to hop on or the moment's passed."

"Trains!" Liam cooed. "I love trains. One train comes and goes and then another comes and goes. I love trains! Choo choo! Choo choo!"

"That's exactly right, Liam. Uncle Stevie should listen to you. **If you miss one train, another will come along.** Just like there's always another stock to buy. In Uncle Stevie's dream, he rides the train of hindsight rather than the train of foresight," concluded Joan.

Steve scowled, pursing his lips together, but a quick rejoinder didn't arrive.

"Another rule extends from this: **History is an excellent teacher**."

"Does history say who'll win the baseball game, Auntie Joan?" Liam asked with a cherubic grin.

"Well, little one, this is just one game, so anything can happen," Joan responded. "But the Blue Jays have never lost to the Mets in the World Series. So how could anyone bet against the Jays?"

"They've never met before in the Series," Steve stated flatly.

"Caught. This is a fine example of why cynicism is a bonus when analyzing a stock," Joan said without losing a step. "The world of stocks is the ultimate big money business, and that brings greed and half-truths and blatant lies to the forefront. It's not nice, but on a happier note, I really believe the Jays will win."

"No way! With Johnson on the mound, the Mets will clean their clock. You're betting with your heart instead of your head!" Steve yelped.

"True," agreed Joan. "Which is something that should never be done with stocks. Especially since, as a contrarian, buying beaten-down shares is the name of the game, which indicates that at some point in the firm's recent history, expectations have not been met."

"Like the Toronto Maple Leafs!" Liam threw in excitedly.

"That's right," Joan responded. "Although their glory years were so long ago, few remember."

"There are some vague memories," uttered Phillip. "Before Vietnam, and the Pill, and disco, and Sri Lanka, and the oil crises, and the breakdown of the Iron Curtain, even before the birth of Lady Di, there was a 'real' hockey team called the Toronto Maple Leafs."

Peter had a distant look on his face. "Yeah, I remember when the team won their last Cup—Sgt. Pepper had just made the scene."

Steve appeared puzzled. "Funny, I never pictured you following military stuff, Peter."

Raj shook his head knowingly and said, "Yeah, under the Toronto regime of Harold Ballard, the tulips couldn't be found for the doo-doo. And now they call it 'The Leaf Nation.' More like a Third World country. But give credit where credit's due. For the Leafs to be this bad for this long defies statistical possibility. Which gets me wondering about aberrations. The stock market seems to do well for long periods of time and then dives. Joan, will a contrarian methodology save me from big wipeouts?"

"Losses should be reduced," responded Joan. "The rationale behind my investing strategy is that a stock's price has already plummeted before my purchase. Therefore, less distance remains to bottom. Plus, if corporations are chosen correctly, undervalued assets are scored—like buying something on sale."

Phillip smiled broadly. "My life's been spent bargain hunting."

"Like Mom's pawnbroker wedding ring?" Tina chirped in.

"That's just a family fable, darling. I actually won it in a poker game." Phillip grinned as the U.S. national anthem began to play. The TV framed a few young people who remained sitting, which immediately changed his tone. "That bugs me. Everyone should stand for the anthem."

"Standing is outdated," countered Steve.

"You do realize the practice of standing started during the war as a show of patriotism," said Phillip.

"No, I didn't know that, Phillip. Maybe back then it made sense."

"What they should do," offered Tina, "is change the American and Canadian national anthems to eliminate references to God and war. After all, anthems should be inclusive. It distances people who don't believe in God, and to glorify war validates violence."

"Point taken," said Phillip.

"Another thing," Tina added. "The sexist machismo in the Canadian anthem offends me. Come on! 'In all thy sons command.' Are there no women in this country? Some traditions are important, but when the values and consciousness of this culture progress, so should our customs."

"Funny, after hearing both anthems so often, the words escape me," remarked Raj.

Peter appeared exasperated. "Are we going to talk about feminism, religion, and nationalism tonight, or discuss stocks?"

"You should listen to your wife, Peter," said Joan. "She's right on topic, applying the contrarian approach to the national anthem. Instead of following the herd and uncritically accepting a flawed status quo, Tina has resisted indoctrination and thinks for herself. It's easier to stand like the rest of the pack rather than sit out on something that doesn't make sense."

Englebert Humperdinck finished singing the anthems as Bucky's voice came booming from the television.

"All right, Tom. The seventh and deciding game of the World Series is about to roll, the first time ever a series between two countries has gone this many games. The driver's seat is all yours, Tom."

"Thanks, Bucky. We're ready to go...but first, a few words from some of our sponsors." And a big gas-guzzling van rolled across the television screen.

Rules
- Avoid crowd psychology
- A contrarian chooses when to go against the crowd
- If you miss one train, another will come along
- History is an excellent teacher

Inning 1
Rookie Hopes and Prayers

Nothing is more frequently overlooked than the obvious.
—Thomas Temple Hoyne

"All right, we're ready to go," said Tom. "Wilson per usual will be leading off for the Jays. Amazingly, this is a cousin of Mookie, a former player for both of these teams. He's not the most patient leadoff hitter but does have that speed needed at the top of the order. Woody winds...the pitch....

The Magic of Compound Interest
Joan crossed her legs and asked, "Liam, can you grab my black case, please? It's time to discuss a few general investment strategies. First, a little quiz: Congratulations, you won the neighbourhood lottery, which in the bad old illegal days was called the numbers game! Because of your competitive nature, you purchased all the tickets for $10,000, but hey, first prize was only $5,000. Imagine those community improvements you helped pay for! Now, you've lent the 'winnings' to 'Mr. Loan' around the corner—you know, the guy in the 'SHARK' T-shirt—so he can reinvest in the neighbourhood's needy. Ten percent interest is yours until eternity if you desire, as Mr. Loan is most generous to his financiers. With compounding, how long before the $5,000 doubles?"

"Compounding?" asked Steve.

"Can I take that, Joan?" Phillip jumped in. "Compounding is earning money on your money or what is known as 'the magic of compound interest.' This is different than simple interest. Here's an example to illustrate the two: Say $10,000 is invested at 10 percent simple interest for two years. At the end of one year, there's $11,000 and after two years, $12,000. With compounding, $11,000 is also in your pocket at the end of year one. But after two years, because interest is also earned on the $1,000 already gained, the grand tally is $12,100. So with compound interest, you end up with an extra $100."

"Cool!" exclaimed Steve. "And imagine if instead of compounding annually, it happens quarterly. The money grows even more rapidly."

"Exactly, Mr. McCleary," agreed Joan. "Compounding offers an important investment edge. Many people either don't know about it or ignore it. It's like some baseball managers who use the bunt a lot. They don't realize that more runs are scored when batters swing away rather than concede an out to advance a runner one base. Which leads back to my quiz: At 10 percent a year, how long before the funds double?"

Everyone was quiet. Finally, Peter said, "A while."

"Very perceptive, Peter, but no cigar. To do this calculation, 'The Rule of 72' comes into play. Divide the number 72 by the expected rate of return. For example, at 10 percent a year, 72 divided by 10 equals 7.2. This means that your money doubles every 7.2 years."

"That's neat," said Raj. "So at 5 percent a year, that would be 72 divided by five, which equals...14.4 years for my initial investment to double."

"Precisely," said Joan. "This system is exceedingly helpful when setting financial goals. Here's a chart to keep in mind when pondering different interest rates."

THE RULE OF 72

Return	Years to Double
1%	72
2%	36
3%	24
4%	18
5%	14.4
6%	12
7%	10.3
8%	9
9%	8
10%	7.2
15%	4.8
16%	4.5
22%	3.3

"Why have you included the 16 percent and 22 percent in that chart?" Tina asked.

"Those last two numbers were thrown in because they're my personal rounded returns over the previous fifteen- and ten-year periods."

"But, Joan, even though this chart gives a barometer of how swiftly, or slowly, our money might grow, the right decisions still have to be made to grow it."

Setting Financial Goals

"Absolutely correct, Peter. Which leads to the next rule: **Set realistic financial goals**. Be it saving X dollars a month, which many experts wisely suggest should be 10 percent of your gross income; or putting away enough money to buy that refrigerator in six months; or setting up an educational fund for Liam, the key is to outline reasonable financial goals. This should be done in conjunction with your budget."

"Get real, Joan. Ten percent might sound like a great idea, but on my puny income, money is non-existent at the end of the month. And that's with Raj's help. Ten percent of diddley squat is squat."

"That's why this rule suggests setting realistic financial goals. If your income is low, then set aside less. An interesting fact: After a war or depression, people manage to save a larger percentage of their income, but it needn't take a catastrophe to make people recognize the necessity of looking after their long-term personal interests."

"Well, government certainly can't be trusted," said Peter. "Who knows if a pension plan will exist by the time my retirement rolls around?"

"Why bother to save at all?" asked Steve. "With nuclear testing, wars, and all the problems in this world, 'live for today' is my motto. Tomorrow, I could get hit by a bus while riding my motorcycle. Maybe when a big TV gig comes along my attitude might change somewhat, but until then...."

"Planning is essential, Steve," Peter interrupted. "Otherwise, you could end up an old impoverished actor frying sardines on a hot plate. Tina and I budget regularly. Joan, when you talk with clients, what budgeting considerations do you suggest?"

Investment Bases

Joan began, "There are four investment bases which must be carefully examined. First, net worth, which are the assets remaining after everything owed is subtracted from everything owned. Second, financial goals, which can be equated to personal needs and desires. Third, risk tolerance, which must be based on reward potential and the ability to be comfortable with the investments chosen. And last, the time horizon, which I quantify as under two years, two to five years, and over five years."

The Risk/Reward Ratio

Joan then handed out the following chart:

THE INVESTMENT QUADRANGLE

GROWTH	SPECULATIVE
• Medium Risk/Medium Reward Potential	• High Risk/High Reward Potential
• Certain Stocks, Certain Mutual Funds, Some Bonds	• Commodities, Junk Bonds, Futures, Options, Penny Stocks

SAFE	CONSERVATIVE
• Low Risk/Low Reward Potential	• Minimal Risk/Minimal Reward Potential
• Money Market Funds, Guaranteed Investment Certificates, T-Bills	• High-Quality Common Stocks, Preferred Stocks, Utility Stocks, Certain Mutual Funds, Provincial Paper, Some Munis, Some, Corporate Paper

"These are various ways to set up a portfolio to match an investor's personality type. The key thing to notice is that as you move from left to right, the financial rewards have the potential to increase tremendously, but at the assumption of higher risk. This is called 'The Risk/Reward Ratio' and can be summarized by the rule: **Higher risk, higher potential reward**.

"Under theoretical circumstances, risk and reward move in tandem. My goal is to find 'holes' in the relationship between them, where my perception of risk is different from the general population's. A correct evaluation can lead to less uncertainty of the benefit. This demonstrates the rule: **Take carefully calculated risks.**

"Now, this next chart shows various investment options. Again, risk and reward are critical considerations. Notice how moving up the quadrangle means more danger, but with the possibility of enhanced financial compensation." Joan circulated copies of the chart and the level of concentration in the room increased dramatically.

After a moment Peter spoke up. "So Tina and I can take moderate risks?" "More than moderate," Joan answered. "A good income flows your way and it continues to increase."

"Not quickly enough. I'm on the slippery slope from forty now."

"It's never fast enough," Joan responded. "But there's a good chance you'll become a partner in the law firm in the next few years. And Tina has mentioned that when Liam and your soon-to-be are both in school, her return to nursing is in order. So income growth in a few years seems promising. Of course, a university education for Liam and the newcomer is becoming a more expensive proposition every year."

Peter groaned. "You can say that again."

"Back on track with a look at 'beta.' Beta compares the price change of a stock relative to market fluctuations. The average stock's beta is 1.0; the higher the beta, the more the stock price gyrates compared to stock indices, such as the Dow Jones. Defensive stocks, which are less risky investments such as utilities and banks, have a beta closer to zero. But I would suggest ignoring beta altogether—I feel it's a vastly overrated measurement tool. Instead, reviewing price variances in specific companies gives tremendous insight into how little or how much a stock's price might fluctuate."

Eggs and Your Stage of Life

"But we're getting ahead of ourselves," continued Joan. "I want to talk about how investment goals and needs change as you move through different stages of life. This should be considered in conjunction with the risk/reward ratio. As in baseball, there are times to take the home run swing, and other times when concentrating on a higher percentage single is more important. Read this to yourselves, while I concentrate on the ball game a bit."

Stage 1: Bachelor/Bachelorette

Typically, this stage features young men and women whose earned income is low but whose discretionary funds—the money they can spend in any manner they choose—are high. Bachelors/bachelorettes usually do not have to support a family and often live at home, so their spending on necessities is limited. Generally, people in this category spend a large percentage of their earnings on vacations, recreation, fashion, music, and—that oldest of pastimes—the mating game. Little money is put aside for investments.

Stage 2: Newly Married Couples

At this juncture are young couples. They are in a better financial position as a couple than they were when single, as expenses can now be shared. This segment has the highest average purchase rate for durable goods of any group. Newlyweds tend to spend a lot of money on cars, furniture, and vacations. And, perhaps, a mortgage. They also begin to analyze various investments more seriously, carefully studying the new ballparks in which they're playing, and hopefully recognizing that playing at Fenway Park requires a different strategy from Dodger Stadium. Initial investment forays might be made during this stage.

Stage 3: Full Nest I
Yee-haw! The baby has finally arrived! But along with all the joys come a number of hardships. The wife often stops working, meaning a loss of family income. In addition to this, furniture, toys, and clothing must be bought for the wee gaffer, and there are all kinds of other financial demands to meet young needs. Space becomes more finite as the little one demands room. Couples with young children are the most dissatisfied with their monetary position and tend to stay home more often to save money and make video stores happy.

In this stage, couples are most susceptible to advertising and new products. There are three major reasons for this. First, because they nest so much, they generally watch more television and therefore see more advertisements. Second, these inexperienced couples start buying many new products and use commercials as sources of information for their choices. Third, they have a tendency to hunt for bargains, be it through newspapers, radio ads, or watching the tube as another evening is passed with baby. As mutual fund publicity flashes before their eyes, the partners ponder more about their family's financial future and how to make more money.

Stage 4: Full Nest II
During this stage, the financial situation generally improves. Although there might be more children, additional income helps as the husband moves up the pay ladder at work. If already back at work, the wife will also likely earn more money, and many women who were stay-at-home moms now return to the workforce. The couple is also less influenced by advertisements, benefiting from additional buying experience. Money tends to be spent on food, cleaning products, bicycles, musical instruments, various lessons for the children, and clothing. The family usually attempts to create a portfolio of investments to be used both for the children's further education and to help ensure enough money for a comfortable retirement.

Stage 5: Full Nest III

At this point, family finances become even better as the husband, usually the wife, and maybe even the children are working. Expenses increase as the family replaces older items with new ones, generally buying goods that are considered to be more tasteful. A large portion of the family's income is spent on travel, cars, dental bills, and magazines. During this phase, the parents are keen on investing smartly and solidifying their twilight years.

Stage 6: Empty Nest I

Yee-haw! The children have left, and with their departure, the couple's financial position is likely the best ever. They are at their optimal earning power and tend to spend their money on travel, recreation, self-education, gifts, and luxuries. A major diversifying of the portfolio takes place here, due to the additional disposable income.

Stage 7: Empty Nest II

At this stage, a reduction in income normally occurs as one or perhaps both of the spouses retire. There is a tendency to stay home more. Additional funds are spent on medical needs, especially health, sleep, and digestion. Some of the investments might be cashed in at this point for ongoing needs, especially if both mates have retired. The security blanket of regular income becomes more important.

Stage 8: Solitary Survivors

In the last stage, one spouse dies. There is the possibility that the home is then sold. If the survivor continues to work, a large portion of that income is used for vacations or health. But if the widow or widower is not working, there may be a drastic drop in income, which may severely curtail a diverse lifestyle. In either case, the surviving spouse desires affection and attention and has numerous anxieties about security. If they did not invest wisely before, or were financially unable to do so, the last stage can become more of an affliction than a pleasure.

"Two rules are drawn from this," Joan began. "First: **Carefully match your personal needs to your investment needs**. Second: **Try to store money for emergencies**. You never know when a batting slump might occur."

Raj snickered. "Surprise, surprise. Steve and I don't fit into any of the categories. Shunted to a dark closet yet again. Seems like the descriptions can use a bit of updating if you don't want to marginalize gay men."

"Excellent point, Raj. You guys would fit best into the Newly Married Couples category. Since it remains unlikely you'll have kids, unless the adoption option is chosen and allowed, your financial position should improve far more swiftly than couples with children. This also applies to childless heterosexual couples, which are becoming more and more common."

"We're not quite married yet, but prepare for the fall wedding of the year," Raj squealed excitedly. "Our time has arrived. Seems like only yesterday interracial marriages were taboo."

"So what do these stages mean for Tina and me, Joan?" Peter interrupted.

"Well, you two are moving into Full Nest II. As the kids get older, your financial situation will improve. Things won't be quite as tight as today."

"That's a relief," Peter uttered.

"So," Joan continued, "When you're young, you can take more chances, as earnings generally increase with age. If you shoot for the moon and miss, it isn't the same disaster it might be later in life, when less time remains to recover from losses. When you're older, more conservative investments become a wiser practice."

"So I can be riskier than grandpa!" Liam said excitedly.
"Exactly," said Joan. "But don't be foolish. Too many people are willing to lose the funds they speculate with."

"I wouldn't do that," Liam assured her.

"Then you're learning already, Liam," Joan smiled.

Diversification

"Now, to broaden your horizons: A crash course in other investments. Always keep in mind that stocks are merely one option, and in a downturn, they're often the fastest way to lose money. Unfortunately, during good times, people fall in love with the market and forget a key rule: **Diversify**. This is critical to any investment strategy."

"Diversify! Our diversification is in diapers and hockey equipment!" said Tina.

"When money is available," said Joan reassuringly. "Soon you'll be well on your way to paying off the mortgage, maybe have a few bonds, some guaranteed investment certificates, and a snowmobile for Peter."

Peter looked excited.

"Constructing a well-rounded portfolio is like piecing together a championship ball team: a variety of pieces is a must. A team of small base-stealing whizzes with no pop in the bat is no more likely to win a championship than a team of big boppers who are slow on the base paths and can't play defense. A few lefties on the mound are needed to complement the righties because statistically, lefty batters hit worse against lefty pitchers. A portfolio comprised completely of high-risk investments will eventually shudder downward, while one made up entirely of low-risk components will only garner nominal gains and perhaps have difficulty beating inflation, especially after taxes."

"Don't some gurus suggest that finding a few top-notch investments and riding them is better than diversification?" Steve asked.

"There's some logic to that. The general rule is: **The greater the diversification, the lower the rate of return**. Of course, this isn't always true. Let's look at baseball. The first-round draft choice is likely to be a better choice than the following picks. Same with choosing investments. But, if your first rounder finally fulfills promise, makes it to the majors, and then gets hurt, that backup is needed to get the team through the season."

"So diversification is critical because if all your funds are in a few areas and they go sour, you're toast," said Steve.

"That's one way to express it," Joan confirmed.

Alternative Investments

"Being an actor, my funds are scarce, but what would I buy in my diversification fantasy land?"

"A gold necklace for me would be nice, lover," Raj said.

"Here's where an interesting division of thought takes place. Gold can be bought in many forms. A few off the top of my head are straight bullion, certificates, coins, or jewelry. A primary consideration is whether the purchase is strictly for investment purposes or actually for wearing or displaying. Money in a bank account appreciates in value, but a painting purchased with those funds gives appreciation value."

"When your footprints are on Hollywood Boulevard, Steve, you can buy a gold necklace instead of a gold certificate for me," Raj suggested.

"This difference is important," said Joan. "Our discussion is about making money, but remember, money is simply a tool to help you achieve a better quality of life."

Paying Down Debts

Peter looked bored. "Tell me then, where should I invest? Let's make some *dinero* already."

"Where to invest? Well this won't be the answer expected. Consider this rule: **Pay off your debts**."

"That's not investing. That's anti-investing!" cried Peter.

"So now you're a wordsmith," responded Joan. "Minimizing debt is the crux of smart financial planning. The number of people who invest in stocks while paying ludicrous interest rates on their credit cards astounds me. Let's say someone is paying 15 percent interest on a card. If their tax bracket is 33 percent, they need a financial return on their investments of 22.5 percent to break even! It's ridiculous when you think about it.

"A good general approach is to first pay down the debts where interest rates are highest and where the interest is not tax-deductible. If both tax-deductible and non-deductible interest rates are being analyzed, calculate the relative rate given your taxation level."

"Peter and I have been discussing whether to pay down our debts further or invest. You're suggesting that they're one and the same: repaying debt is investing."

"Precisely, though that's not readily apparent, given the societal emphasis on expansion rather than contraction. Only when you're very certain that after-tax returns on an investment will beat paying down debt should you even ponder an investment option."

"Listening, Peter?" asked Tina.

"Yes, dear," Peter replied sheepishly. "Should we ask Joan about the mortgage?" Tina nodded. "Okay. At this financial forum we went to, there was this guy who said that mortgaging the home to buy stocks is a good idea. So we're discussing increasing the mortgage on this place. Does that make any sense?"

"One renowned thinker, Jamaica, said, 'You want all, you lose all.' To me, Peter, especially when you have a family, a home is a sanctuary. It lends an assurance, a feeling of safety which exponentially increases your quality of life. Now, an apartment suits me fine, because at this stage of my life, it complements my lifestyle. But for you two, the risks are more significant since you have children to consider. In my opinion, remortgaging to invest is something reputable advisors should never recommend. Slower and surer does have a place."

"Point taken," responded Peter.

"One other thing," said Joan. "Let's say you're shopping for a stove. For someone in the 33-percent tax bracket, paying $100 less for this item is the equivalent of earning $150."

"That's because if I earned $150, $50 of it would go to the government, right?" Steve interrupted.

"Precisely. And for a person in the 50-percent tax bracket, it equals $200. Searching for bargains, if it's not overly time-consuming and a pain in the rear, can be a very worthwhile investment."

Raj was pensively stroking his goatee. "They say a dollar saved is a dollar earned. But in fact, depending on one's tax bracket, a dollar saved can be two dollars earned. That's a lot."

Phillip leaned back in his chair. "Every day after work, I used to go out with the boys for a few beers. One day it finally dawned on me that I was spending too much money, so I cut back to three beers each day instead of four. At four dollars a pop with tip, I saved twenty bucks a week. The annual total was a thousand bucks back in my pocket. That was about $1,500, given my tax bracket at the time, which went a long way to paying down our mortgage. Next thing I did was bring my own coffee instead of buying my morning caffeine fix. Incredible how little things like coffee add up."

"Indeed," agreed Joan. "Okay, let's reverse things for a moment, and instead of trying to save money, imagine everyone has cash burning holes in their pockets. Here are some investment alternatives to rectify that situation." Joan ran down an investment list so quickly that it was obvious she'd done it hundreds of times before. It included real estate, stamps, coins, jewelry, comic books, dolls, glass, antique cars, art, photos, magazines, posters, and sports cards.

"I love baseball cards!" exclaimed Liam. "Twenty-three more and I'll have them all."

"There's the essence of investing. Liam loves baseball cards, and in a few years, some of them might be valuable. In the meantime, he enjoys collecting. But certainly, on a practical level, children should have a bank account to teach them the importance of saving money."

"I don't invest. I win 'em. I'm the school champ at Knock Down the Leaner. Not counting Bobby Armstrong and Mike Spear."

"Some day, Liam, if your winning streak continues, diversification should be a breeze for you," encouraged Joan.

Interest Rates and Inflation

"Now for something that perplexes virtually everyone at some point in their lives: interest rates, which are a major factor in determining your financial returns. Government uses the money supply to control rates: unleashing the flow generally leads to decreasing rates; while tightening the sphincter results in an increase. The goal is to stabilize the economy and avoid the dramatic extremes experienced during severe contractions and expansions."

"That strategy doesn't work very well," said Phillip. "When inflation was a major fear in the eighties, the American and Canadian governments hiked rates to over 15 percent. That should have knocked the heck out of the market, but it didn't. Sure knocked the heck out of a lot of businesses though."

Raj nodded. "My bank loan's at 7.5 percent, and if rates hit 11 or 12 percent, I'll never make a go of the restaurant. Lots of other operations have the same problem: viable enterprises being pushed into the ground by misguided bureaucrats."

"My problem with government," said Peter, "is that the only method they seem to use to combat inflation is raising interest rates. There are numerous other solutions, depending on the situation, but theirs is a one-track mind."

"True," agreed Joan. "But let's be realistic. The government has its own mindset, and while they pledge to help the little guy, you have to be smart and look after your own economic interests."

The Advantage of Investing Early

Joan continued, "Here's one thing to remember that will help you take care of yourself: invest early. For example, take two friends, Julio and Sally. Julio invests $2,000 for 10 years and Sally $2,000 for 20 years. However, Julio starts earlier. Take at look at what happens given an 8 percent annual return."

AGE	JULIO	SALLY
30	$2,000	
31	2,000	
32	2,000	
33	2,000	
34	2,000	
35	2,000	
36	2,000	
37	2,000	
38	2,000	
39	2,000	
40	2,000	
41		$2,000
42		2,000
43		2,000
44		2,000
45		2,000
46		2,000
47		2,000
48		2,000
49		2,000
50		2,000
51		2,000
52		2,000
53		2,000
54		2,000
55		2,000
56		2,000
57		2,000
58		2,000
59		2,000
Total Invested	$20,000	$40,000
Total Value	$145,841	$98,846

"The conclusion is obvious. Where possible, **invest early and often**. Julio invested half as much, but with compound interest, ended up with almost 50 percent more money than his friend."

Steve was at the edge of his seat. "This is exactly what some ball teams do with their farm systems. By investing in players early and having an extensive minor league system from rookie squads right through to Triple A, eventually the major league club benefits."

"So, ideally, money should be set aside now as a building block for our financial future."

"Exactly, Raj. Of course, as Steve mentioned earlier, it's easier said than done. But the earlier you begin, the closer you are to a well-financed retirement."

Hardcore Discipline

"Now, combine this next thought with what has already been mentioned, and the path to financial stability will be sweeter. And if you only take one thing with you tonight, this could be it." Joan opened the case, pulling out a file filled with papers, and passed a page to everyone. On it was written:

WITHOUT DISCIPLINE, YOU HAVE NO METHOD.

"That's all?" said Steve, turning the page over and back again.

"Often the essence of huge ideas is simplicity itself," replied Joan.

Raj agreed. "'Character is simply habit long continued.' Substituting the word, *discipline* for *character* makes sense to me. And then extending it to real-life practice would be logical on both counts. Oh, yes, give Plutarch credit for the first saying. Don't want to steal his thunder."

"Pluto. I love Pluto. Want to see my Pluto poster, Uncle Raj?"

"I'm with Liam, Tina. Pluto over Plutarch any day," Steve said with a scratch of his head.

"Okay. There's a choice," said Joan. "If you're not disciplined enough to manage your money, hand a cheque to a professional and let her do her job. Otherwise, you'll sashay like a grass skirt in the wind, and the returns will be dismal. Naturally, there's a fee for the service, and your results are only as good as the broker's knowledge. But, in handling your personal affairs, discipline is critical."

"That skirt thing sounds like it could be kind of fun," mused Raj.

"Not while you're losing your shirt," said Peter.

"All right." Joan continued. "Now, we're coming to something that should help immensely. At the end of each inning, we will examine the portfolio of the *Contra the Heard* team—the guys who write the investment letter of the same name. These guys have impressive financial returns, which are outlined in a handout you'll receive later [Appendix II]. This is a living breathing example of a portfolio in action, with historical data thrown in. As they buy and sell stocks, you'll be able to follow their logic and participate in their successes and failures. And since I follow their actions to a tee, this represents my portfolio.

"One suggestion: Periodically glance back to compare quarterly portfolios, as this process will help to broaden your perspective on how well they're faring."

"Roll 'em," said Steve.

"We're rolling," returned Joan. "But before the ball moves too quickly, I want to mention one thing to keep in mind when viewing the portfolio. *Buys* mean that the *Contra* people, and I, would still purchase the stock. *Holds* suggest sitting with the shares and doing nothing. And *Sells* indicate that the target has been reached, and normally, part of the shares have been sold. But some of the stock might remain in the stable. Questions?"

Confusion kept everyone quiet.

"So, without further ado, here's the first portfolio," said Joan, who handed everyone a copy of these two sheets of paper.

BOX SCORE INNING 1 — October 15
TORONTO STOCK EXCHANGE

Stock	Purchase Price	Current Price	Initial Target
BUYS			
Bovar	0.95	1.05	4.63
Journey's End	2.01	1.95	7.25
Sears	7.13	7.63	12.50
SELLS			
Agnico-Eagle*	5.75	17.88	12.50
HOLDS			
DomTex	7.50	8.75	16.63
Dylex	23.72	2.30	46.25
Great Pacific	11.30	27.75	41.25
Gulf	3.95	6.00	13.50
Int. Aqua	19.77	2.78	24.00
Laidlaw A	9.10	11.75	21.63
Laidlaw G	14.25	14.88	21.50
Mitel	3.00	7.38	10.38
National Sea	5.94	5.50	21.50
Newf. Capital	1.81	3.65	9.25
Noma	5.13	5.63	12.50
Spar	8.50	14.38	15.38

NEW YORK STOCK EXCHANGE

Stock	Purchase Price	Current Price	Initial Target
BUYS			
Anacormp	2.26	0.56	16.63
Armco	6.85	6.38	11.63
General Host	6.38	5.38	13.60
Grubb & Ellis	2.55	2.125	14.25
Hartmarx	5.94	5.50	18.38
Kaneb	3.25	2.38	15.63
Navistar	31.17	11.25	61.25

SELLS

Acme-Cleveland*	9.99	25.00	18.75
Cinc. Milacron*	10.93	27.50	22.50

HOLDS

Fedders	3.08	6.00	9.40
FeddersA	Div.	4.38	with FJQ
Genrad	4.38	8.88	11.50
National Educ.	4.13	7.50	12.60
Occid. Pete	17.50	21.00	28.75
Parker Drilling	4.75	5.38	9.25
R.J. Nabisco	31.95	32.68	96.50
TesoroPete	8.13	8.00	13.75
Zapata	5.63	4.13	37.58

* partially sold

"Time's up!" Joan called, after giving everyone a few minutes to examine the pages. "Now, my goal is to talk about each corporation during the time frames of these portfolios, when either a transaction occurred or major events affecting the company happened. The past three years are being presented by these box scores, so you'll have to cast your glance back a bit time-wise. Questions?"

There was the kind of silence that results when people don't quite understand but are not sure what to ask. All eyes were focussed on Joan as she said,

"All right then. Near the top of the portfolio is hotelier Journey's End, who took advantage of government largesse to develop a chain of mid- and lower-scale hotels. This was during the 'Wild West' days, when tax benefits were available for all kinds of schemes. An aggressive expansion plan was the result, adding copious amounts of debt and causing major financial difficulties. Once a high-flying stock peaked at $21.75, I purchased it this past quarter for $2.01. The primary rationale was that the organization is cutting debt, big time. Additionally, as the economy improves and this recession becomes history, hotel occupancy rates should increase, benefiting the bottom line.

"Another recent acquisition for my portfolio was Sears. A mainstay of the North American retail scene, with revenues exceeding $4 billion, it underwent a major cost-cutting plan, which included a huge reduction in the number of employees and an improved inventory control program. This once stodgy company appears to be undergoing a renaissance.

"Unfortunately, they have a high debt-load, plus Wal-Mart has caused them problems since entering the Canadian marketplace. Those reasons caused the stock price to plunge."

Tina looked angry. "Wal-Mart is definitely not my favourite corporation. They drive a lot of mom-and-pop stores into bankruptcy. Ethically, I find them difficult to stomach."

"Hey, that's the nature of competition," said Steve. "With my budget, cheap prices and fresh breath are where it's at."

"Ethics and stock," Joan nodded. "There's a loaded question to address later. Meanwhile, on the New York side of the ledger, distance education provider National Education is already proving to be a beautiful purchase, as it's almost doubled in the past few months. That dictated a switch from the buy category to the hold category. Holds are always declared when a stock's upside potential is reduced to less than 50 percent or, as in this case, when the risk/reward ratio has largely diminished. When National Education was in dire need of an extensive restructuring, they hired turnaround specialist Sam Yau as CEO. My purchase, not coincidentally, followed his appointment. Also, their large market share was a factor, as corporations in this position have more power in controlling their industry."

"Maybe this would be a good one to buy for Liam," said Tina. "I recall reading that it's important to get kids involved in finances young."

"That's an excellent idea," Joan agreed. "Now, the next purchase, General Host, was a demographic buy. This organization specializes in flowers, plants and crafts, but is expanding into the Christmas stores and pet food sectors. As the population ages and the boomers' paunches grow, my feeling is that more of them will drive to their local nursery to pass leisure hours that were previously devoted to their lads. Planting gardens, sitting back and watching the tulips bloom will become a regular pastime. This is another corporation coping with high debt and large losses, tempered with potential."

Averaging Down

"I averaged down on the real estate play Grubb & Ellis," Joan said confidently. "This means I bought more at a lower price than my original purchase, decreasing the overall average price per share."

Peter appeared puzzled. "That's a fool's game—throwing good money after bad."

"Many people would agree with you, and unfortunately some of my experiences prove you correct. But if the price remains similar or decreases after my purchase, and the corporate fundamentals remain stable or improve, this can be a wonderful technique to buy more shares at fire-sale prices and achieve additional financial returns.

"Grubb seemed like such a buy. They were hit hard by the excesses in the real estate sector and the economy, but they've now recorded three consecutive quarterly profits for the first time in years. Though this streak was recently broken, a return to normal real estate markets will bode well for Grubb. Plus, Prudential Insurance made an additional investment in the firm, and this was a convincing reason for me to make one, too. The Rock has too much money to let these guys go bankrupt.

"I also dipped into Armco again. I first bought it at $7.13 and then added more at $6.68. The company finally recorded its first profitable year in many with improved productivity—and record shipments for the specialty flat-rolled steel segment to boot. These achievements haven't been reflected in the stock price. Problems still remain, especially with one of the operation's major smelters. But because of the drastic changes, this company appears ready to burst forward.

"The position in Hartmarx, one of the leading manufacturers and retailers of apparel products, was also expanded. The company has a number of key labels including Bobby Jones, Jack Nicklaus, Austin Reed, Pierre Cardin, and Nino Cerruti. The recent stock weakness was caused by the company's deletion from the S&P 500 index, which forced many funds to sell their positions. This increased supply for the stock, thereby negatively impacting on the market price. Back again to those supply and demand lessons from introductory economics."

"Don't remind me," gasped Steve. "Those silly curves got me so bored that I became the class clown. Another catalyst for becoming the fine actor you see today."

"Don't despair, Mr. Olivier. I'm sure you can handle the basic concept. Now, on the sell side of the ledger, a partial position was ejected in Acme-Cleveland. This leader in machine tools had soared past the target price, so it seemed like an optimal moment to take some profits. One-third of the original position was maintained.

"Next, stocks undergoing major transitions in the portfolio include Dylex. This operation is the largest clothing retailer in Canada and was purchased after a few difficult years. Unfortunately, I bought it early, and ongoing bad management led to cumbersome debt loads, which caused major losses. Fortunately, a new investor, River Road, which has a great reputation for corporate turnarounds, arrived on the scene. This led to a management shakeup, a corporate downsizing, and a reverse stock split, also known as a stock consolidation, of about 1-for-52. This means that for every 52 shares I had previously, I now had one. Once you're stuck with less than 100 shares, or odd lot denominations—which means not in multiples of 100—it becomes harder to unload at the best bid price."

"So stock consolidations are negative?" asked Raj.

"They're virtually always negative for investors in the first couple of years after the reverse split takes place. After that, it's anybody's guess. Another similar situation that hurt me was International Aqua's 1-for-20 consolidation. Purchased as a fledgling company in the fish farm industry, this was simply a mistake—and one of the reasons stocks must be listed for 10 years before I'll even consider them. At an even smaller percentage of the portfolio than Dylex, the question is when to take the tax loss on this one. Even with a doubling of the share price, the reduction in the overall loss would be nominal. So the rule here is: **Never buy a stock that you think will undergo a share consolidation**. In fact, if you own one, look to sell just before or very soon after this occurs, before the impact is felt. Then think about repurchasing afterwards at lower prices. About a year after the reverse split, the stock becomes fair game if the price satisfies my other criteria."

"Isn't knowing when consolidations will occur almost impossible?" asked Peter.

"Certainly it's not clear cut," Joan admitted. "But there are clues. Watch if a corporation has been selling shares regularly to beef up their cash, or shares are being used to pay for takeovers, or excessive stock options are granted to management, or simply if the share count becomes ridiculously large."

"Hmm. Never looked for those," mumbled Peter.

"Next, telecommunications firm Mitel—the largest holding in the portfolio, at over 11 percent—has become somewhat overweighted, as the stock price increased almost 150 percent. Therefore the price movement of this issue will have a major impact on the portfolio's returns. The first purchase was at $7.50, while the last, which virtually doubled my number of shares, was at $1.01. With the evolution of my system, a stock would never be purchased more than three times, as the ever-present danger of falling in love with a company exists. This can easily lead to good money being thrown after bad. But in this case, my 'mistake' is proving profitable, as the company enjoys record revenues and near-record earnings in a very competitive telecommunications field.

"So there you have them," concluded Joan. "A rundown of a large number of stocks in the portfolio, along with some of the happenings. Questions? Comments? Answers? Thoughts?"

"I'm confused," said Phillip. "Where's this portfolio from again? Alzheimer's is going to claim me yet."

"I've presented you with the actual *Contra the Heard* investment letter portfolio, which I mirror with my own stock market transactions. By doing this, you can view the management of a real portfolio, which provides a supplement to your learning."

"That works for me," said Phillip. "A stock course that won't cost me a penny."

"And hopefully, Dad, help all of us make more money in the future."

"Exactly," Phillip concurred.

Tom's voice broke through the momentary silence. "So that ends the first inning with the score knotted at zeros. The Jays threatened with men on first and third with no one away, but the heart of the order came up empty. Right back after giving our sponsors their due."

Rules
- Set realistic financial goals
- Higher risk, higher potential reward
- Take carefully calculated risks
- Carefully match your personal to your investment needs
- Try to store money for emergencies
- Diversify
- The greater the diversification, the lower the rate of return
- Pay off your debts
- Invest early and often
- Without discipline, you have no method
- Never buy a stock that you think will undergo a share consolidation

Inning 2
The High-Contract Players

How could I have been so mistaken as to have trusted the experts?
—John F. Kennedy (after the Bay of Pigs)

"...and John Olerud walks for the first time today and the seventh time in the Series. Can't say if that's a record, Tom, but it sure has to be close."

"Don't know either, Bucky, but that's one thing that's often overlooked in this game. Season after season Olerud has one of the best on-base percentages in the league. He waits out more pitchers than any ballplayer except maybe Frank Thomas or Barry Bonds."

"And that's baseball," cried Steve. "Playing the percentages."

"That's also a principle behind the contrarian method," said Joan.

"Strange," Tina returned. "My conception of a contrary person is someone who goes against percentages. The image doesn't fit."

"Percentages are my livelihood," Joan responded. "It's the same for mutual fund managers. Although some play them far better than others."

Mutual Funds Defined

"I'm going to appear naive amongst this group," said Steve timidly, "but what exactly is a mutual fund?"

"That's a good place to start," assured Joan. "A mutual fund is a pool of money to which thousands of people contribute. This money is then invested in a number of areas."

Types of Funds

"Today, there are literally thousands of funds, and in recent years, they've multiplied like weeds. It seems like every day another bank, trust company, investment firm or mutual fund company adds others to the list. Check the financial section of almost any major newspaper to get an idea how broad this sector has become."

"There are more funds in the paper than false prophets on Sunday morning TV," said Phillip. "And that's from a believer."

"Definitely," confirmed Joan. "One more thing: There are two kinds of funds, called 'open-ended' and 'close-ended.' The majority are the former, where money can be invested or cashed at any time, while the latter raise capital by selling shares that are traded either on a stock exchange or over the counter. Here are some handouts for you to examine."

Money Market Funds

Money market funds are designed to offer safety. For this reason, their managers invest in government paper such as treasury bills or bank guaranteed deposits, such as guaranteed investment certificates (GICs). The investor's goal is the preservation of capital with some gain.

Individuals can buy many of these financial vehicles themselves, but by grouping cash in a fund with other people's money, the increased capital can earn a higher rate of return. These mutuals are again sub-divided into groups, the majority of which invest in Canada and the United States, while others are international in scope.

Fixed-Income Funds

Holding assets that pay a fixed rate of return—such as bonds, mortgages, and preferred shares—these are designed primarily for older investors wishing to preserve capital. These funds tend to prosper during times of declining interest rates but generally lose money when rates are climbing.

Mortgage Funds

Conservative in nature, these focus on first mortgages, usually in residential real estate, but some extend themselves to commercial properties. Returns here are primarily in the form of interest income, which means higher tax assessments. This type of fund is particularly advantageous to own when interest rates are tumbling.

Bond Funds

A bond is a loan to a corporation or government agency, repayable with interest. Bond funds invest in these. They can be federal, provincial, municipal, or corporate bonds, or the equivalent in other countries. While some of these funds are country-specific, others are broader in scope and might cover areas such as

North America, Latin America, Asia, etc. As with mortgage funds, bond funds offer higher rates of return than money market funds. Both prosper when interest rates are declining but are to be avoided during upward trends.

Equity Funds
An equity fund invests in stocks. Their major advantage is that some of the earnings are capital gains, meaning the taxation is at a lower rate. There is a broad assortment of these kinds of funds. Again, some invest only in specific countries, such as Canada, the United States, Japan, or India, while some have a broader regional focus. Still others buy into specific industries, such as precious metals, real estate, or oil and gas. The risk of these funds varies dramatically. For example, one that concentrates on North American equities is generally safer than one in an emerging market, such as Eastern Europe.

Dividend Funds
A dividend fund normally focusses on preferred stock in blue-chip top-of-the-line corporations. These often hold a highly weighted proportion of banks and utilities, which typically have high interest yields. This, for example, is far safer than a fund placing money in small capitalization 'growth' companies.

The latter is like the ball player in A ball or Double A who has tremendous potential but might never fulfill it. The blue chipper is a top guy who's already made it to the major leagues, and one can rest virtually assured he'll perform year in and year out: the Vladmir Guerrero of investing.

Depending on the jurisdiction, dividends are taxed at a preferred rate. This favourable tax treatment is a major advantage of these types of funds.

Balanced Funds
Less risky than funds that exist in only one sector, or solely in stocks, are balanced funds, where the money is spread into a number of areas, such as stocks, bonds, and government securities. This diversification typically lowers the potential upside rewards but also reduces downside volatility.

Ethical Funds
These funds concentrate on avoiding unethical areas by shunning sectors such as alcohol or tobacco and organizations that degrade the environment or contribute to military defence (or offence, depending on your beliefs). Different funds have various domains deemed taboo.

Venture Capital Funds

Governments have been using tax incentives to encourage new businesses to invest in venture capital funds. The tax breaks augment the fund's investment results, creating a higher return. Politicians feel that this will stimulate the growth of new corporations, leading to economic benefits and the creation of new jobs. In recent years, there have been fewer of these, as their success has been questionable.

Investment Trusts

Investment trusts originally concentrated on areas such as real estate, oil and gas, and coal, but then moved into such far-flung fields as courier services. They spread like wildfire, as the combination of tax-sheltered income and price appreciation offered excellent returns for investors. However, the government rightly questioned whether they were good for the economy and if it was costing the government tax revenue. They are currently scheduled to be wound up in 2011.

By no means is this an exhaustive list of mutual funds. Other variations exist and new types are continually created. Watch for the latest scoop at your friendly neighbourhood financial institution, a mere phone call away.

"Wow, Joan!" exclaimed Steve. "That's one goitre of a long list. If I had money, it would be almost impossible to choose a fund. Being broke seems like an advantage."

"The choice is daunting. But overall, letting the pros invest for you is simpler than learning and applying my system. The account managers do the leg work, choosing when and what to buy. If they are astute, voila! You get excellent financial returns. But if mistakes are made, it's your cash...."

"Down the toilet!" squealed Liam.

"Good point, Liam. I know. I've been down that road before," Phillip concurred.

"Let's try to be optimistic for the moment," Joan counselled. "Afterwards, we'll discuss the drawbacks. Here, take a ride on this reading."

Advantages of Mutual Funds
Professional Management

A trained, hopefully talented, manager or management team is waiting to invest your money. This homes in on a key rule for purchasing a fund: **Buy the**

management; check their track record. Only consider someone with an excellent long-term track record. A five-year history is an absolute minimum, but ten is even better. However, don't choose a person who is so long in the tooth that he's out of touch with the market.

Diversification
Mutual funds have access to more varied investment opportunities than most individuals do. For example, it's a complex process for an individual to invest in Brazil and Chile, but a Latin American fund will greatly simplify the effort. Also, whereas many people do not have the wherewithal to invest in mortgages, bonds, stocks, T-Bills, et cetera, choosing the correct fund allows them to diversify into different financial arenas.

Time
Managing one's own financial affairs takes time. By investing with a pro, a person can pursue other activities of a more personally desirable nature. Ahh, fishing....

Size Does Matter
Put another way, "It takes money to make money." Funds have huge capitalization, allowing them to throw their weight around to gain higher financial returns. Plus, with substantial assets, their managers can have an impact on some corporate decisions, leading to determinations that are in the fund holders' best interests.

"Mutual funds sound mighty good to me," said Raj. "Maybe Steve and I should sit down and outline a financial plan with these investments in mind. It would mean starting small, but if the restaurant goes well, and my sweetie lands a few plum roles, the gravy train—spiced with garlic and a pinch of basil, of course—should start to roll."

Phillip was shaking his head. "You know, Raj, mutual funds weren't kind to me. Perhaps you should ask Joan about the disadvantages before you get too excited."

"Good idea, Mr. McCleary," Joan agreed. "Definitely time to step up to the plate with those."

Disadvantages of Mutual Funds

Fees

"First, expertise is not provided for free. Annual management expenses, which are skimmed off the top before returns are calculated, range from about 0.5 percent to 3.5 percent. These vary due to the complexity and costs associated with managing the account. For example, a fund that invests in government treasury bills is simpler and less expensive than one that buys into emerging markets. The latter requires flying all over the globe, seeking out targets to buy, while the former can be done over the phone. Naturally, paying for that lowers your return on investment.

"Now for another major cost: funds take a management fee, normally varying between 1.5 and 2.5 percent on every dollar invested with them. This remains constant whether the fund is profitable or not. After all, the suspender-wearing crowd must afford their Porsches."

"So it's in the fund's interest to have as much of your money as possible, for as long as possible."

"Exactly, Tina, which isn't a problem with a good fund. But the majority give sub-standard returns."

"But their advertisements show these incredible returns," Steve protested. "Some are above 20 percent, which is huge compared to the piddling amount from my GIC."

"You bought into the big sales pitch," Joan responded. "Remember, they will only advertise the funds that have done well, not the losers. Keep that critical ear alert."

"Next, the fees paid depend on the nature of the 'load': front-end load, back-end load, and no-load."

"Daddy said Mommy's getting a back-end load," chirped Liam.

"Oh, did he?" responded Tina. "Well, his front-end load more than matches my back-end, doesn't it...honey?"

"Certainly, dear," Peter cowered sheepishly, making a mental note to watch his words more carefully around his son.

"Front-end load means you pay a fee in advance when buying into a fund. Though this amount used to be as high as 9 percent, it has declined in recent years so that paying over 5 percent is unusual. Still, 5 percent creamed off your investment from the get-go is outrageous. Back-end load means you pay when you cash in. This amount works on a declining basis: the earlier the funds are taken out, the higher the percentage charged. This amount can be calculated on either the original sum placed into the fund or the total redeemed. Normally, the former is preferable, but if the fund has declined in value, then the latter would actually be better. After a specified number of years, usually between five and eight, no fees are charged at all.

"Finally, we have no-load funds, which are quickly becoming more common due to the increasingly competitive nature of this field. With these funds, fees are sidestepped altogether. Still, management expenses cannot be avoided."

"This sounds outrageously expensive, Joan. No wonder so many stockbroker types feast at my restaurant on troughs of caviar," said Raj.

"Oh, that's not the end of it. There are also 'incidental' costs. These include setup fees, which are often charged by no-loaders. Transfer costs, annual costs and trustee fees are also too common. But the two that irk me the most are withdrawal and close-out fees, which the managers demand before clients can get their money back."

Raj looked stymied. "So let me get this straight in my head. The firms charge to return your money? That's ludicrous!"

"You got it, Toyota. Not nice. Not nice at all. Now let's look at other disadvantages that are rarely discussed."

Limited Control Over Timing of Buying and Selling

"Portfolio managers have limited control over when they buy. As large sums of money flow into the fund, there is enormous pressure to get it invested quickly. Money sitting on the sidelines, especially in a low-interest rate environment, can lower the overall return of the fund.

"Sometimes, the managers also have difficulties on the sell side. As customers move money from one fund to another or redeem their cash, managers can be forced to liquidate assets at an inopportune time. Since funds buy large amounts of shares, there's a real possibility that there will be difficulty converting investments to cash during a bear market—which is when stocks are in a decline—or worse, when a major stock meltdown occurs."

Short-Term Versus Long-Term Emphasis

"There is pressure not only to do well in the long run but also on a quarter-by-quarter or even monthly basis. Just as with a corporation, where an overemphasis on quarterly results can reduce management's ability to tackle longer-term issues, a solid sensible fund manager may feel pressured into short-term tactical moves to shore up monthly figures. 'Portfolio dressing' is a very tidy term for what are often myopic investment decisions.

"This is contrary to the Japanese methodology, where the long view is prized. Although their short-term results might not always merit glowing reviews, for an isolated country with few natural resources, they produce enviable results. Ultimately, I believe their method is far superior to ours."

Derivative Play

"Many mutual funds use derivatives, which are essentially a security in the form of a contract between two parties, where price depends on the value of an underlying asset such as a stock or currency. The problem is that these are especially fast-moving investments and millions of dollars can be lost in the blink of an eye. Derivatives have already led to the demise of some financial institutions, and they have the ability to play a major role in the next recession or depression."

Milk Bone Rewards

"Here's a favourite of mine. Guessing 'wrong' on stocks is less likely to be punished if wrong happens to be the conventional wisdom of the moment. Choosing to buy shares in well-managed growing companies that are highly competitive within their sector is unlikely to be criticized, even if the companies are overvalued."

Limits to Diversification

"Next, specialized funds can put a fund manager in a straitjacket. Although these category funds have been a marketing bonanza because investors have a better idea where their money is, what happens when an entire sector gets hit? Even the most astute manager can't make money when the fund's mandate precludes a shift to other havens. The irony is that the enormous array of fund choices allows consumers to diversify, but fund managers are constrained in their investment strategy to the detriment of their clients."

Never Say "Sell"

"Here's one more problem with mutual funds," said Joan, "and then we'll move on to more optimistic information. Mutual fund managers, and brokers who push mutual funds, avoid telling clients to sell. The manager might feel that selling is a failure, or perhaps she's concerned that a client exiting a fund might opt out of the manager's umbrella altogether. And, as you know, funds under management create commissions on an ongoing basis. Some advisors don't want to risk losing the money they manage."

"Funds aren't on your love list," Steve stated.

"I wouldn't go that far," said Joan. "Funds can be useful for someone who doesn't have the time or inclination to manage his own investments. But the historical rule is: **Over time, mutual funds perform worse than the overall markets**. So a better strategy would be to throw darts at a board and purchase the hits from a discount broker. All of you—Liam included—in a few years can do better by making your own investment decisions than buying into mutual funds. A bit of time and a modicum of intelligence will serve you better than most managers."

"Hey, what's the score?" said Steve. "I haven't been paying enough attention."

"Zero, zero," said Liam. "Nothing's happened yet. But you wait. John will hit a homer."

"Be patient, Liam, and he just might," his mother responded.

BOX SCORE INNING 2 — January 15
TORONTO STOCK EXCHANGE

Stock	Purchase Price	Current Price	Initial Target
BUYS			
Bovar	0.95	1.02	4.63
DomTex	7.50	6.88	16.63
Journey's End	2.01	1.75	7.25
Sears	7.13	6.25	12.40
SELLS			
Agnico Eagle*	5.75	20.13	12.50
HOLDS			
Great Pacific	11.30	28.00	41.25
Gulf	3.95	6.00	13.50
Int. Aqua	19.77	2.45	24.00
LaidlawA	9.10	13.38	21.63
LaidlawG	14.25	15.50	21.50
Mitel	3.00	8.50	10.38
National Sea	5.94	5.00	21.50
Newf. Capital	1.81	3.50	9.25
Noma	5.13	5.75	12.50

NEW YORK STOCK EXCHANGE

Stock	Purchase Price	Current Price	Initial Target
BUYS			
Armco	6.85	6.00	11.63
General Host	6.38	3.75	13.60
Grubb & Ellis	2.55	2.63	14.25
Hartmarx	5.94	4.50	18.38
Kaneb	3.25	2.38	15.63
Navistar	31.17	11.13	61.25

SELLS

Cinc. Milacron*	10.93	25.13	22.50

HOLDS

Acme Cleveland*	9.99	18.13	18.75
Anacomp	2.26	0.22	16.63
Fedders	3.08	6.63	9.40
FeddersA	Div.	5.25	with FJQ
Genrad	4.38	8.75	11.50
National Educ.	4.13	8.50	12.60
Occid. Pete	17.50	20.75	28.75
Parker Drilling	4.75	5.63	9.25
R.J. Nabisco	31.95	32.75	86.50
TesoroPete	8.13	8.63	13.75
Zapata	5.63	3.25	32.25

* partially sold

"All right," said Joan. "The box score in this quarter shows light trading with two sales recorded. The first was the divesture of Dylex at $2 per share. Though my feeling was that the upside potential was greater than the downside risk, taking a tax loss seemed more beneficial than waiting for a possibility. Plus, the negative repercussions of the aforementioned stock consolidation had shrunk my number of shares to a pittance.

"On a more positive note, SPAR Aerospace was sold at $15.38, a very tidy gain on the buy-in price of $8.50, made in under a year. Even with the yo-yo nature of this firm, the rapid gain was a delightful surprise.

"On the Movers and Newsmakers front, Agnico-Eagle surged forward, as another gold vein was put into production at the LaRonde site. A couple of other prospects showed promising results, indicating that the firm's mineral base would continue to expand. The lesson here is that for mining plays, several exploratory options are better than just one or two.

"The share price of Bovar, the only hazardous waste recycler of its kind in Canada, climbed over 25 percent in this quarter. During the first three quarters of the year, revenues rose by a corresponding amount. Net income per share almost doubled. Some new contracts in both Russia and the U.S. bode well for the company, brightening future prospects substantially.

"The transition at Journey's End continued, with a number of major accomplishments: $13.5 million of debt was forgiven in exchange for subordinate voting shares; $140 million in contingent liabilities was also eliminated along with guarantees of third-party debt. A reduction of debt to clean up the balance sheet is the kind of stuff my method thrives on. In addition, a joint venture with Choice Hotels International was inked. Choice operates the second largest integrated hotel franchise in the world."

"Do shareholders get free accommodation?" Peter was ever the lawyer searching for an angle.

"I wrote them asking for that freebie, but they didn't even have the common decency to respond. Maybe I should have asked Dominion Textile for denim to make a pair of jeans. They reverted from a hold to a buy as the stock slid about $2. They sold their Yarn Company and Specialty Yarns divisions. Also, the firm is setting up plants in emerging markets where labour costs are lower, with an agreement to open a manufacturing plant in India as the initial step in this direction.

"Anacomp is a classic example of overconfidence in management. Their CEO bamboozled me. For years he spoke about the ship finally being righted; the wait continues. These guys are balancing on a weak plank and fighting for survival due to a heavy debt burden. So they were switched from a buy to a hold. But they're a market leader with an enviable product list, specializing in digital, micrographic, and magnetic output. Market leadership catches my eye. Still, being a top firm in the industry might not save them, and regaining my original investment seems dubious. A proposal to pay creditors in full sounds reasonable but might prove difficult for the company to pull off. The near future will dictate whether this firm has the wherewithal to recover and grow in the manner I expected when the first purchase was made. If not, additional stock certificates will be papering the bathroom, and the sole sour benefit will be a tax loss obtained."

"So you got sucked in by management? Bet some of these guys are excellent actors," Steve observed.

"I meet them all the time in my law practice and trust me, they can suck and blow at the same time better than any lawyer I know," stated Peter.

Joan continued without losing a step. "Now, Acme-Cleveland made a remarkable financial turnaround moving to net earnings of $42.5 million from a loss of $23.4 million in the previous year. Sales increased from $77.2 million to $120.7 million. The market initially rewarded the company for this, but then the stock dipped back as manufacturing difficulties at two plants reduced shipments. This will cause a short-term earnings downturn in the first half of the year, but in the long run, the sales will likely occur, with an associated earnings rebound.

"GenRad is a fascinating story. At nine straight years, this stock had the longest streak without a profit in NYSE history. It has been born again. The story is a company benefiting from large investments in R & D, meaning 'research and development' for you non-scientific folks. This is something to watch for when taking a gander at firms that need to invest big bucks to remain at the head of their class. Rule: **High R & D expenditures are a positive long-term indicator.**

"Finally, Zapata remains dogged by vacillation. When purchased, their forte was offshore energy services and marine protein. They got out of those businesses, and natural gas became the primary play. Now that's passé and a reorganization into a food services company is in the cards. Pondering their plans for the millennium remains baffling. An ongoing hold remains in place, but the target price is lowered to $32.25.

"And there disappears another quarter in the life of the *Contra* portfolio. Their investing style should be more evident now and we'll check back three months hence to see where the numbers are at."

"What a catch!" Bucky howled. "Sirisco laced that ball down the first base line and Phillips seemingly jumped six feet in the air to snag it! The famous 'Irving Leap.'"

"Looked like Michael Jordan doing one of his famous dunks on that play, Bucky. An incredibly well-timed jump by Stipl. Sirisco is moping back to the dugout shaking his head on that one. So at the end of the second, the score remains: New York nothing, Toronto nothing."

Rules
- Buy the management; check their track record
- Over time, mutual funds perform worse than the overall markets
- High R & D expenditures are a positive long-term indicator

Inning 3
Hope and Bravado

If it sounds too good to be true, it probably is.

—Canadian Proverb

"...and Walker smashes the ball out of the stadium, giving the Mets a 2-0 lead over the Blue Jays. What irony! Larry Walker is a Canadian beating up on Canada's team. Bet the Jays wish they had him on their squad, Bucky."

"Yeah, Tom. That was one mighty wallop. Walker will be a free agent after this season, but given the show he's put on again this year, he might be a bit too rich for their blood."

"Can't imagine Tampa Bay Rays would pick him up. If they keep cutting their payroll the way they do, soon the players will pay to play. The only thing they've done recently is change their name, taking out the 'Devil.' That will almost make a difference."

"At least their fans can watch baseball. Not like those in Quebec. Unfortunately, while the province always talks about separating, it was the team that upped and left."

"Let's focus on the game shall we?" implored Tom. "Politics can wait for another day."

Steve was busy shovelling popcorn into his mouth.

Raj glared at him. "Can't you eat like a human being?"

His partner gazed at him mischievously. "No."

"You might become famous, Steven, but the Queen will never break bread with you unless you work on those eating habits," Raj scolded.

"The Queen on our money?" asked Liam.

"Exactly," Raj responded.

"Daddy says he hopes that Prince Charles won't be on our money after the Queen dies. He says it would be very sad for Canada. He says it's time Canada grew up. Right, Daddy?"

"Right, Liam. That's what Daddy says."

Politics, Testosterone, and Miniskirts

Bucky and Tom got Peter thinking about the market in a new light. "Joan, how much of an impact would you say politics has on stocks? Obviously it does, but how would you gauge it?"

"That's difficult to measure. In the United States, the market typically sinks in the year after a presidential election. Worse still are years ending in seven after an election. There's a logic to this which extends beyond mere numerology. Often, politicians implement major changes soon after they're elected, and attempt to do what is truly best for the economy. This can lead to tough decisions that have negative repercussions in the short run. But towards the end of a presidential term, the politicians generally carry a softer stick, handing out goodies to bribe voters. Markets typically respond positively. But numerous other factors, which are less clear, also affect the market."

Phillip jumped in. "My favourite is the miniskirt theory: As skirt lengths go up, so goes the market. Kind of like a double positive."

"Obviously a male came up with that one, Mr. McCleary," Joan said. "Guys will say anything to get women to show more leg."

"Maybe," hedged Phillip. "Or perhaps as markets rise, people become financially better off and therefore more optimistic, more playful, and more sexual."

Raj nodded. "Isn't there also a notion that if the National Conference wins the Super Bowl, or maybe it's the American Conference, the stock market goes up? When the other one wins, the market goes down. Which is which, Joan?"

"Beats me. My methodology sticks to more value-oriented models. For example, stocks have a risk element associated with them, so there isn't a specific interest rate, like with a GIC. This is doubly important if losses could have a major negative impact on your standard of living. So, when I'm investing, I postulate that each company could potentially go bankrupt. The rule is: **Imagine the worst-case scenario.** The principle associated with this is: **Don't invest more than you can afford to lose.** These are critical concepts to us when analyzing downside risk."

Steve made a face. "The way my career is going, I can't afford to lose squat."

The Efficient Market Theory

"Well, Steve, the more you learn, the better prepared you'll be when the bucks roll in. And now for a more useful theory—the 'efficient market theory,'" said

Joan. "The essence is that it's impossible to make money from stocks without insider information."

"Insider information?"

"For example," Joan continued, "the CEO of a major mining outfit knows the firm has struck the ultimate mother lode and the information hasn't reached the ears of the public. She buys 10,000 shares of the stock at $10 each, confident that when the data is released, the price will skyrocket. Three days later the firm announces news of the find and the stock doubles. Easy money for the CEO based on inside info."

"Cool," said Steve.

"But not legal," returned Joan. "What concerns us is that according to the efficient market theory, all the news about a corporation is public and dispersed equally, so no individual has an advantage."

"Something doesn't rock," said Steve. "If it's true, why play the market?"

"Exactly," said Joan. "The reality is that markets aren't perfect, and stock valuations are based not only on today's prices but on where rates are heading. One must project, and obviously, people predict the future differently."

"I've seen a lot over the years and one thing is certain, people see things differently," groaned Phillip.

"Even facts," Peter concurred.

Pedantry

"Exactly," agreed Joan, "which leads to my key point: If the market were perfectly efficient, undervalued stocks wouldn't exist. All prices would reflect their fair value. Fortunately for contrarians, this is not the case.

"Back in my university days, I debated this rather heatedly with one of my professors and was worried he might fail me! Fortunately, he didn't, and twice as fortunately, I didn't listen to him. I argued that Black Monday in 1987, when the Dow tumbled over 22 percent, was an example of a panic attack, which refuted the perfectly efficient market theory. My pedantic professor disagreed, positing this as the ultimate proof of the theory! Anyhow, today he continues to pollute innocent minds with his blather, and my bank account continues to swell by taking advantage of undervalued stocks."

"Kind of reminds me of the God-tree argument," stated Steve. "With all this beauty, God must exist."

"I'm not touching that one," returned Joan. "Besides, it's best to stick with what little I know."

The Random Walk Theory

"Which leads to another myth: the random walk theory. This is primarily an academic postulation, which explains why the majority of portfolio managers are unable to outperform a dart board. It suggests that there is no relationship between yesterday's, today's, and tomorrow's stock price, or what statisticians refer to as a 'zero serial correlation.'

"The theory rests on the mathematical analysis of random events. It finds that the apparent 'trends' in the random behaviour of things, like coin tosses and red and black hits in roulette, are exactly the same as what traders call 'momentum.' Put another way, though a batter may be said to be in a streak or a slump, this opinion is of absolutely no use in predicting the batter's chances in the next at bat. Random walk says there is only one statistic that is useful for prediction: the hitter's long-term batting average. The bottom line is that stocks, like dice, have no memory.

"Furthermore, though some statistical analysis does show slight evidence for momentum, the academics point out that these patterns aren't strong enough to overcome transaction costs. In fact, the professors go so far as to say the technical and fundamental analysis industries exist only to give people a reason to make the brokers a commission. The conclusion is that holding a diversified basket of stocks is the optimal long-term strategy to take advantage of the fact that over time, stocks have earned about 8 percent."

"So buy and hold might be optimal. Easier to do and better returns," Phillip mused.

"No, that doesn't make sense to me," said Peter. "There's no doubt in my mind that some people have better returns than others. Random walk doesn't march with me."

"Bad pun, Peter. Joan, if this theory doesn't concur with your ideas, what have you got that's better than pie in the sky?" asked Phillip.

Steve saw his opportunity. "That's exactly my question, Phillip. Certainly the market has some truths. Being an ignorant yutz, the only rule I know is: Buy low, sell high. So does that make me a stock rocket scientist or what?"

"It makes you a what, Steve," Joan responded quickly. "Which doesn't mean that it isn't a great rule. But like a lot of simplistic idioms, it's the end of the trip, rather than the means to arrive. Think about it: How low is low? How high is high? In practice it's almost impossible to quantify, but if you combine buy low and sell high with **Buy on weakness, sell on strength**, you get a better pitch. Call it the double-play ball."

Averaging Up, Up, Up

"I bought Bre-X at $3 on strength and on weakness," Phillip said.

"Bre-X?" Raj chirped. "Wasn't that the gold company with the big play in Indonesia? It jumped from penny stock status to being worth hundreds of dollars a share. When did you get out?"

"Still waiting. Got a share certificate worth more than the stock framed over the toilet."

Joan smiled. "Bought on weakness and strength? You didn't buy on both the way up and down, did you?"

"Uh-huh," Phillip admitted. "A friend touted me on it when the company was new, and as gains mounted and more and more gold was promised, my heart banked on more and more money. So I made three more purchases. This same friend called me a dope for paying more for less, pointing out that I would never apply the 'Buy as it becomes dearer' strategy to anything else. My 'clever' response was that momentum and future earnings were in my favour, complemented with the 'buy high, sell higher' approach. His response, spoken with an excellent W. C. Fields flourish, still rings in my ears: 'Oh, yes. The greater fool method.' If not for stupidity and greed, mega-millionaire status would be mine today."

"Klebouch!" groaned Steve.

"Klebouch is when Bre-X dove to $3, and my mind insisted it was dirt cheap. After all, the stock price had been so high, there had to be some gold. Had to be! So I doubled down on my original investment. Well, it was dirt but not cheap. Did myself in at both highs and lows!"

"The old investment pitfall: 'It's so cheap now that it can't go much lower.' It did. Two rules here. The first one seems obvious: **Don't believe that something cheap is necessarily undervalued**. The second rule, and this is one that goes against the majority of experts: **Never average up**, because that means averaging down on gains. Once a position is taken, if the stock goes up, be happy you got in cheaply."

"But if the position remains undervalued due to a super initial buy or changing corporate fundamentals, additional profits can be made," insisted Peter.

"Many people agree with that methodology, but that technique doesn't fit my style."

"How about a third rule?" suggested Phillip. "Don't buy on rumour as a shortcut to informed decision making."

"I'll buy that," agreed Joan.

"Not again with the puns," groaned Tina. After a slight pause, she said, "Better than dismissing rumour is analyzing it. Amongst the dross, a gem might be hidden."

Dollar Cost Averaging

"Hmm," said Joan. "That reminds me of savvy investor Bernard Baruch, who said that when the shoeshine boy starts giving stocks tips, it's time to exit the market. It's ironic. People will compare microwave ovens for weeks to save $25, and then plunk down $5,000 because a friend heard from a friend that some plumbing outfit in Wawa is a good buy. They don't research it themselves or bother to talk to professionals who might be in the know. As Phillip and Peter mentioned: **Never buy on rumour; do research**."

"I was that close," said Phillip holding two fingers about an inch apart. "Still another of my investment standards differs from virtually all of the experts, be they fundamentalists, technicians, or other. And if you take only one idea from tonight's gathering, this is it: **Do not invest a specified amount in stocks every month**."

"Dollar cost averaging. That always made me suspicious," Tina said.

"Huh? Would someone be so kind as to explain to me what this dollar cost averaging is?" Steve appeared completely befuddled.

"At the law firm where I work," Peter began, "every month, money is subtracted from our paycheques and given to a mutual fund to invest in North American stocks."

"Lawyers are suckers," Tina teased. "The only investors worse than you guys are doctors and dentists. Ironic how professionals with the highest average incomes are so awful at this game. Perhaps this is their idea of charity."

"That's harsh, honey. My financial advisor outlined three ingredients to make it work successfully. One, do it for several years. Two, invest at regular intervals. And three, choose high-quality stocks, because it's a well-known fact that the stock market goes up over time."

"It's an excellent way to save, but not to invest," countered Joan. "The problem is that stocks are purchased irrespective of their price. This eliminates selectively choosing when prices are advantageous and stocks are on sale."

"But it's an excellent way to average on the market."

"Indeed, if averaging the market is all you wish to accomplish, Peter. But consider this for a moment: Do you purchase anything else blindly, regardless of the price, spending the same amount every month? I know you. When post-Christmas bargains appear on Boxing Day, Mr. Long and Lean becomes all elbow, fighting for the biggest shopping cart. That's also the way it should be with stocks. Don't look to buy on the average. Look to steal on the cheap."

"Logical," Raj agreed. "I certainly wouldn't buy bananas at $1.29 a pound when there's a shortage. I'd go for apples or grapefruits instead."

"So why is dollar cost averaging so popular?" Phillip asked after a pause.

"It became nirvana for some stock market advisors and mutual fund managers—regular investments guarantee their livelihood. After all, nothing could be sweeter than obtaining a percentage of a constant cash flow."

Peter's slight facial tic was acting up. "But isn't prosperity assured since markets move up over time?"

"Why average at the top?" Joan responded. "What happens when markets come down? Applying this technique in 1987 to a representative basket of stocks meant waiting two years to recover your investment. Doing the same thing in 1929 would have meant waiting for fifteen years…fifteen years!"

"No wonder it took my father so long to recover," said Phillip.

Short Selling

"Here's another rule to help you understand my investment framework: **Never short a stock unless you're very sophisticated**."

Steve looked puzzled. "I would never do that. Even if I understood what it meant."

"Can I take this, please, Joan?" On her nod, Phillip explained, "Shorting is selling a security that you don't own but borrow from your broker. The short seller makes money when the stock goes down. The major danger with this technique is that the possible loss is unlimited. If the stock keeps spiralling upwards, the investor has to either keep covering his position, by giving the broker more money, or sell. This differs from going long, where price appreciation is the goal, as the maximum loss in that situation would be if the company went bankrupt and the complete investment was wiped out. I know someone who shorted McDonald's in 1971, and lost literally hundreds of thousands of dollars on an investment of $5,000. The stock split and resplit, while this individual remained convinced that eventually hamburgers would go out of style and the stock price would drop."

The Leveraged Margin Dance

"Which leads us to another topic: buying on margin," Joan began.

"Which is?" asked Raj.

"There are two kinds of accounts that can be set up with a broker: a cash account or a margin account. With a cash account, the client pays for all transactions as they transpire. But with a margin account, the investor only pays a percentage of the stock price and borrows the rest from a broker to purchase the securities.

"A few terms apply here. 'Current equity' is the amount of money paid by the investor to the broker. 'Excess margin' is the amount paid above the required minimum. The 'debit balance' is the money still owing. For example, imagine buying a stock worth $10,000 and paying $7,000, when only 30 percent of the investment was needed to satisfy legal margin conditions. The $7,000 represents the current equity, $4,000 the excess margin, and $3,000 the debit balance.

"Here's another rule: **Never buy on margin**. The reason for this is simple. If the stock price goes down, additional funds must be ponied up to meet margin requirements. My method avoids unwanted calls from stockbrokers seeking funds. Also, interest payments are avoided."

"But some of the most successful investors in history use leverage regularly. It's a common way to make high returns," Peter protested.

"Leverage?" queried Steve. "Isn't that a dance term?"

"Leverage in this instance applies in a similar fashion. By placing bodies or equipment in certain positions, more weight can be supported. Buying stocks on leverage allows you to control more shares with less money, so the gains can be far greater. The corollary: so can losses, which are increased further by the interest costs to obtain leverage. Theoretically, I could have made far more money than my 21.8 percent annualized return for the past fifteen years by buying on margin. Plus, a tax benefit would have been thrown in, as the interest is deductible. But big juicy ulcers would have been my fate. Especially in a year like 2000, where over 20 percent of my equity was wiped out."

"My father was ruined by buying on margin when the depression of '29 hit. If I had my druthers, I would banish it altogether because it presents such a huge danger to the economic system. The meltdown possibilities...."

"Just how would you do that, Dad?" interrupted Tina.

"Here's one idea," Joan offered. "Reduce the margin allowable by five percent a year. That would be gradual enough to allow people to gently unwind their positions without harming the economy."

"But wouldn't margin accounts give guys like me more of a chance?" said Steve. "Even with limited funds, the big gain is possible."

"Gambling's in your blood," Tina responded. "With Liam, a second baby on the way, and a mortgage, risks aren't for us. Plus, even though our income is higher than yours, so is our cost of living, meaning our disposable income is probably lower."

"Sometimes I suggest to Tina that we should take a few more chances. There's one lawyer at the firm who made megabucks by buying options on this little mining company. At one point, it appeared he was going to completely lose his investment as the option expiry date neared. But then they hit this find in Chile and the share price catapulted."

"It happens, Peter. As I stated before, many roads lead to Rome. Mine is one path. Warren Buffett's buy and hold and hold and hold strategy is another."

"Any road would have been better than investing in Bre-X," added Phillip.

Luck

Tina looked bored. Obviously, she had heard the Bre-X story numerous times before. "Oh, Dad, maybe luck wasn't on your side."

"Luck? I hate when people talk about luck that way. I got suckered into a hollow story along with the rest of the herd. Plain and simple."

Joan smiled knowingly. "My belief is that luck is a short-term phenomenon. My rule: **Over the long term, luck balances out**. After all, Las Vegas can be beaten on a weekend junket, but those huge casinos weren't built by giving money away. One very successful professional tennis player said, 'The more I practice, the more luck I seem to have.' Do your homework and warp the odds in your favour." She passed out another box score.

BOX SCORE INNING 3 — April 15
TORONTO STOCK EXCHANGE

Stock	Purchase Price	Current Price	Initial Target
BUYS			
Bovar	0.95	1.24	4.63
Cineplex	1.77	1.74	3.85
DomTex	7.50	6.38	16.63
Journey's End	2.01	2.08	7.25
Noma	5.13	4.30	12.50
Sears	7.13	6.50	12.40
Stelco	5.88	6.75	23.25
Trizec	9.75	9.25	22.38
HOLDS			
Great Pacific	11.30	39.00	41.25
Gulf	3.95	7.00	13.50
Int. Aqua	19.77	2.15	24.00
LaidlawA	9.10	14.38	21.63
LaidlawG	14.25	16.25	21.50
Mitel	3.00	8.88	10.38
National Sea	5.94	5.00	21.50
Newf. Capital	1.81	3.15	9.25

NEW YORK STOCK EXCHANGE

Stock	Purchase Price	Current Price	Initial Target
BUYS			
Armco	6.85	5.63	11.63
General Host	6.38	3.63	13.60
Grubb & Ellis	2.55	2.25	14.25
Hartmarx	5.94	5.88	18.38
Kaneb	3.25	2.63	15.63
Navistar	31.17	10.13	61.25

SELLS

Acme Cleveland*	9.99	30.63	18.75
Cinc. Milacron*	10.93	25.25	22.50
Genrad*	4.38	12.25	11.50

HOLDS

Anacomp	2.26	0.13	16.63
Fedders	3.08	6.50	9.40
FeddersA	Div.	5.63	with FJQ
National Educ.	4.13	12.50	14.38
Occid. Pete	17.50	24.88	28.75
Parker Drilling	4.75	7.75	9.25
R.J. Nabisco	31.95	30.00	96.50
TesoroPete	8.13	9.38	13.75
Zapata	5.63	3.25	37.58

* partially sold

"How 'bout starting with the portfolio's real estate stocks?" suggested Peter. "We bought our house in the spring of 1996, when prices appeared ready to recover, and they did. My guess is that real estate stocks did the same."

"I remember in university you followed housing prices mighty closely, planning the optimal moment to purchase a home. Given your overly expanded state of consciousness of the time, it's hard to imagine anything stayed in that head of yours."

"Talk about obsessive. I read at least a dozen books on the subject."

"That demonstrates, in a roundabout way, one stock market philosophy: 'Buy what you know.' So as a testament to past fortitude, real estate is it. As a matter of fact, I added Trizec to the portfolio this quarter. Two primary reasons led to its purchase. First, I was convinced the real estate cycle was turning around."

"Isn't that sectoral analysis, Joan?"

"Exactly, Phillip. Glad to see someone's thinking. Second, applying our recent lesson, management appeared very able. Plus, debt had recently been retired to the tune of $1.1 billion. That is billion. The corporation was escaping a debt straitjacket.

"The diversification principle was front and centre when considering Trizec: Was too much money being placed in the real estate sector? As only about four percent of my assets were in this sphere, another dive seemed reasonable."

"What about Grubb & Ellis?" Peter asked anxiously.

"Boring time for G & B. Went down somewhat. But one aspect to ponder is the impact using a margin account would have had here. A broker might have called to get me to cover my position, but because it was a cash purchase, I can wait, cool my heels, and remain confident that one day my faith will be rewarded.

"A couple other Canadian stocks entered the stable, including Cineplex Odeon. Everyone who has gone to the movies knows this company. In some ways, this was another management buy. Garth Drabinsky, the CEO who co-founded the company and was instrumental in creating a huge debt load, was removed. Eliminating him made this organization instantaneously far more attractive, as it appeared that the new leader would do a better job reviving the firm.

"Next purchase: steel producer Stelco. This company had recently stared bankruptcy in the face, with the price of the stock falling under $1. But with the debt level reduced over $850 million in 1989 alone and $135 million of debentures having also been redeemed, risk had been dramatically reduced."

"Any profits, Joan?" Peter inquired.

"Indeed. On the sale side, partial positions were jettisoned in Acme-Cleveland, Fedders, and GenRad. Agnico-Eagle also departed at $22.38.

"Acme-Cleveland was the target of a takeover bid. During this type of event, holding to tender is normally preferable, hoping that a higher offer will appear. Remember: **no commission is payable on stock tendered in a takeover.** But I was a bit leery as to whether the deal would transpire, so some profits were grabbed at $30.38, which was well over the takeover bid of $27."

"Is this where arbitrage comes in?"

"Wow! Bonus points, Peter!" Joan remarked. "One type of arbitrage is the simultaneous purchase and sale of two different but closely related securities to take advantage of a price differential. The gains are minute but can be substantial with large amounts of money. Arbitrage is extremely difficult to do and normally reserved for experts with souped-up computers. But, as Peter indicated, takeovers present this type of opportunity, as investors gamble that the buyout will occur, and the narrow gap between the buy and tender price makes the risk/reward ratio worthwhile.

"Next, Fedders was planning a merger with Nycor, a unit they previously divested. This meant a 20-percent increase in outstanding stock would occur, which normally depresses a stock price. Plus, a joint venture in China had me worried. While labour costs would be low, and half of the product was designated for the local market, corporations new to this country often get burned. My wariness led to an additional sale.

"GenRad, another purchase decision because of strong management, was reduced by half after a gain of 163 percent. Orders in the fourth quarter were up 23 percent, earnings 114 percent, and revenues 11 percent. Still, the stock seemed to have legs left."

"Joan, I'm getting dizzy. Stop already," moaned Raj.

"This could be fun. Maybe I should talk faster," Joan replied gleefully.

"Now, in the Movers and Newsmakers category, Great Pacific Enterprises jumped to almost $40. The packaging sector had been in the doghouse due to environmental concerns and stiff competition, but it was becoming popular again. 'Packaging will never go out of style,' I reasoned on the purchase, and this simplistic insight was proving fruitful.

"But offsetting some of these fine moves was the blunder on Anacomp, which was now in receivership and delisted from the NYSE. The terms to stay alive were messy, and a tax write-off was definitely in sight."

"So you pick losers, Joan," Raj said.

"Absolutely," she admitted, "And one never knows when it might happen. Fortunately, Anacomp was only one small holding in my portfolio. So even though money was lost, my compensation is the fact that so many of my purchases are winners. At the end of the day, the overall percentage return is the ball score."

"Joan, how do you recognize a market top?" Peter inquired.

"You're lurching too far ahead, Peter, but just this once I'll let you jump the gun. Ready?"

Peter nodded. Joan looked him straight in the eye and said, "I don't."

"Oh?" a confused Peter replied.

"Don't tease Daddy, Joan. It's not nice," said Liam, who until that moment had been focused totally on the ball game.

"Okay, Liam. I'll give your father two crucial rules: **Always set a sell target**. Out of this comes the second: **The target price must be a minimum of 50 percent higher than the buy price**. Normally I look at 100 percent minimum."

"Always?" asked Peter.

"Always," Joan responded. "Two contrasting philosophies are at work here. One stems from the old LA Dodgers rule of baseball. Maury Wills would hit a single, steal second, be bunted to third, and then sacrificed home. With Koufax and Drysdale on the mound, that was a viable strategy. But the problem with playing for one run is that odds dictate that more than one won't be scored. Stock pickers looking for the nimble in-and-out of ten percent gains are akin to the Dodgers. I prefer former Baltimore manager Earl Weaver's strategy of 'two bloops and a blast' because this creates the opportunity for big innings. That's why 50 percent is a minimum gain. Often, 300, 400, 500 percent and above are common targets. Of course, this appears quite presumptuous when Mitel is purchased at $1.01 and the goal is $10.38. The point is, the vast majority of the investing public has no plan when to exit a position, and this leads to bad decision making. Remember this adage: **Beat the market, not yourself**."

"I remember hearing about Wills and Koufax and Drysdale from Steve, but who's this Weaver guy?" Raj wondered.

Steve hopped to respond. "Weaver was considered by many to be the god of baseball managers. He loved having big boppers in his lineup. Which reminds me of a joke. When did God invent the home run? In the Big Inning."

Peter groaned. "The Blue Jays will never have one if they keep swinging at bad pitches. Johnson throws it a mile out of the strike zone and they swing. I'm embarrassed for them."

"That's because the hitters are constantly anticipating what will happen in a very short time frame," Joan replied. "Johnson throws at 100 miles plus, and the decision to swing must take place in a millisecond. Lots of people react this way to the market, sitting at the end of their converter while anticipating an up or down move and rallying to buy or sell on momentary impulse and conjecture. That's why the majority of my rules are very specific and designed to limit choice. This enforces discipline."

"What time frame do you have for the 50 percent?" Phillip queried.

"Again, 50 percent is a minimum gain. Ideally one year, but normally it doesn't happen that way. Still say my timing is off and four years elapse at the minimum 50 percent target. That's still a 12.5 percent return per annum. Definitely better than a kick in the head. Remember, returns should be compared to other investments for a more comprehensive picture, with the associated risk."

"For me, making that big score is smart," said Steve. "And 12.5 percent per year doesn't cut it. If I bought Microsoft or Yahoo in their infancy, we'd watch this game on a huge TV screen at my beach mansion."

"He's got wannabe star syndrome," Peter said with a pat on Steve's head.

"Lottery syndrome," suggested Tina.

Fear, Greed, Loathing

Joan continued, "Two overriding human characteristics cloud judgement when dealing with the market: fear and greed."

Tina glanced over at Joan, removing her gaze from the game. "This is my realm. As a nurse, I saw how people reacted during their best and worst moments. Fear is a powerful force."

Joan concurred. "There are two kinds of fear. The first is the terror of losing money, where people panic to get out of a plummeting market. Here, the lemming mentality corrupts, and an initial stock drop often leads to further decreases, with the market typically dropping more quickly than it rose. A few reasons often contribute to this swift downslide: a sharp increase in interest rates; low cash reserves amongst institutional investors; heavy selling by insiders; inflated inventories; and, last but not least, high margin and general debt."

"Losing doesn't scare me as much as not winning when everyone's making money and this guy isn't. It's like the whole world's getting further ahead of me and leaving me behind," Peter said.

"My darling suffers from the fear of missing out," Tina said. "When the Blue Jays were winning World Series in the early nineties, Peter would fight everyone at the office for tickets. Then when they fell to the scrap heap, ducats couldn't be given away. Now, once again, it's almost impossible to get a ticket."

"Again, the bandwagon effect," Joan said. "Definitely to be avoided. As a contrarian, try to lead the bandwagon, not hop on. Remember, when the bandwagon is loaded, no one is left to push it."

Steve furrowed his brow. "Which means?"

"Which means the end of the trend and almost assuredly a switch in the pendulum's direction. Human nature dictates that when someone screams, 'Fire!' everyone automatically runs with the crowd. If all your neighbours are getting rich, the tendency is to react quickly, leading to irrational decision making."

"And you wouldn't?" Steve asked trying to sound cool and aloof.

"I'm human," said Joan. "My suggestion is to try to remain calm and clearheaded. Often the best solution is to **take periodic breaks from the market.** Go fishing or something. Allow the subconscious to re-establish reason. It's tough to beat the market, but if you're relaxed and can step away from the action, long-term perceptions become clearer."

"Easier said than done," Phillip kicked in.

"I know," agreed Joan with an instinctive tug where her shoulder pads would be on a business day. "Which leads to the second major motivator: greed. Many people look for the big killing and don't recognize when to take a profit."

"I learned that the hard way," concurred Phillip. "If I'd cashed in some Bre-X instead of being a greedy pig." His voice trailed off with a sad shaking of his head. "When that stock dove, sleep was impossible. Twenty percent of my assets were in that suckhole."

"Perhaps everyone here can profit from your misfortune. Because two more basic principles come from this, which are absolutely pivotal," said Joan optimistically.

"Joan's rolling," Peter sang.

Health and Welfare

"Number one: **Invest so you can sleep at night**. Many people take risks that not only have a negative impact on their financial future but also ruin their quality of life due to stress. The key is to acknowledge personal temperament. **Know thyself.** What works for Peter won't necessarily appeal to Raj. Me? I like sleeping at night. That's why I steer away from options, puts, calls, and anything fast, and I suggest that if you wish to dabble in those areas, another advisor would be preferable. Remember, don't place yourself in a dubious position because something works for someone else. This is critical to both your financial health and emotional well-being. My road is a slower but ulcer-free path to gains."

"These are health tips, not financial lessons," noted Peter. "This from the person who went 52 hours straight without sleeping before two exams and earned the nickname Burnout."

"But I wouldn't do it again, Peter. Anyhow, consider the free health advice a bonus. But rest assured that financial and emotional health are definitely interrelated and the lure of money can act as a false prophet. As they say, 'Money often costs too much.'"

"Wow," Peter gaped. "To think I'm hearing you quoting the—"

"I was miserable," Phillip interrupted. "Food had no taste. Art had no value. Everything was Bre-X, Bre-X, Bre-X. If I could get a hold of those owners in their swank Caribbean mansions...."

"The CEO died, Dad," Tina informed him.

Phillip paused, and it appeared he might burst into laughter. Then he pulled out a hankie, and wiped his brow where a few beads of sweat had appeared. He said very slowly, "That's unfortunate. Hopefully it wasn't too, too painful."

"Remember," warned Joan, "this is your money. You are the final arbiter of how and where it is spent. Other people might have your best, or worst, interests at heart, but at the end of the day, you make the bed you sleep in."

Just as Raj was about to say something, the doorbell rang. Phillip had a sudden burst of optimism. "Must be the pizza, and since Joan is going to make me all kinds of money, I'll spring."

He went with Peter to the door and returned a minute later carrying pizzas stacked above their heads. "How many pizzas did you order?" asked Tina.

"Two," said Peter. "But I forgot how two-for-one pizza became three-for-one pizza. Now they appear to be six-for-one."

On the TV, Tom's voice was picking up steam. "A two-two count on Goldberg. Bases loaded, 2-0 the score. Goldberg has been hot, hitting four homers in the playoffs on top of the thirty-eight he slammed during the season. Johnson's in motion. Outside. Three-two count. Imagine Johnson will throw a fastball. Goldberg had one of the highest strikeout ratios in major league history, rivalling numbers put up by guys like Dave Kingman. He's an all-or-nothing swinger. Johnson rears back. He checks Winters on second. In motion. The pitch. Goldberg swings and misses. Johnson has struck out the side."

"We're witnessing an incredible pitching performance, Tom. You're dead-on about Goldberg. He's a classic big swinger. Seems to either hit it over the fence or strike out. Not the kind of player who advances the runners when he doesn't hit the big one. We'll be back after many words from our sponsors."

Joan saw an opening for the next lesson. "While your mouths are all full, this might be the ideal moment to bore you with perhaps my most important rule, which I'll repeat again and again ad nauseam. So much so, you'll likely get impatient with me."

Joan waited as everyone except Liam stopped eating, shifting their sight lines to her. Phillip even muted the sound on the TV. The place was so quiet, the spider in the corner could almost be heard spinning her web.

Finally, Peter blurted, "Okay, what's this most important of important rules?"

Joan was quiet. After a few more seconds, Peter blurted out, "What, already?"

Joan sat quietly for another second before saying, **"Patience."**

"Patience?" Peter and Steve harmonized. "That's it?"

Joan paused a moment further before repeating, "Patience."

Rules

- Imagine the worst-case scenario
- Don't invest more than you can afford to lose
- Buy on weakness, sell on strength
- Don't believe that something cheap is necessarily undervalued
- Never average up
- Never buy on rumour; do research
- Do not invest a specified amount in stocks every month
- Never short a stock unless you're very sophisticated
- Never buy on margin
- Over the long term, luck balances out
- Always set a sell target
- The target price must be a minimum of 50 percent higher than the buy price
- Beat the market, not yourself
- Take periodic breaks from the market
- Invest so you can sleep at night
- Know thyself
- Patience

Inning 4
The Long-Term Contract

A thief believes everybody steals.

—Edgar Watson Howe

Joan distracted the group from a typical beer commercial—silicone girls and steroid boys frolicking about—to keep things moving.

Traders Versus Investors

"Time to get back on track. Two types of people buy into the stock market: traders and investors. Traders are in and out of various stocks and other investments like crazy, seeking nimble short-term scores. Brokerage firms adore them because their method generates lots of commissions, but for the most part, traders lose money. The rule is: **Don't be a trader; invest for the long term**. If you're fortunate, maybe the short-term exit sign will light up sooner than expected."

"Sounds idealistic," Peter said, unconvinced.

"Ideally, you should almost be able to forget about your funds, although every three months or so, each of your holdings should be re-evaluated. Then, just before the stock hits the target price, consider whether or not to cash in."

"Cashing...." Peter said in a Homer Simpson–esque manner.

Steve emitted a low cry of distress. "You guys are already cashing and I can't even read the stock tables in the newspaper."

"All right," said Joan. "Maybe the pace has been a mite quick, but we'll get there. The key point is: It's difficult to gauge when markets are topping or bottoming out. But it is identifiable if you're trading too much. That's why every stock has a definite sell target in my system. That way, once the purchase is made, it isn't necessary to face a whole flock of decisions. I just relax and wait."

"Why do I have this sinking feeling that your system misses great buys?"

"Opportunities are always missed, Peter. What won't happen with my method is out-thinking yourself by reacting to every gyration and news event. As the cartoon character Pogo said, 'We've met the enemy and he is us.'"

"The enemy?" Raj said. "When I read about some organizations' incredibly insensitive actions, management appears to be the enemy. Perhaps CEOs should be traded like baseball players, with the worst of them banished to the minor leagues."

"That would be very cool," Steve said. "Bill Gates of Microsoft for Steve Jobs of Apple plus a second round draft choice. Very cool."

"Management can be a double-edged sword, which brings us to another dictum: **Check how much of the corporation management owns**."

"That's a double-edged sword? In fact, management owning stock is preferable," stated Peter. "The more they own, the more their interests are served by a high stock price."

"Makes sense to me," said Tina. "Best that shareholders' interests correspond with management's. Otherwise, the big cheeses might only do what's in their personal interests. Witness the outrageous salaries and stock options of some CEOs today as testament to their greed. How can shareholders determine if management is serving my best interests as a shareholder, Joan?"

"That's a toughie and one reason of many to look at annual reports and review management compensation. No question, many executives are vastly overpaid, some making mega-millions of dollars while their minions toil at minimum wage. That's where government should step in to create equity."

"There's already enough government intervention for me," stated Phillip.

Beneficial Laziness

"Here's my story about getting rich while avoiding the responsibilities of being a CEO. When I was a wee lass of fourteen, my goal was to make lots of money, but working hard wasn't my idea of a fun time. Hoping to emulate Richie Rich, I wrote away for a book called *The Lazy Man's Way to Riches*. For ten bucks, this book was mine. Now, ten bucks was a lot of money for me, and as Phillip reminds us, ten bucks then was worth a lot more than ten bucks now. But there was an enticing money-back guarantee: If I wasn't completely satisfied, the book could be returned for a full refund. What a stupendous deal, I thought. So I plopped my ten bucks in the mail, and a month later, my outline to fortune arrived."

Peter smiled. "Bet you got one of those phony eight-page things, telling of other wonderful books, all at a very nominal price, and business opportunities extraordinaire, like swampland in Florida? That scam is as old as the Bible."

"Actually, it was a real book. Not a particularly insightful one, nor one full of amazing opportunities that would make me rich quickly. It provided some basic ideas with a nice cover."

Peter sounded like he was searching for a class action suit as he asked, "So you sent it back and they never returned your ten bucks?"

"I planned to, but I kept putting it off. Laziness defeated me."

"So the author of *The Lazy Man's Way to Riches* scored at the bank on your laziness!"

"Afraid so," said Joan.

"That's so not like you, Joan," said Tina. "You're always so conscientious."

"That was then, this is now, but that's not the moral of this story. The moral is: **Be lazy and let others do research for you.** That's where services like Value Line, who provide all kinds of corporate information and calculate all sorts of financial ratios, come in. Subscribe to this or similar services or do what a cheapo like me does: go to the library or scan the Web for info."

"I go to the library," said Liam. "What's next?"

Technical and Fundamental Analysis

"Next are two common investment methods: technical and fundamental analysis."

"Huh?" said Liam.

"Double huh?" added Steve.

"This isn't as complex as it seems or as difficult as many professionals would have you believe. First, fundamental analysis. People following this method pore over reams of numbers and facts and figures. They lovingly gaze at profit and loss statements and balance sheets, calculate current earnings versus future earnings, orgasm over increasing dividends, and party down over all kinds of aberrations and permutations. For them the proverb 'A picture is worth a thousand words' is apt, as they can sit and study charts for hours. But they do extend their research to places like luncheons, where they'll press the flesh and avidly listen to presidents spill their gourds on every wonderful thing the company is doing, while garnering profiles and positives and abstracting negatives to evaluate corporate potential."

"Doesn't sound like I want to invite these guys to my next party," said Raj.

"Imagine what they'd wear," responded Tina. "Probably woven skinny neckties." Peter shrunk at that comment.

"No," Joan responded. "Those are technical analysts. They try to spot overall market trends and ignore general market psychology. They pore over price movements of stocks and copious mathematical indicators that turn their cranks. Technicians believe that fundamental analysis is a distraction. And, of course, to complete the circle, fundamentalists aren't high on technicians either."

"Which investment method do you subscribe to?" asked Phillip. He turned down the television's volume, edging forward in his seat, and peered as if the gospel was to be spoken.

Chartists and Market Timing

"Well, I'm not done yet," Joan responded. "I haven't even touched upon chartists. These guys use momentum theory while adding a technician's slant to the equation. As a general rule, a market moving upwards should prolong the trend; a market on a slide should continue downwards. These guys scout for different sorts of formations with fancy names like 'spike top' or 'head and shoulders' formation. The latter is illustrated in this chart."

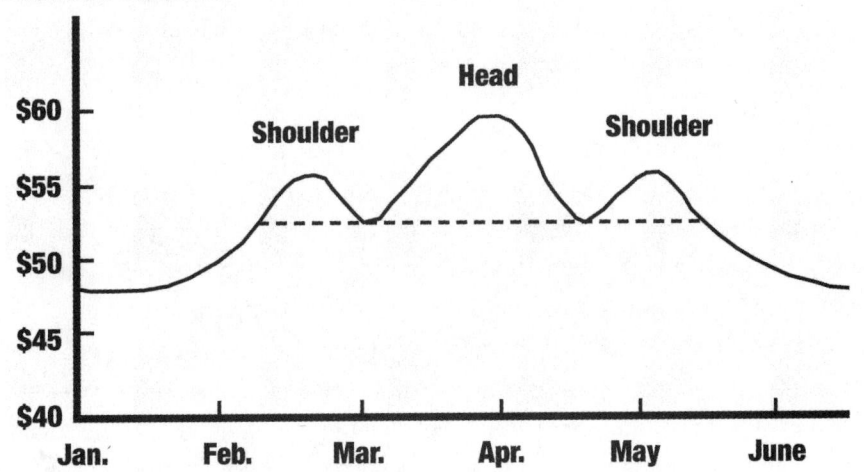

Head and Shoulders

Head and Shoulders Formation

"Now, there are multiple reasons why charting works. Chartists love talking about 'resistance levels.' An example: Peter buys a stock at $18. It falls to $7."

"Sounds like he's adopted my methodology," chuckled Phillip.

"He waits and waits and finally, after four long years, it rebounds to $18. Peter and all his cronies at the law firm who bought in at the same price decide to dump, ecstatic to get their money back. This creates a 'resistance point.' Now a flock of diners at Raj's restaurant saw the stock at $7, thought of buying, but didn't. They watched it move to $18, and then lo and behold, it rolled back down again. Well, when it hits $7, they hop in to avoid missing the boat yet again. This becomes a 'support' level."

"Resistance? Support? Sounds like terms from a bra manufacturer, not a stock market," Raj said.

Joan rolled her eyes. "Now, these are merely a couple of examples of charting and market timing in a huge list that the proponents of this method watch for. Certainly it has some validity. In my system, charts are only glanced at, but my numerical studies indicate the same thing—only the manner of looking at the data is different."

"My broker always uses charts and says there is a specific 'food chain' that they display," began Phillip. "For example, a prospector discovers a major find and insiders buy-in big time. The stock moves. These guys tell their family and friends. The stock moves up some more. Next, the professionals latch onto this information. The stock moves even more. The pros tell schmucks like you and me to buy-in. The stock moves up yet again. Unfortunately, after us, no poor slobs are left to bail us out, so the stock price barrels down."

Trading Volume

"Good scenario, Mr. McCleary. Critical to this methodology is trading volume, which for many market timers is a key indicator of where a stock is heading. For example, these players like to see a base form at the bottom end of a stock's trading range, knowing that this is likely to lead to a surge. But when markets are still trending downward, they fear increasing trading volumes as investors become inclined to take profits by dumping stock, often seeking safer havens for their money. Some players consider understanding trading volumes to be one of the most important, if not the most important, indicator of a stock's direction. I feel that it's important, which is why I established the rule: **Watch trading volumes**.

"But one key reason why charting might fail should be discussed. Buying is normally done after a price move is established. Because of this, sharp, quick changes in value can be missed, letting major buying opportunities fall by the wayside."

"There aren't any perfect systems, are there, Joan?"
"I wish there were, Tina. Mine certainly isn't."

Top-Down, Bottom-Up, and Sectoral Investing

Joan paused, wondering about the creation of the ideal system. Smiling inwardly at the impossibility, she continued, "I want to discuss a few more methodologies for you to think about. One is the top-down approach, where the economy is the focus and the goal is to forecast how it will perform in the short-to-medium term. Then, stocks that will perform well, given the economic outlook, are chosen.

"The bottom-up methodology is almost the inverse. Undervalued stocks with excellent long-term potential are identified. A macroeconomic view is considered but remains secondary.

"Sectoral investing concentrates on areas that appear primed for a surge. An example of this was the real estate sector, which reached unsealed peaks in the late eighties, tumbled through the mid-nineties, and then underwent an upswing."

Growth Investing

"Then there's what I call the 'doomsday' strategy, which others justifiably refer to as 'growth.' This one isn't as negative as I'm making it sound, and it's practiced very successfully by some of the world's top investors. These individuals buy very few stocks per annum, concentrating on undervalued growth situations. Then they sit and hold, often for years. This technique creates a compounding situation, where instead of selling part of the portfolio and paying tax, the investor can potentially make additional money on money already earned, thereby compounding returns. I refer to it in doomsday terms because these companies often fall precipitously, sometimes never returning to former glories, when the market turns sour."

There was a slight pause before Phillip said, "Can we get back to my earlier question, please, Joan? Of these methodologies, which one do you subscribe to?"

"All of them, to various degrees. The fact is, the so-called experts want to specify a domain as theirs, otherwise they disappear into the crowd. Very similar to establishing a market niche to differentiate a product or service.

"Many people want to be pigeonholed, be it as Catholic or Muslim, Republican or Democrat, but a survey showed that the most educated voters regularly switch their party allegiance. To me, this supplanting makes sense. When leadership and members in the upper echelons of the brain trust change, so does the party philosophy. If the left have some good ideas, don't ignore them because you lean right. Likewise, if fundamentalists have effective strategies, then technicians should adopt them, too. And vice versa. Borrowing various successful strategies from different camps is what my system is all about."

The Full Service Versus Discounter Conundrum

Joan could see that Peter was anxious. "Spill it."

"A friend of mine buys stocks and has done very well. He swears by his full-service broker. Tina often kids me about how I'm convinced everyone should avail themselves of a lawyer's services from cradle to grave, but paying for the expertise of others is against my religion. Except for a couple of trades a year, which I do with a full-service broker, discounters receive all the commissions from my minor market forays. But maybe full service is the way to go. What do you think, Joan?"

"Okay, I'll try to field the question of full service versus discounter with neutrality. Start with a comparison to lawyers: It's a given that many lawyers make their living by holding people's hands, as clients are desperately fearful of making a mistake. Of course, expertise and skill are also a part of the equation, with some of these lawyers highly skilled, and others less so. Clients judge how good that expertise is. Evaluating a lawyer is more difficult than a broker. The latter's expertise is largely, but not completely, measured in a number, i.e. the financial return. If a broker's advice is followed and $10,000 invested in stocks becomes $10,400 a year later, the 4 percent rate of return can easily be compared to alternative investments. If the rate of return on GICs was 5 percent, the advisor took greater risks for a lower reward. If his return was 10 percent, then the return ratio was twice as good as a low-risk investment. But if the Dow Jones Index rose 20 percent, then he didn't do well compared to the average."

"That sounds almost too simple," said Steve.

"Well, it is and isn't," responded Joan. "An important consideration is the time frame. For example, corporations must report their financial situation every three months. While two years is longer, it remains short-term. In fact, in accounting, less than two years is considered to be short-term.

"Let's gander at my financial results. In the fifteen or so years I've been investing, which goes back to before my financial advisor days, I've only had one losing year. It was an absolute disaster, as almost 25 percent of my equity was lost. My best year, on the other hand, saw a return of over 75 percent. The key is the long-term annualized average, which for the past fifteen years has been 21.8 percent. Judging a broker by short-term results is unfair."

"You blew almost 25 percent?" asked Phillip, quickly rethinking whether this system was for him.

"Yup," responded Joan. "And immediately afterwards the whole system was re-evaluated and modified somewhat."

"Hopefully big time. That is ugly," said Raj. "How can a person like myself find out an advisor's track record?"

"How does someone know if your restaurant is any good? Or if a plumber can plumb? A doctor can doctor? Ask family or friends. Check who they use. If they're happy with the broker they use, call him or her up. Sit down over a cup of coffee and discuss your investment needs and inquire in detail about their service. Consider your compatibility. Ask about their track record but listen with a jaded ear.

"If your account is large enough, perhaps two brokers would be even better. One's expertise might be in mutual funds, while the other is a stock maven. Also, having brokers from different institutions creates diversification, thereby reducing risk. The number of people who have all of their savings with one investment firm or bank astounds me, especially when the balances exceed the insurance limits set by the government. The rule here is: **Split assets between different institutions for safety**."

Phillip scratched the side of his nose as he said, "Joan, my money is all tied into a major bank I've been with since I deposited my first pennies as a child. As far as I'm concerned, they're as safe as Canada."

"The argument that big banks are so secure that they can't ever go bankrupt is naive. The failure and near failure of numerous financial institutions, both large and small, in the recent and distant past, clearly indicates this. And the assumption that if a huge bank such as Bank America meets its demise that no one will be safe is specious at best. One financial institution can go under without affecting other banks, as has happened before and will undoubtedly happen again. So if there are enough assets in your portfolio to merit it, diversify. Back to the question of full service versus discounter. Here are a few handouts for you."

Full-Service Brokers—Advantages
Specialized Training
Brokers must take specialized investment training to offer professional advice in their field. This education creates a range of knowledge to aid the search for investments appropriate to a broad spectrum of people. But the key to success is not only book learning, it's also active time spent in the guts of the industry, hence the rule: **Search for a broker with experience**. Five years is fine, but someone with at least ten years under her belt is better. Ideally, it's someone who has seen the market through a number of cycles. This is a far superior selection to your friend Johnny's son, who passed his security commission exam by a whisker and is wet and foamy behind the ears.

Access to Information
Historically, brokers had access to all kinds of information that was unavailable to the general public. Behind your contact at the firm are research departments and analysts who scour various markets for opportunities. But this knowledge advantage has diminished due to the Internet, as it is much easier today for the individual investor to access data in a timely way.

Still, business people seeking financing arrive at the major firms' doorsteps with transactions that might prove profitable for your portfolio. Without these middlemen, their options would remain unavailable to you.

Service
If something needs to be accomplished quickly, the full-service guy generally responds more quickly than the discounter. This can vary from sending info to transferring money to returning calls. Working on a name-to-name basis is virtually always more effective than with a no-name generic brand. Face-to-face is even better, as long as you don't get in each others blowers.

Two Heads Are Better Than One
A good full-service broker offers another mind to play off of. Even if financial opportunities are discovered independently, a pro can offer the second opinion to persuade or dissuade an investment decision. This can prove invaluable.

Overall Planning
A broker can outline an overall investment strategy and help oversee your investments, making certain that the investment goals and needs envisioned in

your short- and long-range plan are being targeted. She can help to ensure that the portfolio accurately reflects both your stage of life and personality type.

"Very convincing arguments," said Raj. "Especially for a bumblehead like me who can't be bothered with the humdrum of investing. My idea of a fabulous evening is pursuing the perfect lemon bisque."

"Mmm...eating your perfect lemon bisque is mine," Steve nodded.

"Perhaps a full-service broker is your optimal solution," concluded Joan.

"Then time can be spent doing what turns your crank. But there is a flipside. Take a quick gander at the skylines of the big cities. Which buildings are the tallest?"

"Churches?" responded Steve.

"In small towns, certainly, but in Gotham and other major metropolitan cities, large financial institutions, banks, and investment houses have their names pasted on the monolithic skyscrapers that are the most expensive pieces of real estate in town. Who pays for these monoliths? John and Judy Q. Investor.

"A story about Mitel. When I was acquiring my position in the company, discount brokers were debuting in Canada. At the time, my broker was a likable enough but—unbeknownst to me—not completely reputable fellow named Larry. As I contemplated a dip into the stock, I inquired about his commission schedule and was told that in this case it would be about $85. This seemed high given that the charge at a discount broker would be about half that. He gave me the song and dance about the value of his service, sending me items as I needed them, calling to confirm my transactions, yadda, yadda, yadda. My problem was simply this: the research was my own. Did I want to give him an extra 40 bucks or so for his camaraderie? This expanded to the larger question: If twelve trades a year transpired using his services, was an additional $500 worthwhile? Absolutely not, I decided. It was time to can Larry. Which leads to the next handout on discounter pluses."

Full-Service Brokers—Disadvantages
Price
Even though discounters are often owned by the same institutions as full-service brokers, they cost the client a smaller piece of change—and prices have dropped dramatically. Originally, their fees were lower because of reduced service, but prices declined further because of telephone trading, which eliminated the need for layers of staff. Now the cost has dropped even more because of the Internet. A stock transaction today can be made for less than

one-tenth the price of a few years ago, and while full-service brokers have reduced their fees in many instances, on a price basis they remain uncompetitive. Still, as a general guideline, the odds of being "lucky" increase as commissions decrease.

Groupthink
Ye olde bandwagon effect. Contemplate a group of mostly guys, top-flight salesmen sitting side by side on their heinies day in and day out. Think of shysters in the snake pit. Imagine the diminishment of free will as groupthink festers. Watch them gradually be taken in by their colleagues' pitches. Research has found that an individual who sees a commercial featuring a spokesperson he detests will immediately brand the product as suspect. But if the same person is exposed to that same advertisement again and again, belief often sets in gradually.

Tickeritis
Tickeritis is the need to make a deal. This can be caused by working around people who seem busier than you all day or the line of stock quotes whizzing by your eyeballs every second, distorting time. The need arises to make a deal rather than rest patiently. Action feels like a decision, while inaction—though often the best action—resonates as failure. Patience, as stated before, is a primary market virtue.

Churning
Churning is quite different from tickeritis. While both normally hurt the client, tickeritis is at least done with the customer's best interests in mind.

Churning is when a broker constantly turns over an account to accrue commissions. La Churn is designed to fill a broker's pocket with lucre, and numerous legal cases have been lost by advisors who manipulated accounts like pizza dough.

Remain vigilant. Commissions are the bread of life for brokers. If a mortgage payment is coming due, a new mouth needs feeding, or a Florida vacation is in their blood, looking out for number one might prove overwhelming. This underlines a firm rule: **Never give a broker discretionary power**.

Product Pushers
Some brokerage firms encourage their dealers to push their products specifically, as this pads their bottom line. This risk is exacerbated when the research

department of a brokerage has a recommendation that needs selling. They tell the broker. He starts at the top of his list and, after running through the major clients, dingles little-guy you. Meanwhile, other brokers have been busy working their phones. By the time the deal arrives on your table, your premium price is another person's bargain. And remember the historical data: As with mutual funds, **stockbrokers' results typically lag behind the market averages**. Two well-documented sad-but-truisms. As Samuel Hopkins Adams said, "A broker is a man who runs your fortune into a shoestring."

Joan waited patiently for everyone to finish reading. When all eyes were back on the ball game, she said, "My contrarian system is for the independent investor who makes her own decisions and is seeking prime turnaround candidates. If this is you, by all means use a discounter. But it's only fair that if a full-service broker recommends something you buy, the deal should be placed through that person."

"C'mon, Joan, don't be so self-righteous," interrupted Peter. "A full-service broker gives advice at his risk. My method is to place just enough trades through mine so he'll continue feeding me information while I save on the commish with Mr. Discount."

"Your husband can be incredibly duplicitous, Tina," said Phillip. "For me, a second account with a discounter will be opened to complement my full-service one. Once your system is clearer to me, I'll pick a few stocks myself."

Opening an Account

"I've got a question, Joan. How does someone open an account?"

"Good question, Steve. It's amazing how many people, including professionals, fear doing this."

"There's really less than nothing to it," Peter interjected. "I got the application form from another broker last week. There was the basic stuff such as name, address, phone number, occupation, and employer. Then they wanted to know if the account was cash or margin, my investment objectives, risk tolerance, total assets and the usual banking info, including account and address. That was pretty well it. All in plain English instead of legalese."

"That will only take about ten minutes to do," stated Steve.

"Well, a bit longer," responded Joan. "And hopefully understanding this next portfolio will be as uncomplicated. Here are a couple of handouts from our not-yet-paperless society."

"Beautiful," said Tina. "More dead trees."

BOX SCORE INNING 4 — July 15
TORONTO STOCK EXCHANGE

Stock	Purchase Price	Current Price	Initial Target
BUYS			
Bovar	0.95	1.14	4.63
DomTex	7.50	7.50	16.63
Journey's End	2.01	2.38	7.25
Noma	5.13	3.85	12.50
Sears	7.13	7.70	12.40
Stelco	5.88	6.20	23.25
Trizec	9.75	10.25	22.38
HOLDS			
Cinepiex	1.77	2.60	3,85
Great Pacific	11.30	40.00	41.25
Gulf	3.95	7.70	13.50
Int. Aqua	19.77	1.92	24.00
LaidlawA	9.10	13.10	21.63
LaidlawG	14.25	16.50	21.50
Mitel	3.00	8.50	10.38
National Sea	5.94	5.25	21.50
Newf. Capital	1.81	2.90	9.25

NEW YORK STOCK EXCHANGE

Stock	Purchase Price	Current Price	Initial Target
BUYS			
Armco	6.85	4.63	11.63
General Host	6.38	3.00	13.60
Grubb & Ellis	2.55	4.00	14.25
Hartmarx	5.94	5,75	18.38
Kaneb	3.25	2.88	15.63
Navistar	31.17	10.25	61.25
NovaCare	6.50	7.20	18.50
Unisys	6.00	6.38	18.50

SELLS

Genrad*	4.38	13.63	11.50
National Educ.*	4.13	15.13	14.38

HOLDS

Cinc. Milacron*	10.93	21.00	22.50
Occid. Pete	17.50	23.75	32.50
Parker Drilling	4.75	6.50	9.25
R.J. Nabisco	31.95	30.50	86.50
TesoroPete	8.13	11.13	13.75
Zapata	5.63	3.63	37.58

*partially sold

"To start with, I bailed out of Anacomp. The original purchase and the doubling down were divested at a fraction of the original value. An immediate evaluation of where the error occurred was undertaken. The problem appeared to be too much faith in the president's lip service to an impending turnaround and not enough attention to the debt load. Lesson learned and filed away for future reference as the system's evolution proceeds.

"On the upside, though, there were numerous developments. The last portion of Acme-Cleveland was sold for over $30. Since it was purchased at under $10, this helped take the sting out of the Anacomp fiasco. Fedders was also dispensed with, the common stock sold at $7.25 and the dividend freebie, Fedder's A shares, at $6.50. The questionable flip-flop on Nycor, accompanied by the aforementioned move into China, made me wary."

Stock Dividends

"Are stock dividends common?" asked Tina. "No pun intended."

"Common enough," said Joan. "In one sense they're better than cash because tax doesn't have to be paid on them until they're sold. A negative is that an odd lot of shares often results. Plus, the number of outstanding shares increases, which, in a perfect world, should decrease the stock price in a percentage tango. Normally, though, a net gain for the investor is recorded here.

"A couple of stocks were purchased. One was Unisys, a mainframe computer manufacturer that was transforming itself into an information technology company. This business had downsized by almost 8,000 jobs, a very significant total even in a corporation that had a sales reduction from $8.5 billion to

$6 billion. Naturally, the write-offs were substantial, pushing the annualized loss to $625 million. Talk about cleaning out the cobwebs. Savings from these actions were estimated at $500 million per annum. As well, 42 percent of the corporation's units were expanding at double-digit rates. And key alliances were formed with a bevy of leading corporations, including: Hewlett-Packard, Lotus, Microsoft, and Siemens Nixdorf.

"NovaCare, a demographer's delight, given the aging population, was also purchased. This is the world's largest provider of medical rehabilitation services, with over 2,100 nursing facilities, 375 outpatient clinics, 125 orthotics and prosthetics centres, treating over 40,000 patients per day. From under $400 million of revenues in four years previously, sales had grown to over $900 million in a market expected to grow by 10 to 12 percent per annum. This leads to another rule to add to your list: **Check demographic trends**.

"The primary cause of the stock's descent was the firm's largest client moving services in-house, which reduced revenues at NovaCare by about $35 million. A kick in the butt, but definitely surmountable.

"On the Movers and Newsmakers front, Grubb & Ellis had almost doubled due to finally turning a profit after a decade. Talk about a long wait!

"The negative side of the ledger featured General Host, which was slipping eighth-by-eighth in an almost innocuous fashion. I became antsy because of the amount of time this one had remained in the catacombs, but I did retain hope that it would eventually turn. This firm also appears to be a demographer's delight, being a leader in garden and nursery products. All those boomers have to find something to do when Alphonse and Gaston go to college."

"Alphonse and Gaston?" asked Steve.

"Mmm...David and Jennifer," Joan corrected herself.

Rules
- Don't be a trader; invest for the long term
- Check how much of the corporation management owns
- Be lazy and let others do research for you
- Watch trading volumes
- Split assets between different institutions for safety
- Search for a broker with experience
- Never give a broker discretionary power
- Stockbrokers' results typically lag behind the market averages
- Check demographic trends

Inning 5
The Draft Pick, The Veteran, The Hanger-On

Never confuse a bull market and brains.

—Wall Street axiom

"...and that ball is going, going...it's gone. John Olerud hits his fourth home run of the World Series to give the New York Mets a 3-2 lead over the Jays in the top of the fourth inning. Man, this Olerud is awesome."

Steve raised his hands excitedly. "Man, that guy can hit. I can't believe the Blue Jays gave him up for a Triple A pitcher. Plus, throwing five million smackers into the bargain to cover most of his salary was bona fide idiocy. The Mets are gonna do it! The Mets are gonna do it!"

"He's the best," screamed Liam. "Too bad he isn't with Toronto anymore." Phillip put a potato chip in his mouth and warned, "Like Knute said, 'It ain't over till it's over.'"

"Oh, Dad. Stop quoting dead people all the time. It's so tiring."

"Not dead," Phillip deadpanned, grabbing a big handful of chips. "They're merely living in a place beyond sight. Old Knute is probably looking down right now, observing the game on a freebie ticket."

Tina appeared exasperated, "You're scaring me, Dad."

Gurus and Has-Beens

"Well, hopefully this won't scare you," said Phillip. "Joan, with all due respect, why should we follow your system instead of the thousands of others out there?"

"Let me start with an end around on this one, Mr. McCleary. One of the most respected investors in history, John Templeton, talked about how he and his cronies would get the buy wrong one time out of three. Even with this record, Templeton was revered because of his long-term success. Plus, his philosophy on life was admirable, perhaps a credit to his religious learning. But other 'once gurus' have fallen into disrepute because of some major boo-boos.

When I entered the profession, Joseph Granville was an icon. The man literally moved markets. However, after he made some bad market calls, his popularity dropped significantly. Robert Prechter, a disciple of the Elliott wave theory of stock market movement, had his day in the sun, but after missing a boat or two, he's been relegated to the lightweight category. More recently, Elaine Garzarelli became a superstar by calling the crash of 1987 just days before it happened. Since then, various goofs have rendered her a mere player on the financial scene, a shadow of her former self. Even more current, the Beardstown Ladies, who apparently had phenomenal financial returns, which they spun into five best-selling books, have been discredited. Hoping to become a respected elderly woman myself, I prefer to excuse rather than pick on them. Let's just say the incredible returns they publicized were actually more cellar than stellar. But, hey, it was a great story while it lasted."

Joan's Skeletons

"Enough of fallen gurus, Ms. Beliveau. Your very personal skeletons please. Ahem."

"You'd enjoy that, wouldn't you, Peter?" Joan replied. "We've talked about my mistakes before."

"Pray tell," said Raj.

"Well, the worst was the travesty of Northland Bank, which occurred early in my investment career. When Northland was a relatively new institution, I purchased it as the share price was sliding. As the value tumbled further, I made additional forays on three other declines. Each buy was larger than the preceding. Convinced that the Canadian government would never let a bank go belly-up, since that hadn't happened since the twenties, my confidence remained unshaken until the Conservative government of the day pulled the plug. This situation contributed to a number of rules, the first and foremost being: **Analyze your mistakes**. This is critical to improving methodologies and avoiding inertia so you won't use faulty techniques on an ongoing basis." Peter started to say something, but Joan cut him off. "Unfortunately, I'm not finished. Another major error was amassing shares in real estate entity Bramalea. This corporation had been around for years and was one of the most successful land and mall developers and operators in Canada. But when the real estate downturn arrived, the company was nursing a huge debt load from overpriced properties purchased during the halcyon days of rampant speculation. It appeared to me that corrective actions were working and the CEO of the corporation assured the investing public not only that the battle for survival was being won but also that prosperity was around the corner. I became a believer and purchased shares in the mid-30-cent range.

"A stock consolidation followed. The objective was to push the share price above $5, the minimum level at which numerous institutions will even consider buying shares. And it worked—momentarily. Quickly, though, the debt house of cards unravelled, and the stock price streamed down to worthless. I received nada as a return from my investment.

"There were other disastrous plays, most made as I learned and fine-tuned my craft. Honourable mentions as failures included: American Ship, Anacomp, Cygnal Technologies, Dylex, and Pacific Aqua, the forerunner to International Aqua. But even with these, my overall returns have proven stellar, with recent results proving that I can learn from my mistakes.

"According to the Bondei, 'The journey of folly has to be travelled a second time.' My record shows multiple infractions. So why follow my system? With any advice, put it in your mouth slowly, chew it carefully, and only swallow if it's palatable. Otherwise, a humongous spittoon is what this doctor orders."

"Same advice goes for investment letters?" Peter asked.

"Absolutely. Some are excellent, some are merely better than others, and others are just plain bad. An excellent research technique is studying past issues. See if advice given in the past five years has panned out. Be especially wary of Internet newsletters with pie-in-the-sky promises and small-print caveats.

"The upshot is, there are no infallible experts, and anyone who self-describes this way has snake oil in her back pocket. Everyone makes mistakes."

Liam piped up. "Does that mean God makes mistakes, since we're created in God's image?"

"Oh, Liam," his mother said. "We'll talk about that tomorrow. Tonight is for baseball and investments."

Cycles

"Liam, how would you like to help me?"

"Okay, Auntie Joan. What can I do?"

"Please pass this handout to everyone and then read it aloud. It might be a bit difficult, but I'm confident you can handle it."

Liam scooted across the room and grabbed the papers, handing them out quickly before racing back to his seat. "Cycles," he began. "Before buying a stock, it is very important to consider the cycles that will have an impact on your venture. Seasonal, business, and product life cycle should all be considered."

Seasonal Cycles

"For some businesses, especially those that produce necessities such as bread, seasonal cycles do not exist, as people purchase the product throughout the year. On the other hand, some industries are dictated by the seasons—take skiing. The vast majority of skiing occurs in the winter months, with some autumn and spring skiing in certain areas of the country. These seasonal variations must be planned for, as revenues outside of the winter months will be negligible or non-existent; ski resort owners, ski equipment vendors, and hotels and caterers who depend on the industry must prepare themselves so they have sufficient cash to survive the lean months.

"The Christmas months of November and December comprise about 50 percent of annual sales volume for many retailers. To prepare for this, consideration must be given to short-term financing to buy inventory in the fall, seasonal employee hiring, promotion schedules, and numerous other factors. Adjusting a business to these seasonal fluctuations is a key reason for success.

"Many stock prices follow fluctuations corresponding to the reporting of earnings and revenues during this annual cycle. Though these cycles are not identical every year, astute investors can often take advantage of the similar patterns."

Liam paused. "How'm I doing?"

"Very well," was murmured from different corners of the room, although it was readily apparent that the ball game was more interesting to some individuals than hearing a child stumble over numerous words.

"Should I keep going?"

Phillip broke in, "Joan, don't most major stock drops happen in fall?"

"The worst do, Mr. McCleary."

"It's interesting," began Peter. "More crime and violence occurs in summer than any other time of the year. Heat seems to be a major factor. My feeling is that the market should be more volatile in summer. If this was a law, it could be, 'Most stock market tumbles should happen in summer, might happen in summer, but more often in fall.'"

"My obtuse husband returns from the past. The reason I lusted for you."

"Really?" uttered a befuddled Peter.

"Back to stock market revelations. There's something important to be explained here. Liam, what's the last month of the year?"

"Christmas!" he yelled. "And presents!"

"The last month. Not the last event."

"Oh. December?"

"Good. And that's important for buying stocks. Rule: **Carefully consider buying in December.** Here's the rationale. December is tax loss selling season, when people and institutions bail out of losers. This pushes down stock prices, meaning buyers can gain an extra percentage point or two. While others are selling for no reason that has to do with corporate fundamentals, you can buy and receive an early Christmas present of sorts."

"Sounds lovely," remarked Phillip.

"Here's another bonus. Historically, stocks go up the last two days of the year and the first four days of January. So if the past serves as an indicator of the future, there's an advantage on the buy, and then a New Year's boost as a reward."

"Like batteries included!" Liam shrieked.

"And this happens annually," Peter said, sounding as excited as his son.

"Not annually. Some years, yes. Some years, no. But overall, it represents a definite historical trend. Another example of crowd psychology at work."

"If this is common knowledge, why doesn't everyone gain from it?" asked Tina.

"It's not necessarily common knowledge. Plus, when people sell for tax reasons, there's a tendency to wait until the last moment. Kind of like doing an assignment at the office. The due date is known months ahead, but inevitably, you spend the last night slaving to finish."

"Been there, done that," said Peter.

"Human psychology and activity don't seem to change much over time. For smart investors, this creates opportunities. Consider doing your tax loss selling in September, before the October dangers arrive. That means being ahead of the pack, rather than getting dragged down by it. Plus, if the stock remains a good investment, consider repurchasing it in December when others are kicking it out of the kennel at even lower prices."

"Sell losers in late summer or early fall and buy in December. That'll be an entry in my new stock file," said Phillip. "When holiday advertisements start, I'll be planning ahead."

"All right," Joan said. "Why doesn't everyone continue reading on their own. This way I can save my voice a bit and concentrate on the ball game for a few minutes."

Business Cycles

Within the economy, there are also business cycles. These cycles vary in their duration and intensity but include a number of prominent phases. In the expansionary portion of the cycle, production and spending levels increase and unemployment levels fall. Businesses generally prosper and bankruptcies are at their minimum relative levels. This culminates in a "peak" when the economy is functioning at its best levels before a "contraction" begins. This contraction can result in either a recession or depression, depending on the severity. During this phase, spending, production, and profit levels fall, and unemployment and bankruptcies increase. The base of this period, before expansion begins anew, is called a "trough."

Numerous factors can induce waves of expansion and contraction. Some of these factors include: the government's economic and monetary policies, inventory levels, and people's expectations.

It is important for the corporation to prepare for the contractionary phase of the business cycle when times are good. This will help ensure that the business survives through difficult times to enjoy the benefits of the next recovery. Keep in mind that stock prices will vary to some degree with this ephemerality, and investing near the tail of a trough, when corporations are survival-tough and earnings are ready to ladder upwards, can offer a definitive profitable advantage.

This cycle has been in place for eons. Periodically, economists, politicians, or other prognosticators suggest that a new economy is in place and that this rhythm has reached its demise. Be it "voodoo economics," a "technocratic front," or another rationale, ignore the repetition of history at your peril.

The Business Cycle

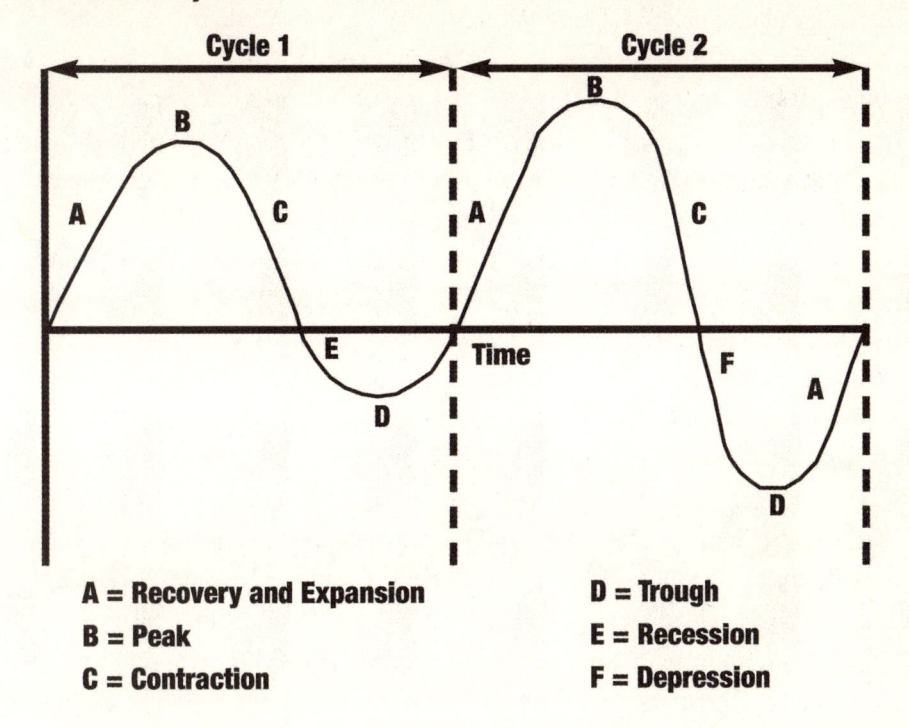

A = Recovery and Expansion
B = Peak
C = Contraction
D = Trough
E = Recession
F = Depression

Product Life Cycle

The third major cycle to consider is the product life cycle. Products go through four phases within this cycle: introduction to the marketplace, growth, maturity, and decline. Each of these stages is associated with certain events and business strategies.

A new product entering the marketplace will either have to create a demand or serve the needs of "pent-up" demand—demand that exists but is not currently being met. Sales in this initial stage are usually slow, while production costs are quite high because of a lack of economies of scale: the larger the organization, the lower the cost per unit. For this reason the product price is usually quite high, and the lack of competitors in this introductory stage allows it to remain that way.

Many people like investing in new companies that have innovative technologies to bring to market. The financial rewards can be exceedingly high if the firm succeeds, but more often than not, young companies with new ideas fail, as brilliant as they might be.

If the product finds and satisfies a market need, then demand often increases quickly. In this growth stage, sales expand quickly, allowing economies of scale to be realized. Often, though, the savings realized are not passed on to the consumer. Instead, the firm uses the increased margin to recoup costs or simply obtain larger profits. If this is the case, competitors often enter the marketplace, sometimes refining the product to carve their own market niche. As growth continues, new market segments are targeted with the establishment of new channels of distribution to reach the consumer.

It is less risky for investors to buy into a company that has reached the growth stage, as public acceptance of the product has already been received. Still, many firms fail at this stage by expanding too quickly without sufficient capital to meet new demands. Overall, though, the risk of purchasing this stock has dropped, albeit in conjunction with the reward level.

The third phase is the maturity stage, which contains three subsections. First, sales growth continues, but at a reduced rate. During "saturation," the market has reached its potential, with the vast majority of customers being repeat purchasers. In the third subsection, "decaying maturity," sales levels begin to drop. This can lead to industry overcapacity, which results in increased competition as businesses battle for a shrinking market. Both price and promotional battles intensify during this latter phase. These pressures lead some corporations to reduce output or vacate the field, while others are forced into bankruptcy.

Finally, the downturn leads to the decline stage, where sales decrease, companies withdraw from the market, and promotional budgets are usually slashed. Corporations that stay in the field are sometimes rewarded by increased revenues, gaining clients from firms who have left the industry. Depending on the product or service, though, it is possible that demand might completely disappear. This is not like the Edsel car, where demand was never created.

"Edsel?" said Steve, looking up from the handout.

Phillip jumped in. "It's good to know you're reading, Steven. Sometimes I wonder if anyone in your generation still does. The Edsel was a car that defined technology and beauty to the company producing it but only attained junk heap status in consumers' minds. Its marketers predicted the car was poised to outsell all automobiles for all time, but instead it was a flaming bust. Hype doesn't always create a marketplace."

"Liam, why don't you finish reading this for us?" Tina asked. "From 'To avoid the decline stage....'"

The lad responded instantly. "To avoid the decline stage, firms often try various strategies to prolong the growth period or lengthen the period of maturity. One method used frequently is 'market modification.' Market modification is a search for new market segments that might potentially buy your product, or a repositioning of the product so that existing buyers will increase usage. For example: by convincing the public that eggs are not merely for breakfast, but also ideal as a dinner, eggs were repositioned in the marketplace.

"'Product modification' is another technique used to avoid a decaying marketplace. Here, the product is changed so that people are convinced that it is 'new and improved,' 'stronger,' 'more powerful,' or a host of other wonderful and silly adjectives advertisers present. Consumers often believe these messages are important, and product sales are boosted to stem the decline. As the product or service of the company you're thinking of purchasing is evaluated, make certain that you give consideration to the poor person who invested in an operation producing slide rules just as the calculator was introduced to the masses.

"And now we have one more pretty graph and I'm finished."

The Product Life Cycle

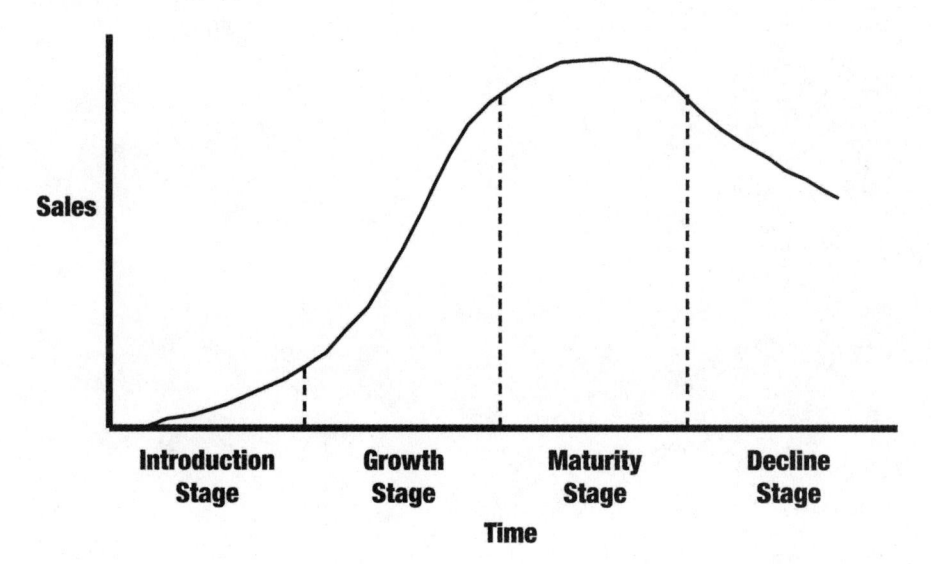

"Liam's the number student in his class in reading," Peter bragged.

"Number one," Tina repeated.

"Oh, that was last month," Liam said with a trace of sadness. "This month I was fourteenth."

Peter collected himself briefly, then said, "Competitions for kids are dumb anyhow. Recently we've been thinking that a private school would be preferable for our boy."

Joan interrupted him. "For the moment, let's analyze companies in the decline stage that have the wherewithal to reinvent themselves. The advantage of these firms is the existence of an established infrastructure, which needs only to be modified rather than built from the ground up like in a new business. This is a primary reason why my technique is so successful: I avoid fledgling companies and their almost inevitable mistakes. Take a good look at the firms listed in the portfolio to see illustrative stories of decline, rebirth, and turnarounds."

BOX SCORE INNING 5 — OCTOBER 13
TORONTO STOCK EXCHANGE

Stock	Purchase Price	Current Price	Initial Target
BUYS			
Bovar	0.95	1.09	4.63
DomTex	7.50	7.30	16.63
Journey's End	2.01	2.25	7.25
Noma	5.13	3.00	12.50
Princeton	0.29	0.31	1.05
Roman	1.20	1.16	2.85
Sears	7.13	8.10	12.40
Stelco	5.88	6.75	23.25
SELLS			
Great Pacific	11.30	45.00	41.25
HOLDS			
Cinepiex	1.77	2.07	3.85
FCA	2.21	2.50	10.75
Gulf	3.95	8.90	13.50
LaidlawA	9.10	15.90	21.63
LaidlawG	14.25	17.50	21.50
Mitel	3.00	9.25	10.38
National Sea	5.94	6.10	21.50
Newf. Capital	1.81	2.90	9.25
Trizec	9.75	12.80	22.38

NEW YORK STOCK EXCHANGE

Stock	Purchase Price	Current Price	Initial Target
BUYS			
Armco	4.63	4.13	11.63
General Host	2.38	2.75	13.60
Grubb & Ellis	2.55	4.25	14.25
Hartmarx	5.94	4.38	18.38
Kaneb	3.25	3.13	15.63
Navistar	31.17	9.25	61.25
Unisys	6.00	7.13	18.50

SELLS

Genrad*	4.38	16.13	11.50
National Educ.*	4.13	18.00	14.38

HOLDS

Cinc. Milacron*	10.93	19.50	22.50
NovaCare	6.50	8.63	18.50
Occid. Pete	17.50	24.38	32.50
Parker Drilling	4.75	6.75	9.25
R.J. Nabisco	31.95	27.63	86.50

*partially sold

Joan cleared her throat. "I'm not used to doing this much talking."

"Daddy says you love talking," disagreed Liam.

"Daddy was just joking," Peter said with his best on-the-spot laugh.

Joan rolled her eyes. "Sure he was."

Penny Stocks

"Anyhow, enough chit-chat. The *Contra* portfolio awaits eyeballing. Four new buys were made in this quarter, and they provide an example of stocks that are only suitable for a more aggressive portfolio. Perhaps the riskiest is Princeton Mines, which owns one major copper play in the north of B.C. The stock was purchased below $0.30, and as a general rule: **The lower the stock price, the greater both the risks and rewards**. But the payoff if the company reaches the target of $1.05 is quite impressive, and the nature of the business is such that when their mine comes on stream and reports earnings, an increase could happen quickly. Princeton is certainly not for empty nesters or solitary survivors unless they have lots of spare cash and really want to chance a bit of a flyer. But for younger people with risk capital, this one should prove very beneficial.

"Another in almost the same category is Denison Mines. This company was once one of the largest uranium producers in the world, but problems with their major client, a large land reclamation project, and questionable management decisions cost them dearly. Currently, the top brass is working briskly to restructure the business, and debt was reduced from $62 million to $30 million. Also, some creditors were issued common shares, thereby eliminating preferred shares, a move that was accompanied by $103 million of undeclared cumulative dividends. Now, an interesting part of the potential cyclicity of this play is nuclear energy. Even with the recent problems Denison had in this field, their most hopeful play is another uranium project called McClean Lake. Will nuclear power and uranium go out of style? My bet is no.

"At the same time that Denison was picked up, Roman Corporation, which owns 5 percent of Denison but is most active in the paper field, was also purchased. This is another penny stock, which cost $1.20, indicating major risk. But historically, Roman was priced far higher and my belief is that management has learned from past over-leveraging mistakes."

"Isn't buying two related companies hurting diversification?" asked Raj. "Like inbreeding? We all know what that can bring about."

"A wise consideration," agreed Joan. "But in this case, Roman's main business is not the same as Denison's and the 5 percent ownership position is not very significant.

"Now, here's one thing you might have already picked up on if you noticed the price levels of stocks I purchase. I have a rule: **Never buy firms with a share price over $25.** In keeping with this dictum, I use an anomaly of mathematical logic and completely ignore the reality of percentages. Consider: stocks that cost over $25 have further to fall than those under, but the lower the firm is priced, the greater the chance that the complete investment will be lost. Additionally, it's easier to double the value of a cheaper stock than a more expensive one. These are definitive reasons for purchasing lower-priced stocks."

There were a few confused faces as Peter stated, "But there are some stocks in the portfolio purchased at over $25."

"Those were companies that were purchased under $25 but had share consolidations," Joan explained. "Also, keep in mind that the $25 level used to be $20, but with inflation and the general rise in the market, the nature of my initial corporate screen changed. Keeping the system static for the sake of sameness is madness. Discipline and inertia are not the same thing. Although, truth be told, I rarely acquire a stock for over $10 now."

Corporate Stock Repurchases

"Finally, I bought another company that profits most when the business cycle is at a low ebb. FCA International is a dreaded collection agency, so when firms have difficulty paying bills, these guys prosper. This company was established in 1926 but had recently fallen upon hard times as margins in this competitive field were shaved to the bone. The company was also locked into some agreements at sub-standard rates that would soon expire. But on the plus side, management was quickly slashing costs, consolidating operations, and repurchasing stock, which should prove beneficial in the long term."

"How so?" asked Tina.

"Well, if the company has the same earnings and fewer shares outstanding, the earnings per share, or EPS, rises. This makes every share outstanding worth more."

Tina stroked Liam's hair as she mulled this over. "So if a company has a million shares outstanding and they make a million dollars, their EPS is $1. But if they buy back half their shares, the EPS becomes $2."

"Precisely," confirmed Joan. "Therefore, the stock price should increase if the price/earnings multiple is to remain similar. Unfortunately, these movements aren't completely congruent, so they remain difficult to predict, like trying to see 'next' before next happens. But the buyback procedure is a common way to meet this end.

"Next, Kaneb was doubled down on at $2.75 as the stock price trended downward. It appeared to be a particular bargain at this price, as sales were increasing, revenues were improving, and debt was dropping. A fine triple-play combination."

Kissing-Off Losers

"Any stocks sold?" asked Phillip.

"Glad you asked," answered Joan. "Put on your thinking caps for this one because it gets a mite complex and is your preview to taxation. Seven stocks were sold: International Aqua Foods ($1.70), Zapata ($3.75), Armco ($4.25), General Host ($2.50), Hartmarx ($5), Navistar ($9.63), and Noma ($3.70). All were lower than their purchase price with the dogs used to offset gains, thereby reducing income. This means that less tax will be paid."

"I'm a tax neophyte," said Steve. "In fact, the tax woman and I have never gotten acquainted."

"You've never paid tax? Never?" uttered Raj. "But you've worked off and on for years! You're the number one server/actor I know, and the tips showed that big time."

"Actor/server. Please get that right. Under-the-table payment, babe. Talk to your business partner who writes the employees' cheques."

"Never declared a penny?" screeched Raj. "You could go to jail!"

"The system isn't fair. The richest people and corporations hardly pay any taxes," said Steve. "Instead they chase after small fry like me."

"I practiced a bit of tax law in my younger days," Peter warned. "It's true. Often the smallest fish are nabbed for the biggest payments. Maybe you should open a bank, Steve. Then you can evade tax big time."

"Avoid," corrected Joan. "Not evade."

"Semantics," returned Peter.

Joan shook her head. "Back to the matter at hand. Our goal is to avoid taxes, not evade them, by selling losers to create write-offs. For example, if you paid $5,000 in total for 1,000 shares of company ABC and they're now worth $2,000, a loss of $3,000 has occurred. This loss can be written off against gains on other stocks but not against regular income. If a gain is not available this annum, it can be applied against profits of recent years. If it's still no dice, the loss can be carried forward against future gains. So I sold seven stocks but re-purchased five after waiting for thirty days. If I'd bought back the companies earlier, the tax loss could not be declared."

"Interesting," Phillip said pensively. "In all my years of investing, I've never done anything like that. My crop of losers has been held for eons. The list is rather extensive."

"Better get a new accountant, Mr. McCleary. Someone with a clue. Dump losers to offset gains."

"So few gains to offset. Oh well, live and learn."

There was an appropriate moment of silence as everyone commiserated with Phillip. Then Peter said, "I apologize, Joan. That 'talk too much' comment was uncalled for."

"Oh, cut it out, Peter. I know I talk a lot. I've always talked a lot. I like talking a lot. That's one of the primo reasons I took this job—because I get to talk to people all the time. And I can talk a lot because they want to hear what I have to say."

Peter assumed a boyish grin. "Uh-huh. So the apology isn't necessary?"

"Absolutely necessary," said Joan.

Bucky's voice came from the TV, "Wells leans back to fire. Oh, that hit Treice on the elbow! That one smucked off him and he's doing the grimace dance."

"That one could be felt up here," replied Tom. "It appeared to be a screwball targeted for the inside part of the plate, but it got away from Wells. That's one pitch he didn't throw during that perfect game in '98."

"Didn't need to. But that's one way to stop Toronto's hottest batter from hitting with men on second and third. Manager Johnson is coming from the dugout. He's saying that Wells threw intentionally at Treice. Can't imagine he would ever do that," Bucky said sarcastically.

"Ever call for that kind of pitch in your active days, Bucky?"

"That's a while ago, Tom. Tough to remember. But rest assured that if the stats are checked, nowhere is there a box score showing that this catcher called to intentionally hit a batter."

"It wouldn't show up in the box score," returned Tom.

"Back to the action at hand," Bucky said with a laugh. "Johnson is returning to the dugout and it appears his efforts, as expected, will be for naught."

"Canseco is up. The pitch. He slams that ball. It's deep, deep, deep. Tishman up against the wall. What a catch! What a catch! Tishman thrust his arm over the wall to bring that one back into the park or Canseco would have had a grand slam. Tishman makes a career catch that will rank up there with Mays and White in World Series history. What a play! Incredible."

"That was some catch, Tom. That ball gets out of here and this Series might've been over."

"What a catch! And this Tishman is part of a brother combination, with the younger one currently lighting up the lights at Triple A. He could be in the bigs next season. Be right back after a word or two from our sponsors."

Rules

- Analyze your mistakes
- Carefully consider buying in December
- The lower the stock price, the greater both the risks and rewards
- Never buy firms with a share price over $25

Inning 6
Scouting

Everything should be made as simple as possible, but not more so.
—Albert Einstein

Refining the Search

"...and it's one, two, three strikes you're out at the old ball game."

"That was wonderful, Liam," Tina cooed, as only a proud mother can.

"What a wonderful little singer. Wasn't that beautiful, Dad?" Tina's father was sitting with his hands covering his ears. "Dad, Dad, wasn't that beautiful?"

"A beautiful finish. One of the most priceless endings ever heard. Thanks, Liam."

"Thank you, Grandpa," Liam blushed,

"Now, Joan," Phillip began, "this background has been useful, but tell us specifically about your magical system. At my age, beating around the bush leagues is trying. Time for the show."

"But this isn't a magical system, and a number of key components have been discussed. Take notes, Mr. McCleary, for now the stage is ripe for expansion and integration."

"I'm with ya," Phillip said.

"All right. Choosing stocks for a portfolio is akin to scouting to fill positions on a ball team. There are common places where everyone looks, like the top leagues in other countries and university teams in the States. And then there's beating the bushes, trying to find that golden gem on a sandlot where other seekers aren't seeking. There are the basic drills prospects, like the forty-yard dash, fielding and throwing, and taking some cuts with the bat. But often ignored are the tests for the intangibles: baseball smarts, a willingness to work hard, ability to learn, and loyalty to an organization. The trick is to examine beyond the obvious for the edge, or a terrific ballplayer like Pete Rose would be bypassed."

"To step away from the crowd, so to speak, and pick with an independent eye," Raj said.

The Bargain Bin

"That's the ticket," Joan agreed. "Remember the conversation about manias. People move in herds. When analyzing stocks, upswings tend to be overvalued, while downswings tend to be undervalued. So my first step is to seek companies that might have been devalued too far, the 'fallen angels.' To do this, I study the financial section of the newspaper and find stocks trading within 30 percent of their 52-week low. At the same time, the high for the year must have been at minimum 50 percent greater than the current price. Take a look at this." She reached into one of her seemingly bottomless briefcases for more papers.

Reading Stock Tables

When Steve received the handout, he was clearly discouraged. "These stock tables are a mystery to me. Every day I make a beeline away from the business section to make sure I avoid this stuff. And they talk all this mumbo jumbo about the different indexes like Dow Jones and Standard and something. What is all this stuff?" He swung his curly blonde locks from the front of his face.

"Now's the time to learn," Joan said with an encouraging smile. "But one small piece of advice first. For a neophyte like you, Steven, an investment club might prove worthwhile. These groups talk about investment methodology, have speakers visit to talk on various financial topics, and often pool money to buy a few stocks. This can be an excellent way to get a taste of the market.

"All right, let's start with the mumbo jumbo first. The Dow Jones and the Standard & Poor's are indexes that measure how stock markets are performing. There are numerous others, including the Russell 2000, the Russell 3000, and the TSX 300 index. The Dow is the most widely followed but only covers thirty stocks, whereas the Russell 3000 includes 3000. My personal feeling is that the more companies recorded, the more comprehensive the indicator. As for stock tables, here's one from the local newspaper, which is fairly typical, although they do vary from one journal to another."

SAMPLE OF NEWSPAPER STOCK LISTING

52 WEEK HIGH	LOW	STOCK	SYM	DIV	HI/BID	LO/ASK	CLOSE	CHG	VOL	YIELD	SHARE PROFIT	P/E RATIO
0.80	0.15	Denbridge	DNB		0.49	0.45	0.45	+0.03	525		-0.43	
34.00	19.00	Denbury	DNR		24.10	23.75	24.00	-0.10	2718		0.74	22.7
0.48	0.28	Denison	DEN		0.32	0.29	0.31	+0.01	4825		0.07	4.4
3.90	2.80	Denning	DEH	0.10	3.65	3.65	3.65	-0.25	17	2.74	0.28	13.0
6.40	3.60	Derlan	DRL		5.25	4.95	5.05	+0.20	876		0.02	

"It's funny," Steve said. "Standing in front of 500 people making a fool of myself is as easy as pie, but reading stock tables is freaky enough to make me pee my pants."

"It's not that horrendous," Joan said encouragingly. "A ten-minute lesson and this knowledge is yours for a lifetime.

"All right, here we go. For those of you who already know this, please bear with me. First, there is the '52-week high/low,' which indicates the stock's price range for the past year. Next, under 'Stock,' you all recognize the name of a corporation. 'Sym' is simply a short form for 'symbol,' used to easily identify the company for purposes of buying and selling. The 'Hi/Bid' and 'Low/Ask' are the price range for the day, with the 'Close' price being where things finished. 'Chg' is the price change from the final trade the day before. 'VoP was the volume of shares traded—in this case with two zeros added. So Denbridge's '525' actually represented 52,500 shares. 'Yield' is the dividend paid relative to the stock price. Of these five companies, Denninghouse is the only one paying a dividend, so at the close price of $3.65, the dividend of 100 works out to a yield of 2.74 percent. 'Share Profit' shows how much money the company earned in the previous year, with Denbridge being the sole firm in the group to lose money. 'P/E Ratio' stands for 'Price/Earnings.' This compares the stock price to corporate earnings and acts as an indicator of how much in income the corporation receives relative to the stock price. Generally, growth companies have higher P/E ratios and utilities and banks much lower. And that's all she wrote. Got it?"

Steve was nodding his head slowly. "There has got to be more. Really, for years I've been afraid to even glance at those pages."

"You could have asked me, sugarplum," stated Raj.

"This kind of thing has never been your forte."

"Yeah, but listen up. The only stock that satisfies Joan's criteria is Denison. A quick learner, aren't I?"

"Impressive," assured Joan. "It's trading within 30 percent of the annual low, and has 50 percent room on the upside. None of the other stocks pass this initial test. At any time, it's difficult to say what percentage of stocks will pass through this initial hoop, as it depends on the recent market performance. But as a general guideline, in up markets, less stocks meet the criteria than in down markets.

"Which leads to the second weeding-out process: Where has the stock price been for the previous ten years? Here, corporations eliminate themselves for two reasons: first, not being listed on a public exchange for ten years, and second, the stock price being high compared to historical bottoms. Corporations that don't qualify here are immediately crossed off my list of buy possibilities. Those which pass this test are established firms with a track record."

"Example, please?" asked Peter.

"Well, there's Noma, which was purchased this quarter. And what do you know, I have this page on its stock prices for the past ten years."

NOMA

Year	1	2	3	4	5	6	7	8	9	10
High	$20.75	18.63	18.38	12.88	8.50	7.50	7.75	7.50	6.13	5.88
Low	$8.88	9.75	11.75	4.05	4.20	4.75	4.50	4.10	4.35	2.69

"This one has really dived," observed Raj. "If the pattern ensues, there will be nothing left."

"Exactly, which is the reason why past performance is not indicative of future performance. Will the trend continue, or has the moment arrived for a change in direction? This is where it gets very tricky. Glancing backward, you'll note that Noma was originally, and prematurely, purchased at $5.13. Then it was sold at $3.70 for the tax loss and repurchased at $3.40. The company responded like a dead duck, but I was convinced that an upward move was in order, so I quadrupled my number of shares at a price of $3.55."

"That's a major purchase," said Raj flatly.

"Truly," Joan agreed. "It's obvious from past data that until year four, Noma was experiencing some glory days, and then the shit hit the fan." Tina checked to make sure Liam was still absorbed in the baseball game and raised her eyebrows at Joan.

"Oops, forgot the kid," she apologized. "Now, back to Noma. The major question here was: Will the stock's downdraft continue? Certainly, if the boat could be levelled, dramatic upside potential was possible. Sales revenues, which had been shrinking, were on an upswing, with cash flow following a similar pattern. Debt, though not decreasing on an annual basis, was on an overall downtrend. So based on these numbers, things were looking better."

"But didn't they also look better in year six when the first buy was made?" observed Tina.

"Exactly," said Joan. "Quite frankly, my investments are often premature. This is not by design, and wishful thinking is that my system would better predict the timing of turnaround points. Unfortunately, it doesn't."

"I've read of people who call market turns," Peter said "No one is consistent. Bar none. And timing when a stock is ready to turn is incredibly difficult. There are so many intangibles."

"I'm not so sure you're right," Peter mumbled.

"Now, for a firm that I previously owned and am watching again. A quiz: What would be reasonable buy and sell targets for Bethlehem? Think about this and we'll check it out later."

BETHLEHEM STEEL

Year	1	2	3	4	5	6	7	8	9	10
High	$19.80	25.50	28.50	21.10	18.50	17.30	20.90	24.10	19.10	15.90
Low	$6.40	15.30	15.30	10.60	10.80	10.00	12.90	16.30	12.60	7.60

Phillip was staring at the paper where he had started making notes, and rubbing the side of his head with a pencil. "So let me make sure these three rules are straight in my head. Number one: **Only consider stocks trading within 30 percent of their 52-week low**. Number two: **Only consider stocks that have traded at least 50 percent higher in the past 52 weeks**. Number three: **Only buy stocks that have been listed for a minimum of ten years**."

"Bull's-eye," commended Joan with a clap of her hands. "Now for the fourth: **Examine the ten-year price range**."

"But, Joan," Peter said with uncharacteristic softness. "That rule would have precluded making tons of money on Internet stocks when those companies were newbies."

Steve was nodding his head. "Peter has an excellent point. I had one buddy, a struggling actor, who bought Google and made so much dough he bought a theatre for him and a few friends to perform in."

Joan shook her head. "It happens. Choose the right numbers and the lottery jackpot might be yours. Certainly lots of money can be made with new companies and other stock market methods which differ completely from mine. With that in mind, this next rule certainly won't sound good to you: **Only buy stocks listed on major exchanges**. As Steve's friend will attest, mountains of money can be made on the over-the-counter market or Vancouver or other minor league exchanges. For me, major exchanges automatically filter corporations, eliminating the riff-raff, although certainly some weak companies and scams sneak around their watchdogs. Although I confess, the odd time I'll make a foray into the stock exchange minor leagues."

Phillip was looking serious. "So effectively, by not looking at the minor league exchanges, you let the majors weed out the dross for you. And by only buying stocks that have been listed for a minimum of ten years, you increase the odds that the firm isn't a fly-by-nighter."

"Precisely," Joan responded. "Follow these rules and you'll avoid the phelp out there."

"Phelp?" asked Phillip.

"Phelp is the diddley squat you pick from your jacket pockets, or pieces of belly button lint, or, in this case, stocks surrounded by hype and hoopla that are ultimately bogus companies."

Corporate Contact

Joan unravelled her methodology further. "Next: **Write to the corporation for information**. Ask to be sent annual reports from the past four years, quarterly reports since the last annual, recent press releases, and to be put on their mailing list for upcoming literature. Got all that?"

"Maybe. Will they? I had no idea."

"They will for the most part, Mr. McCleary, although some corporations do prefer you just go to their websites or SEDAR or EDGAR to save paper and money," responded Joan. "Overall though, it's in their best interest. If more people feel the company's a good investment, that increases the demand for shares, and the price moves upwards. Again, the supply/demand relationship."

"How do you contact them?" asked Peter.

"Very simply. To begin with, I have a form letter, which sits on my computer. Find the corporate investor relations person on their website and let if fly by email. Love that technology.

"Here's a sample of the letter I send." She took copies from her briefcase and passed them around.

Dear Sir/Madam:

Please send me your four most recent annual reports. Also any quarterly reports that have been issued since the last annual.

Also, if you could put me on the mailing list to receive all future annual and quarterly reports and news releases, that would be greatly appreciated.

Thanks,

Joan Beliveau
18 Jupiter-Orion Cres.
Toronto, Ontario
M5P 1M4
Tel: (416) 410-4431
e-mail: jbellwoods@blowtorch.com

"Now, let me toot my own horn for a second in terms of time efficiency. The date isn't at the top, nor is the corporate address; the letters aren't directed to anyone in particular, and none of them are signed."

"How do you know if they ever get to the right person?" Tina queried.

"I don't, but when I'm sending these e-mails to fifty companies or so, missing one or two is no big deal."

"Huge job," said Steve.

"Yup, but investing isn't all sitting around and drinking iced cappuccinos. There's grunt work, too. And it's way easier than the old days of snail mail and stuffing envelopes and placing stamps. Hard to believe sometimes I took the time."

Phillip was smiling. "But out of the depths of the mine come the jewels. Have you ever calculated how much time this contrarian system should take, and your salary per hour, Joan?"

"Actually...no. But let's say someone averaged a portfolio of $50,000 over the last fifteen years. She would have earned around $11,000 per annum following my picks. If the average time spent using my method is one and a half hours per week, and it needn't take more than that, she'd be earning over $140 an hour. Not bad, if I do say so myself. And as we'll discuss later, these gains are taxed at a preferred rate."

"Sounds good to me," Phillip said. "Where do I sign on?"

"For this task, at the post office so to speak. Then sit back and wait for the mail. As everything arrives, start doing your homework by studying the data."

"Why do I have the feeling you're not the posties' favourite customer?" asked Tina.

"I'm not. My mail arrives in quantity, and the packages aren't light. The postie does lots of work before my opening, sorting, and filing commences. I use two filing cabinets with four drawers each. Fortunately, I have a locker in the basement of my building because without it, I would need a larger apartment. And in my home office there are two drawers in my filing cabinet reserved for stocks already owned."

"You must do a shitload of reading," Steve observed.

The Stock Watch List

Joan nodded. "In truth, I do more skimming than reading, but there is a method to my madness. When mail from new companies arrives, I place the stock price from the day I first researched the firm on the front of their information. Then I put the name of each firm on my Stock Watch List. This is like my minor league farm team, where players are trained for the majors. This roster gets divided into two sections: those companies being watched most intently as short-term potential buys, and those of a longer-term interest."

"More work!" screeched Steve. "Doesn't it stop?"

"Steve, money doesn't get handed over to you on a silver platter. Besides, it's not as much work as you might think," Joan responded. "But no, it doesn't stop, and this is another rule: **Write a Stock Watch list**. The modus operandi has been simplified so that the amount of time and effort required is quite reasonable. This review should be done at least quarterly, although my pattern is to do it about every six weeks. It should only take a few hours each time."

"All this, plus you have to watch the stocks previously purchased!" Steve said in an exasperated tone.

"Here's part of the beauty of my contrarian system. Once a stock is purchased, you don't need to watch it on a daily basis. The most important times to keep tabs on it is when the sell target nears, or when the share price drops quite a bit and tax loss selling becomes an issue. Or, of course, at earnings time or when major events happen."

"So after all of the corporate info is in your hands, and the companies' names have been added to your Stock Watch list, then you buy, buy, buy," said Peter anxiously.

"Not so fast. Here's another spot where the patience rule enters the fray. A newcomer brought into the fold isn't even considered for six months."

"Six months!" gasped Peter.

"Six months is the minimum. Sometimes years pass after an initial evaluation before I purchase a stock. And most corporations never move beyond the preliminary examination stage. My assumption is that since the stock price has dropped, there are a number of corporate happenings unbeknownst to me. So I'm like a detective searching for clues. Scrutinize the letter from the president for leads, normally found at the beginning of annual reports. By starting with the annual from three years ago, it's evident if what has been said panned out. For example, let's say record earnings were predicted, but the company actually incurred losses. The head honcho's credibility should be questioned. On the flip side, let's say two years earlier she proffered that the company was going to have a couple of bad years, which they did. Then, if in the most recent report the CEO states that difficult decisions have paved the way for a bright future, this organization might be worth a buy if the stock price hasn't already jetted upwards. Of course, I'm also checking numerous other sources for news about the company and watching the corporate finances."

Steve made a face. "Like I know where to look."

"Numerous sources show corporate statistics for ten years. Value Line remains my personal favourite, but plenty of websites are now gathering this information. Here's a list of a very few sources."

Before Joan made a move, Liam raced to her, waiting eagerly to pass out the papers. "Raj, are you secretly training Liam to become a server?"

Raj laughed, petted the lad on the head as he came by and suggested, "Kid, join the Marines."

THE INTERNET AND OTHER SOURCES

Daily Newspapers
Globe and Mail
Wall Street Journal
Financial Post
Investor's Digest

Weekly Magazines
Barron's
Business Week
Forbes
Fortune

Other Sources
Value Line
Standard & Poor's

Websites
For Canadian Stocks:
Canoe Money *www.money.canoe.ca*
Advice for Investors *www.adviceforinvestors.com*
E-trade *www.canada,etrade.com*
Globe Investor *www.globeinvestor.com*
Sedar *www.sedar.com*

For the U.S.:
Bloomberg Online *www.bloomberg.com*
Edgar *www.edgar-online.com*
Google Finance *www.finance.google.com*
Guru Focus *www.gurufocus.com*
MSN *www.moneycentral.msn.com*
Market Watch *www.marketwatch.com*
Worth Online *www.worth.com*
Yahoo *www.finance.yahoo.com*

"This is a bare-bones list, with the investment content varying from source to source. It's worthwhile to take a bit of time and explore, both at the library and on the Net to see what's kicking around. Many of these resources have 'Company Indexes,' so perusing there quickly to see if any firms you're following are in the news saves time."

"At my age, saving time's a bonus," said Phillip.

"Well, then the Internet is the place for you. Stock quotes are available in real time. Annual reports, quarterlies, and other corporate financials are only a few keystrokes away, along with Security Exchange Commission filings.

You can also check into analysts' opinions to refute other people's outrageous views before chatting with other investors about your favourite and most despised stocks. And last, but certainly not least, buying and selling stocks and mutual funds is simple. These are just a few of the offerings on the Internet now, and it will change and broaden dramatically in the next few years as a fuller range of options and linking technologies are explored."

"I love the Internet now," said Phillip. "I remember when I was afraid to use it."

"It has developed quickly. Hard to believe that less than twenty years ago it was unknown. Now, a new scenario. It's December and rich Aunt Wilma died, leaving you $10,000. Figuring it's found money, you pull out the Stock Watch list and examine the top four entries to see if any are ready to be brought up to the big leagues. Three companies look ripe. So you pick up the phone and follow the next rule to obtain a better feel for the corporation: **Talk to management**."

"Right. Like the bigwigs will talk to us ordinary Steves?"

"You'd be surprised, Steve," Joan said. "Management will often talk to you. Sometimes even the head honcho, but otherwise a VP of finance or someone in shareholder relations, will often get the nod. Naturally, the nearer to the decision-making throne you speak, the better the information imparted."

"C'mon," implored Phillip. "I'm with Steve. CEOs have better things to do than talk with nobodies like us."

"Often that's true," agreed Joan. "But my experience is they like talking to us little people. Corporations feel that by talking to the public, and spreading word-of-mouth goodwill, benefits will accrue to the company and the stock price. And if the designated mouth is also a shareholder, he'll receive the direct benefit of an increased price."

"Sure, Joan. I'll dingle Mr. President of IBM and have a gabfest." Peter snickered at the thought.

Joan ignored him. "This strategy is way more cost-effective than it was a number of years ago. Back then, being the tightwad I am, I always used to call during off-hours, knowing the office was vacant. Firms would then return the call on their nickel. Today though, talking at peak hours can be done for only pennies a minute. A twenty-minute call often proves a very worthwhile investment."

"Sneaky," said Peter. "If you ever decide to become a lawyer, our firm has a place for you."

"When calling, make sure that you have a shopping list of questions ready. At the end of the call, hopefully your contact will have relayed answers to those queries as well as additional information you hadn't previously considered. Later, call periodically for updates, and once more before selling your position. This method keeps you attuned to recent developments."

"Sounds too easy," Raj said.

"*Easy* isn't the word to express it. One has to muster up the guts to get on the blower, find the time, and be willing to spend a few bucks. But as a form of due diligence, it pays off."

"Due diligence?" Steve asked.

"A fancy term for research that proves what you believe," explained Peter.

"Remember, though, management doesn't always deliver the straight goods. Keep the raven of cynicism on your shoulder. And with that caveat comes another rule: **Study management**. Remember, these people will make the decisions that will determine your future fortunes, or lack thereof."

"Don't you find that getting a feel for someone over the phone is next to impossible?" inquired Peter.

"Not at all. Think about potential clients who call you. Don't you find that speaking to them on the phone brandishes an image in your brain? Whether or not they're intelligent, their personality types, axe-murdering capabilities, et cetera. Some people conduct business for years on the telephone without meeting the voice at the other end. A close friend of mine became so intrigued with a woman he talked to almost every day for business that he flew from Toronto to Halifax for a date."

"Ooh. That's so sweet. And they got married?" Raj said, eyes glazing over.

"No. Short guy syndrome. Maybe if he'd been a wee bit taller. The point is, one forms an opinion on the phone, and more often than not, the impression is correct. I reiterate: talk to management. Heck, gab with a couple of people in the ivory tower. Then decide if these are the people with whom to invest your dollars."

Insider Trading

"Now, here's another management related rule: **Check for insider trading**."

"What's that?" Steve asked, beginning to feel like a broken record.

"Insider trading is when top management is buying or selling shares. This often indicates their perception of upcoming corporate performance. Simply put, if management is buying, the outlook is likely to be rosy; selling suggests that things are not so good."

Joan took a sip of white wine while Peter said, "That sounds too easy."

"It is too easy," agreed Joan. "Do a further analysis to discover if management is buying at current prices or using options to buy stock at lower prices than the current trading level. Also, the bigwigs might be selling for many reasons. For example, the chief financial officer might be paying down his mortgage, or surprising his wife with a luxurious necklace for her birthday. One person's actions can be deceiving, but if a number of execs are selling, be on red alert. Don't buy, or if you're already an owner and the target price has been passed, think about bailing out."

"And this information is available to the public?" asked a surprised Peter.

"It is. Although certainly in the U.S. they're more forthright about getting it into the hands of John and Joan Q. Public. Some of the sources previously mentioned provide this data, and numerous organizations specialize in covering insider trading."

Numbers—Oooh, Scary

"So that finishes the qualitative part of our analysis. Ahead is the quantitative area. This is where a lot of people get nervous and fail."

"Give them a test," said Liam.

"Not a bad idea," she responded with a smile. "Maybe when they know more. Now, let's take Liam's favourite ball player, Frank Thomas."

"Frank Thomas is the best, Auntie Joan."

"Probably not the best, Liam, but certainly a good one. He hits for a reasonable average and with power. Behind the obvious stuff, look at Thomas' on-base percentage, which consistently dwarfs the vast majority of ballplayers. Frank knows how to take a walk, and while walking isn't as exciting as even a single, it gets the job done and creates runs. On-base percentage is one of the most underestimated numbers in baseball."

"I rarely glance at that statistic," Steve admitted.

"Indeed," agreed Joan. "Almost everyone who follows baseball even semi-closely knows the names of the big boppers, the guys who hit lots of homers. Many people know the names of the players who consistently have high batting averages, although sometimes the best among them are relatively ignored—like Tony Gwynn was—if they're not on playoff teams. The problem here is more than simple ignorance. It's my experience that a large segment of the population is afraid of numbers."

"A rule is coming," said Peter.

"Indeed. **Do not fear numbers**. They might seem initially complex, but after a few look-sees, you'll realize they're not that difficult."

"This guy isn't a believer," said Steve. "In fact, numbers make me feel sick. I don't even count my change. Even if I was willing to learn, my career must take precedence."

"Can't break away from your busy audition schedule," Peter said sarcastically.

"You use numbers, honey," Raj protested. "You devour those baseball statistics like I inhale mango ice cream. How many of those rotisserie baseball leagues are you in now, anyhow?"

"Just two. You're right though, Raj. I don't consider baseball stats numbers."

"They definitely are," said Joan. "And if you can play with those figures, then the next rule won't be that difficult to follow: **Learn to understand financial statements**. If you're not willing to do this, then leave stock picking to the experts.

First up, a sample income statement, also known as a profit and loss statement. Afterwards, we'll examine balance sheets. Read this handout through while these annoying commercials break up the game."

The Income Statement

The income statement is the financial information that indicates the profit or loss for a company. As the "bottom line" for the business, this statement is of particular significance.

In the annual report published by publicly traded corporations, the income statement normally covers a period of one year. Sometimes, because of special circumstances, such as the changing of the year-end, the time frame can be longer or shorter. It is also mandatory to produce reports with quarterly income statements.

At the top of the income statement is the name of the business (see sample income statement below), followed by "Income Statement" and the time period covered. After this, "Gross Sales" (1) appears on many income statements. This is the total of all the revenues in this respective period, even those sales for which cash has not been received. Following gross sales is "Returns and Allowances" (2). This allows for items that were returned because they were unsatisfactory, or an allowance made because a person was dissatisfied with the product and a discount was therefore given. This leads to the "Net Sales" (3) category, which is derived from subtracting the returns and allowances from the gross sales.

The next category on the statement is the "Cost of Goods Sold" (4). Cost of goods sold appears on the statement for non-manufacturing operations. It does not appear on the financials for a service, as this type of business has no cost of goods sold. To calculate this is fairly simple; it is the cost that the company pays for its product, including freight, duty, and other accompanying expenses. For example, if a business sold five stuffed teddy bears at $50 each, and the cost of each bear was $25, sales would be $250 and the cost of goods sold $125; then, by subtracting the cost of goods sold from the net sales, the "Gross Profit" (5) is derived, which, in this case, would be $125.

"Operating Expenses"—the costs of running the business—appear next on the income statement. There are far too many of these to indicate here, but some of the most common include: "Salaries" (6), "Rent" (7), "Promotion" (8), "Transport" (9), "Hydro" (10), "Depreciation" (11), and "Miscellaneous" (12).

"Total Expenses" (13) is the sum of the operating expenses and appears next. By subtracting this from the gross profit, the "Net Profit Before Tax" (14) is derived. After calculating the "Income Tax" assessment (15) and subtracting this from the net profit before tax, the "Net Profit After Tax" (16) figure is the result, and the statement is finished.

As was mentioned previously, an income statement for a manufacturing firm differs slightly from that of a non-manufacturing business; the "Cost of Goods Sold" becomes the "Cost of Goods Manufactured," and this requires additional detail. In the income statement chart, the inventory at the beginning of the accounting period must be calculated. This includes "Raw Materials" (3), "Work in Process" (4), and "Finished Inventory" (5). To define these, think of a car manufacturing plant. Raw materials are waiting to be placed on the line, work in process is that being done on the line, and finished inventory is the cars waiting to go into the showrooms.

To this total (6) must be added the sum of "Purchases" (7) made within the accounting period, the "Direct Labour" (8) that helped to create the product, and the "Factory Overhead" (9), which includes all of the other costs of production. This sum gives the subtotal (10); then by subtracting the "Ending Inventory" (12) from (11), which is the sum of (6) and (10), your "Cost of Goods Manufactured" (2) is calculated. After this, the income statement is identical to that of a non-manufacturing firm.

SAMPLE INCOME STATEMENT
MANUFACTURING BUSINESS

Bounty Lifts Ltd.
Income Statement: Year Ending December 31, 2007

Net Sales	$150,000 (1)	
Cost of Goods Manufactured (2)		
Inventory, December 31, 2006		
Inventory	$10,000 (3)	
Raw Materials	6,000 (4)	
Finished Inventory	<u>12.000</u> (5)	
		$28,000 (6) = (3 + 4 + 5)
Purchases	55,000 (7)	
Direct Labour	12,000 (8)	
Factory Overhead	16,000 (9)	
		<u>83.000</u> (10) = (7 + 8 + 9)
		111,000 (11) = (10) + (6)
Less: Inventory, December 31, 2007	<u>31.000</u> (12)	
		<u>80.000</u> (2) = (11)-(12)
Gross Profit		70,000 (13) = (I)-(2)
Operating Expenses		
General and Administrative	9,000 (14)	
Selling Expenses	15,000 (15)	
Depreciation	6,000 (16)	
Total Expenses		<u>30.000</u> (17) = (14 + 15 + 16)
Net Profit Before Tax		40,000 (18) = (13)-(17)
Income Tax		<u>10.000</u> (19)
Net Profit After Tax		$30,000 (20) = (18)-(19)

The Balance Sheet

While the income statement shows how well the business has done over time, the balance sheet demonstrates how the operation is doing at a particular point. This is done by showing the assets, liabilities, and net worth of the business for a given date.

The balance sheet derives its name from the fact that it must balance, as the total assets always equal the liabilities plus the net worth. The simplest definition of assets is what the business owns. Liabilities are what the business owes. Net worth is the difference between the two, which represents the owner's stake in the business.

It is imperative to understand the meanings of other elements on the balance sheet. "Current Assets" are assets that the business expects to turn into cash within one year. They are stated at their present value or cost, whichever is lower, and are listed in order of liquidity: the most liquid items being those that can be turned into cash most quickly. "Cash" is the amount of money that the business has on hand, usually in a bank or trust account. "Accounts Receivable" is the cash that the business expects to receive from customers. On many balance sheets, accounts receivable is followed by "Allowance for Uncollectable Accounts," which is the amount that the management assumes will not be collected from clients. Inventory is the goods on hand for sale and in storage for non-manufacturing firms; for a manufacturer, raw materials, work in process, and other finished products that have not been sold must be included.

Fixed assets are items that will last longer than one year, and items that are to be used in the operation of the business but are not intended for resale. Fixed assets should be recorded in the books at their original cost, less depreciation, and stated in order of permanence. Examples of fixed assets include land, buildings, machinery, office equipment, and automobiles. Items depreciate over time as value is lost due to wear and tear. For example, a car is worth much less after a year on the road than when new.

One area of the balance sheet that is sometimes difficult to grasp is the depreciation of a building. A building bought this year for $1,000,000 will often be listed for $950,000 next year on the books. This is because of the depreciation rate, in this case 5 percent, which companies normally use as quickly as possible to reduce profits, thereby lowering taxes payable. In reality, the building might have increased in value, but because of the accounting principle of conservatism, this lower value will be stated. This is of particular importance for an individual scouting stocks, as calculating the present value rather than the worth on the balance sheet enables a smart shopper to purchase undervalued assets.

The next part of the balance sheet is the liabilities section. "Current Liabilities" is the amount of money that the venture owes and must pay within one year. These liabilities often include the following: "Accounts Payable" is money owed to suppliers, "Notes Payable" are the funds owed to other lenders, "Accrued Expenses Payable" are owed for goods or services, and "Taxes Payable" must be paid to the government.

"Long-Term Liabilities" are the funds that a business borrowed and must repay at some point after one year. Common examples of this are "Notes Payable," which is the portion of the bank note due after one year, and a "First Mortgage Bond," which is a bond that the business might have issued to buy a building.

The last section of the balance sheet is the "Net Worth" portion, also referred to as "Equity" or, in the case of shareholders, "Shareholders' Equity" or "Stockholders' Equity." As stated previously, the net worth is the owner's stake in the business.

For example, say you purchase a car for $10,000, $4,000 of which is paid in cash and $6,000 with a bank loan. If you were creating a simple balance sheet for this transaction, it would look like this:

Assets		Liabilities	
Car	$10,000	Bank Loan	$6,000
		Equity	
		Equity	4,000
		Total Liabilities & Equity	
Total Assets	$10,000		$10,000

The equity in this case is $4,000, the owner's actual stake in the car. Notice that, as with all balance sheets, the assets ($10,000) equal the liabilities plus the equity.

Entries in the net worth section of the balance sheet include "Equity" which can include "Capital Stock," "Preferred Shares," and "Common Shares." Capital stock is the original investment by the owner plus any additional funding in later years. Preferred shares and/or common shares are the components of this capital stock. The former give the owner preference in receiving dividends ahead of common stockholders and money if the firm is liquidated, while also usually guaranteeing a fixed dividend. Normally, though, preferred shares "carry" no voting rights. Common shares, on the contrary, almost always allow shareholders to vote, but they don't often pay a dividend, and if so, it is not guaranteed. Common shareholders are also the last creditors to receive funds if the company is liquidated, which normally means they will receive nada. "Retained Earnings" are profits earned by the operation and reinvested in the business, rather than being paid out to the owners. Retained earnings are adjusted annually, increasing or decreasing by the profit or loss of the business.

Balance Sheet Rules
1. The balance sheet always balances. Assets = Liabilities + Equity.
2. The company name and date are at the top.
3. Assets are on the left side, liabilities and equity are on the right.
4. Current assets are listed first and then fixed assets. Current liabilities are listed before long-term liabilities.
5. Items are listed in order of liquidity and/or permanence.
6. Items are stated at cost or market value, whichever is lower.

For both income statements and balance sheets, planning for the future leads to "pro forma" statements. These are forecasts derived by making educated estimates based on the numerous transactions in which the corporation will engage. These help the investor recognize whether the company has the potential for upcoming success. Though this is not a simple process, anticipating the assets, liabilities, and equity position of the firm alongside the future revenue and income streams increases the prospects for a good investment.

Ratio Analysis and Other Critical Numbers

Book Value
"This is tiring," groaned Steve. "Mr. Party Hearty's brain is exhausted."

"Good," responded Joan. "All this thinking helps prevent cerebral atrophy. And since I'm a sadist at heart, here are a few more critical numbers for you to consider when buying stocks. Then, the nitty gritty of ratio analysis will be proffered. First: book value."

"Book value? Unless it's for a part, reading isn't my gig," Steve returned.

"Cute, Steve. The book value is one method of measuring the value of a share. It's calculated by starting with the assets of a company, subtracting the liabilities to give the equity, and then dividing the equity by the number of shares outstanding."

"Huh?" uttered Steve, reviving the only line he spoke in his last role.

"Here's an example. Company A has assets of $250 million. Their liabilities add up to $200 million, which leaves their net worth at $50 million. Now, let's say they have 5 million shares outstanding. That means, you take the $50 million, divide it by 5 million, and the book value per share is $10. Here's a formula."

EQUITY/TOTAL SHARES = BOOK VALUE PER SHARE

"I think I've got it," said Steve, pausing to turn it over in his mind once more. "Okay, I got it. Book value per share of $10. Next."

"Say the stock is selling at $5 per share, or, expressed another way, at 50 percent of book value. Purchasers obtain an undervalued asset at half price."

"That's too easy, especially if Steve understands it that quickly." Raj gave him a playful pinch.

"Remember," Joan continued, "to be wary of companies with ongoing losses, as this not only makes the company less stable but also lowers book value."

Cash Flow

"Next, a critical tool for analyzing corporate health: cash flow. This is money moving in and out of a business, and can be compared to a budget. More funds going out over a long period of time eventually leads to major problems, potentially bankruptcy. For a business to flourish, positive cash flow is a necessity, although I have purchased some corporations with negative cash flow when I believed the trend was improving."

Goodwill

"Now, let's boogie into the realm of goodwill. This is created when one company pays more than the book value for another, feeling that the corporation being acquired either has assets unrecognized on the balance sheet or certain intangibles that make it worth more than the shareholders' equity. An example might be if a company bought Coke, where the purchaser would pay a premium for the name. This extra would be valued as goodwill on the buyer's balance sheet. Sometimes, though, companies overpay for goodwill and then write down its value, taking a loss that ultimately lowers their book value. You might consider picking up an accounting book or taking an introductory course on understanding financial statements to comprehend this better. It might prove a very beneficial investment."

"There isn't enough time in my lifetime for that. Another job for my accountant, when I can afford to hire one," said Steve.

"My accountant is a financial wizard," began Peter. "I complained to him about paying too much tax. 'No problem,' he responded. 'How much do you want to pay?' My income then dropped incredibly with no change of dollars in my pocket, if you know what I mean."

"Nudge, nudge, wink, wink, say no more," responded Joan. "Perhaps, Peter, they'll be enough room in Steve's cell for both of you."

Phillip's laugh lines were in full bloom. "Well, in that case, Raj and Tina can go together on visitor's day."

"My point is that my accountant could probably do something with book value," reiterated Peter.

"He could certainly dance around with it to some degree. Accounting is an inexact science and, for some, a ride into pure fantasyland.

"So, with that, how about some real fun? I present, for your pleasure and amusement, ratio analysis. This will be confusing, but after a couple of ganders, the major thrust will become clear. If it truly tickles your fancy, calculate some equations on your own. For those of you who don't get off on numbers, check some of the sources previously outlined, which have already produced most of these figures. Quite frankly, knowing how to work these equations is not very important, but understanding what these figures mean is critical to grading corporate performance. Examine the pages Liam already gave you."

Everyone grabbed them and began reading to themselves.

One area of business analysis that is often ignored or avoided by investors is ratio analysis. This provides a wealth of data, information that can establish the groundwork for the majority of future business decisions. Ratio analysis indicates where a business has been and where it is now, and it can offer insight into the corporation's future. By taking the time to examine the balance sheets and income statements of the operation, and by working through the following equations, an investor can determine strengths or weaknesses within a company's operation.

A) Liquidity Ratios

The liquidity ratios demonstrate how easily the firm can turn its debts into cash and therefore pay accounts as they become due. This is critical, because if a business cannot pay its debts, bankruptcy is a couple of steps around the corner.

1) Working Capital

Working capital is the amount of money the business has on hand to pay its debts and is determined by calculating the difference between the current assets and current liabilities. Since it is the current portion of the balance sheet being evaluated, this ratio indicates the financing requirements for the upcoming year. Corporations experiencing a shortfall of current assets to current liabilities will often have difficulty meeting their monetary needs.

WORKING CAPITAL = CURRENT ASSETS - CURRENT LIABILITIES

2) Current Ratio

The current ratio also compares the firm's current assets with the current liabilities, but instead of dollar figures, a ratio format is used. Though standards vary from industry to industry, a healthy current ratio is generally considered to be 2:1. This means that the business should be able to cover what it owes in the upcoming year by a factor of two.

CURRENT RATIO = CURRENT ASSETS : CURRENT LIABILITIES

When analyzing ratios, it is worthwhile to examine the trend to see if it is positive or negative. For example:

ABC COMPANY	2006	2007	2008
Current Assets	$80,000	90,000	100,000
Current Liabilities	$40,000	70,000	100,000
Current Ratio	2:1	1.29:1	1:1

These figures show a negative trend: the 2:1 in 2006 is a healthy ratio, but that decreases to 1:1 in 2008. The analysis should then lead to an examination of the current assets and liabilities on the balance sheet to determine which factors are causing the difficulties and what action should be taken. This type of analysis is critical for all of the ratios. For an individual who does not have historical data to work with, this type of comparison is impossible, and the analysis would have to be done relative to industry standards, which can be found in reference books at the library or on the Internet. These standards are extremely useful guidelines against which to measure corporate performance.

3) Acid Test Ratio

The acid test ratio is exactly the same calculation as the current ratio, except that inventory is not included. There are two major reasons for doing this test. First, inventory is often difficult to liquidate quickly. Second, if it is sold, there is a tremendous likelihood that the seller will only receive a percentage of the payment price. Therefore, in some respects, this ratio is a truer measure of the liquidity of a business than the current ratio.

ACID TEST = (CURRENT ASSETS - INVENTORY) : CURRENT LIABILITIES

4) Debt-to-Equity Ratio

Debt to equity illustrates the amount "invested" in the business by creditors, as compared to the owner(s). The higher this ratio is, the larger the creditors' claim on the business. The major danger here occurs if the creditors' portion becomes so high the business cannot pay the debt and the creditors demand their money.

Philosophically, there is a major business debate involved here—that of conservatism versus risk and leverage. The higher the debt-to-equity ratio, the greater the business' leverage; the operation uses other people's money, rather than the equity of the owners, to make a profit. While greater leverage does increase the potential for a higher return on investment, it can also greatly increase the operation's chance of bankruptcy.

There is not an ultimate answer as to whether one should be a conservative operator or engage in high-leverage practices. Many extremely successful corporations are completely averse to debt and will finance everything internally. Alternatively, numerous major corporations have high debt-to-equity ratios and remain successful. But remember that banks can develop hair triggers during a recession or depression. In the past recession, many businesses went bankrupt due to this deadly combination: a high debt-to-equity ratio and a nervous banker. A key rule: **Avoid debt-laden companies**.

DEBT TO EQUITY = LONG-TERM DEBT : EQUITY

5) *Age of Accounts Receivable*

The age of accounts receivable demonstrates how many days on average it takes for the business to collect on a sale. This is critical, as one of the reasons businesses fail is that clients take an unreasonable amount of time to pay, or do not pay at all. The corporation must make certain that it obtains receivables as quickly as possible, with 30 days being a business standard. For calculations such as age of accounts receivable, 365 days is most commonly used, although 360 days is also a norm.

$$\text{AGE OF ACCOUNTS RECEIVABLE} = \frac{\text{ACCOUNTS RECEIVABLE}}{(\text{SALES}/365)}$$

6) *Age of Accounts Payable*

This ratio demonstrates how long, on average, it takes a company to pay for the things it buys. There is an interesting balance here. On the one hand, it is worthwhile to "stretch" accounts payable. By paying more slowly, the company maintains cash for a longer period of time and therefore can use the funds toward the business or to earn interest. Conversely, if accounts payable are stretched too much, suppliers might become disenchanted and treat the enterprise shabbily or, worse, cut off credit and supplies.

$$\text{AGE OF ACCOUNTS PAYABLE} = \frac{\text{ACCOUNTS PAYABLE}}{(\text{SALES}/365)}$$

7) *Age of Inventory*

The age of inventory indicates how many days it takes to turn over the goods for sale. Ideally, this should happen as often as possible, while avoiding stockouts that might encourage customers to seek out competitors. Ordering more goods to obtain a volume discount or reduce shipping costs can be worthwhile business decisions, which will lead to holding higher inventories.

$$\text{AGE OF INVENTORY} = \frac{\text{INVENTORY}}{(\text{COST OF GOODS SOLD}/365)}$$

B) Profitability Ratios

As the name suggests, profitability ratios indicate the bottom line for the enterprise. Remember the importance of comparing current results to prior years to see if the trend is positive or negative.

1) Gross Profit to Sales

The gross-profit-to-sales ratio demonstrates the difference between the cost of goods sold and their selling price. If the percentage is increasing, this indicates that the selling price has increased or one or more elements in the cost of goods calculation has decreased. A percentage change could be the result of more astute purchasing, higher labour productivity, or perhaps lower plant overhead. If a negative situation is noted, buyer beware.

$$\text{GROSS PROFIT TO SALES} = \frac{\text{GROSS PROFIT}}{\text{SALES}}$$

2) Net Profit to Sales

This outlines the percentage of each dollar of sales that becomes profit. It should be analyzed in conjunction with the gross-profit-to-sales ratio. For example, if the gross profit to sales is increasing and net profit to sales is decreasing, this indicates that the firm might be losing control of its expenses. In this instance, costs should be monitored carefully to see which ones are rising and whether this increase is justifiable.

$$\text{NET PROFIT TO SALES} = \frac{\text{NET PROFIT}}{\text{SALES}}$$

3) Return on Investment (ROI)

The return on investment illustrates the percentage payback that the owners are receiving on their equity in the business. This equity is equivalent to the owners' original investment plus the retained earnings that the venture has generated since its inception.

For many investors, the ROI ratio is the one that will be analyzed first to see if funds are being used wisely. For example, if the business has an ROI of 3 percent, while an option is to place money in the bank at a guaranteed rate of 9 percent, the latter could be the more attractive investment.

Generally, if another company in the industry has a higher ROI, over a prolonged period of time, then it is probably doing a more efficient job of operating their business. This state of affairs should lead the management of the laggard to analyze operations and improve current business practices.

$$ROI = \frac{NET\ PROFIT}{(TOTAL\ EQUITY\ YEAR\ 1 + TOTAL\ EQUITY\ YEAR\ 2)/2}$$

C) Growth Ratios

Growth ratios indicate how quickly the business is developing. Many people equate swift growth with success. This is not necessarily the case. The expansion of a firm is often brisk, but other ratios could suggest that bankruptcy looms near. Therefore, do not rely strictly on size as an indicator of prosperity.

1) Sales Growth

This shows, quite simply, how quickly sales are growing. The ratio is derived by taking the sales increase this year and dividing it by last year's sales. Retrenching firms often see a decrease or levelling off here before an upturn can be accomplished.

$$SALES\ GROWTH = \frac{(SALES\ THIS\ YEAR - SALES\ LAST\ YEAR)}{SALES\ LAST\ YEAR}$$

2) Profit Growth

Profit growth illustrates how quickly profit is growing. It should be analyzed with revenues in mind. If sales have doubled in the past year and income has only increased marginally, there might be problems.

$$PROFIT\ GROWTH = \frac{(NET\ PROFIT\ THIS\ YEAR - NET\ PROFIT\ LAST\ YEAR)}{PROFIT\ LAST\ YEAR}$$

3) Asset Growth

Asset growth indicates how quickly the business is acquiring assets, sometimes through takeovers. An increase is usually a positive trend, unless the owners are investing money foolishly or the accounts receivable are not being controlled.

$$\text{ASSET GROWTH} = \frac{\text{(ASSETS THIS YEAR - ASSETS LAST YEAR)}}{\text{LAST YEAR'S ASSETS}}$$

4) Debt Growth

Debt can be assumed by an enterprise for two primary reasons. The first is for growth, and unless the expansion is too rapid, this can be a wise decision. But often management tacks on debt in an imprudent manner, and this is a major danger for corporations. This ratio should be considered in conjunction with the debt-to-equity ratio.

$$\text{DEBT GROWTH} = \frac{\text{(TOTAL DEBT THIS YEAR - TOTAL DEBT LAST YEAR)}}{\text{LAST YEAR'S DEBT}}$$

Ratio analysis is a wonderful tool when examining a business. When this technique is first encountered, it often seems difficult, and therefore many people choose to avoid it. But after just a few hours of work, the mysteries of ratio analysis should begin to disappear, and applying this methodology to investing will become far simpler.

After a lengthy pause, Steve said, "You don't really expect us to follow all of that and, even if we could, to actually use it?"

"Hey, this isn't for everyone. But remember, it's not critical that you do the calculations yourself, just that you understand what the numbers are indicating. And, again, numerous sources have already calculated them for you. There are shortcuts."

"Joan, advocating shortcuts as a policy disturbs me."

"I appreciate that, Mr. McCleary, but with time limitations being as they are in this sped-up world, I cheat the clock where I can. You're probably the most religious one here. Think about what Matthew said in the Bible: 'Consider the lilies of the field, how they grow; they toil not, neither do they spin.'"

"Laziness," Phillip concluded.

"Precisely, Mr. McCleary. I fully admit to laziness as long as I can still do an excellent job."

"Maybe the time has arrived to move onto something more familiar, like another box score, Joan."

"Let's do that, Tina. Another box score coming right up."

BOX SCORE INNING 6 — January 12
TORONTO STOCK EXCHANGE

Stock	Purchase Price	Current Price	Initial Target
BUYS			
Bovar	0.95	0.85	4.63
Cinepiex	1.77	2.00	3.85
DomTex	7.50	6.85	16.63
FCA	2.21	1.63	10.75
Markborough	0.43	0.57	7.65
Noma	5.13	3.70	12.50
Princeton	0.29	0.40	1.05
Roman	1.20	1.21	2.85
SELLS			
Great Pacific*	11.30	53.70	41.25
HOLDS			
Breakwater	1.93	2.50	6.25
Gulf	3.95	11.85	13.50
Journey's End	2.01	4.90	7.25
LaidlawA	9.10	17.45	21.63
LaidlawG	14.25	19.00	21.50
Mitel	3.00	9.10	10.38
National Sea	5.94	6.25	21.50
Newf. Capital	1.81	4.70	9.25
Sears	7.13	10.25	12.40
Stelco	5.88	8.45	23.25
Trizec	17.91	30.05	40.25

NEW YORK STOCK EXCHANGE

Stock	Purchase Price	Current Price	Initial Target
BUYS			
Armco	4.63	4.38	11.63
Bethlehem	8.75	8.88	17.75
General Host	2.38	3.13	13.60
Hartmarx	5.94	5.25	18.38
InterTAN	5.75	4.13	9.63
Kaneb	3.25	3.50	15.63
Navistar	31.17	9.75	61.25
Unisys	6.00	6.88	18.50
SELLS			
Cinc. Milacron*	10.93	23.25	22.50
Genrad*	4.38	22.00	11.50
Parker Drilling	4.75	6.75	9.25
HOLDS			
Grubb & Ellis	2.55	6.38	14.25
National Educ.*	4.13	14.25	14.38
NovaCare	6.50	10.25	18.50
Occid. Pete	17.50	24.88	32.50
R.J. Nabisco	31.95	32.25	86.50

*partially sold

"So where's the portfolio now?" demanded Peter "How are you and those *Contra* guys doing, especially after all those tax loss sales and the decision to buy so many losers back."

"Well, four of the five were up about 10 percent, which in three months is darn good. Although these short-term results can be more of an aberration than true indicators of success. Still, I got about as close as ever to hitting the nail on the head when I bought Breakwater Resources right before it turned upwards. Take a look at this one."

BREAKWATER RESOURCES

Year	1	2	3	4	5	6	7	8	9	10
High	$270.00	127.50	97.00	57.00	14.40	15.00	6.40	6.60	2.90	2.85
Low	$80.00	74.00	40.00	11.60	3.40	2.40	1.90	2.00	1.50	1.53

"Interesting, isn't it? Ten years ago, this stock traded at an 'equivalent' rate of $270. I picked it up at $1.93 per share. Now, there's a story here. In Year 2, after having gone through some terrible times, they did a 1-for-20 reverse split. Year 5's loss of $8.4 million looked mighty promising after the $37 million and change of the previous annum. More red ink followed to the tune of $24.1 million in Year 4. Year 3's loss was $2.5 million with Year 2 at $3.4 million. Sales figures for the period were moving southward to the tune of $63.960 million in Year 6; $54.267 million in Year 5, $33.900 million in Year 4; $40.900 million in Year 3 and $26.700 million in Year 2. This looked like a dying company."

"So naturally, you coughed up funds for it," Phillip scoffed.

"They appeared to be making the right moves. From the financial reports it was evident that their debt load was radically reduced as shares were exchanged for liabilities. Some of their mining properties appeared very promising, and metal prices appeared to be on the upswing. A new management team was also put in place.

"But here's the kicker: Patience dictated waiting over a year after the reverse split to buy the company. As I mentioned previously, after reverse splits, stocks have a tendency to approach or break previous lows."

"What about share splits? Aren't they good for a company?" asked Phillip.

"In most cases they are bullish," agreed Joan. "As an example, consider a stock which trades for $100. A 4-for-1 split is announced, meaning that afterwards, each shareholder will have four shares. *Ceteris paribus*—all things being equal—the stock price should be $25. But because a split is virtually always done when stocks have upward price momentum, and more people will be able to purchase board lots of the stock at lower prices, the price might rise from say, $100 to $110 after the announcement, and go up to, say, $28 to $30 when the split is done. This makes for a lovely gain."

"Is that because splits are a recognition of corporate prosperity and mean that there's a good chance for an increased dividend payout?" asked Peter.

"Hey, someone's got his thinking cap on," said Joan. "Next, and still on the Canadian side of the ledger, Markborough Properties was purchased. This real estate firm had been over $10 in six years prior, and was now dangling at a purchase price of $0.42. They were hacksawed during the real estate crisis but appeared to have the potential to reclaim their former glory, given their excellent real estate assets.

"On the U.S. side is the answer to the previous quiz about Bethlehem Steel, if you remember it, but first, a few other reasons for that purchase. Debt had shrunk from over $750 million to less than $500 million. Additionally, the company's unfunded pension liability was reduced by $750 million in the previous three years, another major reason for the improvement in the balance sheet. Plus, a $370 million write-off for mills that were to be shutdown or sold had been announced, disseminating a block of bad news.

"Now, on to the answers. Bethlehem Steel was purchased at $8.75. It seemed like an excellent acquisition price, even though the book value per share was only a tad over $3. The target was set at $17.75, a figure that seemed very reasonable given past performance and the size of the enterprise. Now it was time to sit back and wait and hope."

"Joan, I don't understand this $17.75 number. Why not round it to $18 or $20?"

"Good question, Raj. It's a bit of a guessing game. One reason $17.75 was chosen is because the stock had reached that level eight of the previous ten years. Also, $20 is too common as a target. Now, as I mentioned before, if and when the price approaches the target, a re-evaluation is done to see if the fundamentals changed and a higher target price, and longer wait, is in order. But at the purchase time, a ballpark sell figure is established.

"Another purchase was InterTAN, of RadioShack fame. These guys, who specialize in consumer electronics such as audio and video systems, phones, games and, of course, radios, have about 1,750 stores in Canada, the U.K., and Australia. Recently, though, their operations were performing badly, leading to a large loss of $3.61 per share, and the shuttering of their continental European stores. This drove sales down from $630 million to a sliver over $450 million.

"A few key moves made me optimistic. Rogers Cantel, a huge phone and cable TV operator, had agreed to open 70 to 100 stores in Canadian malls in conjunction with RadioShack. Part of the deal is the exclusive rights to sell Cantel's products and services. Additionally, the company was teaming up with Royal Bank of Canada in a Visa loyalty program, where points can be traded for merchandise.

"The last buy was Mesa, Inc. This was partially a 'partnership' purchase, as Richard Rainwater had recently invested $133 million in the company, accompanied by existing shareholders who showed their confidence by anteing up another $132 million. While the balance sheet remained highly leveraged, these moves improved it substantially.

"And, finally, the firm had its first quarterly profit since...about a decade! Now, there's a wait. T. Boone Pickens, the high-flying CEO who had been shunted to the sidelines, could only watch from his new perch—a place that made us even more comfortable with our buy.

"On the sell side, more GenRad went out the door at $21.63. Their CEO, James Lyons, was talking about a potential price of $40 and takeover possibilities, so some was kept. Plus, half the position in Parker Drilling was released at $9.50, as the upswing in oil drilling was leading to major demand for their equipment."

Bucky's voice was at a fevered pitch. "Gonzalez picks it up deep in the hole. And that's a double play! What an amazing pickup by Gonzalez at short! Amazing!"

"This Jay squad has been using the 6 to 4 to 3 all season long to get the job done. They were number three in league history, doing that this year with Gonzalez to Ossea to Geris the pat hand. Incredible. That finishes the sixth, and it's into the top of the seventh with the Mets still leading 3-2."

Rules
- Only consider stocks trading within 30 percent of their 52-week low
- Only consider stocks that have traded at least 50 percent higher in the past 52 weeks
- Only buy stocks that have been listed for a minimum of ten years
- Examine the ten-year price range
- Only buy stocks listed on major exchanges
- Write to the corporation for information
- Write a stock watch list
- Scrutinize the letter from the president
- Talk to management
- Study management
- Check for insider trading
- Do not fear numbers
- Learn to understand financial statements
- Avoid debt-laden companies

Inning 7
The Pitch

Remember Patience...patience to buy...patience to hold...patience to sell....

The Buy Decision

"This contrarian method is becoming somewhat clearer," began Steve. "It has me thinking about a way to make a ton of money. Here's the plot. Nine months after a blackout, the birth rate skyrockets, as once TV screens go blank, people need to find a way to fill their time. So here's the plan. We short a utility stock. Then we blow up some of their equipment, causing the price of the shares to come careening down, making us a ton of money. Next, with the profits, we invest in items pertaining to babies and children, such as baby food and clothing and daycares. The price of those stocks should go out of sight and we're resting on easy street."

Everyone glared at Steve, who had a distant look in his eyes, perhaps viewing his beachfront house.

"Interesting idea for a TV plot, Steve," Joan said. "But now, time for another rule: **Before buying, test your idea on people you respect**. Ask around a bit. For example, before developer Markborough came into my stable, I asked a few people their opinions on the real estate market. One person was a friend of mine who develops shopping centres, another was a real estate agent, and still another is one of those well-rounded individuals who seems to know lots about lots. Two of the three thought it seemed like a good buy. My opinion skewed the ratio to three out of four. The bid was placed; the stock was bought."

The Bid

"But I'm jumping ahead of myself. Here's the process. An excellent prospect has appeared on the sunny horizon via the Stock Watch list. You get a quote and find the bid for XYZ Corp. is $10 and the ask is $10.25. A major error many investors both seasoned and neophyte make is buying at what is known as the market or offer price. Don't! Check where the stock has been for the past week, concentrating on the spread for the last few days. Plan a bid near the bottom range of the spread."

"Isn't that both time consuming and cheap?" Peter asked.

"Wrong on both counts," returned Joan. "While the majority of people place a day order, meaning, as you'd suspect, that it expires at the end of the day, my bids are normally placed to lapse at the end of a month. This way, they're easier to keep track of, as I know they all terminate the same day. And, more important, my place remains reserved in the bidding queue. Normally, the bid is filled during this time frame.

"What does take time are the daily checks to see if the shares have been purchased and money must be sent to my broker. Or if a partial fill has occurred. For example, let's say an order is placed to buy 5,000 Mitel. An 'all or nothing' order is used, meaning that the transaction will not occur unless all 5,000 shares are bought. Without this restriction, any portion of the total might be purchased. The reason the order is placed with this restriction is to avoid a 'partial fill,' where, say, only 1,000 shares are purchased. In this scenario, the commissions normally increase dramatically as a percentage of the shares purchased. Once, on Newfoundland Capital, my fill on an order of 3,000 shares was only 100 at $1.81. The commission in this case tallied an outrageous 20 percent of my order.

"Tricky," said Raj. "So which do you normally choose, an order without restrictions or an 'all or nothing' placement?"

"It depends. If the stock is 'thinly' traded, which means that not many shares are bought and sold every day, an all or nothing order is my modus operandi. Otherwise, an order with no restrictions is used.

"Oh yes, one other little thing. Virtually all of my orders are placed when the markets are closed. This discipline works for me because it limits rash decision making. In fact, by placing my order soon after markets close, I have an earlier position in the order queue. And if I sleep badly on the bid, I can pull it first thing in the morning."

Playing Percentages

"As for Peter's second point, about being cheap, most investors and a large percentage of brokers are overanxious, jumping at the offer. Applying patience, I wait for the market to come back to me. Take the previous example. Odds are that my bid price would be less than the current $10 for XYZ Corp., which is even more distant, of course, from the $10.25 offer. Say $9.75 is my bid. On 1,000 shares, the 500 saved works out to $500, and that's better than a kick in the behind. Not so long ago, even more was earned if the deal was in American funds, given the old exchange rate.

"Here's a key rule: **Always think in percentage terms**. By buying at $9.75 instead of $10.25, the saving works out to around 5 percent. Now say the stock is held for three years before selling. When the position is sold, the same strategy is applied, economizing another 5 percent. That means a financial gain of 10 percent over three years or 3.3 percent per annum. Obviously numbers like this add up."

"Point made," said Peter. "But buys and sells can be missed altogether. That's bad business."

"That happens, but on 100 transactions, maybe 5 are missed. Certainly, though, a week or two passes before some deals transpire."

Peter was shaking his head in a dismissive fashion. "My ex-broker told me that placing a bid under the market is questionable because pros can exploit this strategy. For example, you lowball the bid. A negative development occurs, leading other investors to dump their stock on you. You're caught. Also, he mentioned that experienced market players can gamble that the price of the stock will go up, confident that your bid, and those of other suckers, will provide a floor to the stock price. Would you play poker with your cards face up? Absolutely not! Leave your orders on the books for as short a time as possible!"

"Those are valid points. There are certainly dangers to lowballing bids, especially in oscillating markets, but overall this is generally a sound strategy."

Peter shook his head. "This takes so much patience, Joan. I want to make a buy decision that sees it happen *now*. Sitting back and waiting is not my style."

"People like you, Peter, make money for people like me. So a heartfelt thanks from us to you, especially for financing that vacation to Amsterdam last spring."

"I'm not sure I like the sound of that," Peter mumbled.

"One other thing to show how percentages clarify thinking," Joan said. "Years ago, when the Dow Jones Index was at 5,000 points, a 100-point drop was huge, clicking in at 2 percent. But when the Dow's at 10,000, this same drop is only a 1 percent fall, and therefore only half as bad."

"I hear you," Tina said. "The other day on the financial news it was talking about how markets fluctuate way more today than 10 years ago, and 100-

point moves were specified as a barometer. But the report ignored the percentage element altogether. I don't like the sound of half-stories."

Order Ratios

"Well, maybe the sound of this will tickle your fancy. Here's an important strategic move. When my first investments were made, my funds were severely limited. Since I'm a percentage player, the idea of putting $1,000 in a stock, paying an 8 percent commission in, watching the stock double, and paying another 7 percent out, didn't appeal to me. This, of course, was in the days predating discount brokers and trading on the Internet, when higher commissions were the norm. So a minimum pledge of $2,000 was established on every investment. Then as my financial returns mounted, more funds were available. Taking into account that one stock often appealed to me more than another while both seemed like worthwhile investments, my system evolved so that every foray would be rated on a per-dollar basis. This weighting took a ratio format of 2:1, meaning twice as much money would be placed in companies with a more tantalizing risk/reward ratio. Later, as my cash reserves grew further, a 3:1 ratio became my standard. After the stellar returns of the past few years, a 4:1 ratio is the system's backbone. The rule: **Divide your funds into weighted investment packages**.

"One slight clarification here. The risk/reward ratio is more like a curve than a straight line. Any investment that seems exceedingly dangerous, even if it has tremendous reward potential, would receive the minimum, or close to the minimum, investment."

"That's a crazy system for someone like me," said Steve. "Maybe by the year 3000, I'll have enough funds to make some real investments. But now...."
"It does take time, Steve, but my method should shorten this wait."

Order Quantities

"Now for a tad more detail. One item most people don't ask about is the order quantity, which shows how many shares are being bid for and how many are offered. Orders are in board lots of 100. So in the scenario outlined before, say there are 120 bid and 850 offered, which means 12,000 shares at $10 and 85,000 shares at $10.25. This indicates more sellers than buyers at current levels and is another good reason to lowball the bid. Isn't this fun?"

"Is a lowball bid for stocks the same as throwing a lowball pitch in baseball?" asked Liam.

"Kind of, Liam, especially if the batter has an oh-two count and is digging in, ready to swing at just about anything. Now consider checking these quantities further by looking at the quantities behind the bid and offer. Perhaps at the $9.50 level, there are 25,000 board lots. If your bid was set at this level, the wait to buy would likely be long. Plus, there's a good chance that this quantity would form a price base for the stock, unless some of those orders were pulled. So, **before buying, check the order quantities**."

"So I buy the stock," said Steve. "Then what?"

"Then the 'settlement date' to pay is three days away. After, sit back, wait, and hope for appreciation."

"I like 'preciation," said Liam.

"A different type," corrected Peter. "This is the kind of appreciation where something goes up in value. Like the *Contra* portfolio. What's been happening there, anyhow?"

"Good question," responded Joan.

BOX SCORE INNING 7 — APRIL 13
TORONTO STOCK EXCHANGE

Stock	Purchase Price	Current Price	Initial Target
BUYS			
Bovar	0.95	0.70	4.63
Cinepiex	1.77	1.84	3.85
DomTex	7.50	5.85	16.63
FCA	2.21	1.61	10.75
Markborough	0.43	0.56	7.65
Noma	5.13	3.90	12.50
Princeton	0.29	0.40	1.05
Roman	1.20	1.20	2.85
HOLDS			
Breakwater	1.93	3.90	6.25
Gulf	3.95	9.80	13.50
Journey's End	2.01	3.81	7.25
LaidlawA	9.10	17.75	21.63
LaidlawG	14.25	18.20	21.50
Mitel	3.00	7.05	10.38
National Sea	5.94	6.30	21.50
Newf. Capital	1.81	5.50	9.25
Stelco	5.88	7.45	23.25
Trizec	17.91	30.70	40.25

NEW YORK STOCK EXCHANGE

Stock	Purchase Price	Current Price	Initial Target
BUYS			
Armco	4.63	3.88	11.63
Bethlehem	8.75	8.00	17.75
General Host	2.38	3.38	13.60
Hartmarx	4.63	6.63	18.38
InterTAN	5.75	3.88	9.63
Kaneb	3.25	3.88	15.63
Mesa	4.50	4.75	12.75
Navistar	31.17	9.63	61.25
Unisys	6.00	5.88	18.50
SELLS			
Genrad*	4.38	14.63	11.50
National Educ.*	4.13	14.63	14.38
HOLDS			
Cinc. Milacron*	10.93	18.13	22.50
Grubb & Ellis	2.55	9.00	14.25
NovaCare	6.50	12.13	18.50
Occid. Pete	17.50	22.75	32.50
Parker Drilling	4.75	8.125	9.25
R.J. Nabisco	31.95	30.63	86.50

*partially sold

"All right. Now let's have a look at a buy decision that appeared wrong for too long: the purchase of Dominion Textile at $7.50. As of January 15, the stock was sitting at $6.85, but it then gradually slid downwards. I tripled down at $6.30. This simply seemed like too good an opportunity to pass up. And it certainly fit my rule: **Buy when a stock has few friends**. Now, unfortunately, the company sits at $5.85. Oops."

"Looks like you blew it," stated Peter.

"It doesn't look very intelligent, but it's only been about a month since the buy. Remember, avoid getting trapped in short-term results. A year remains a relative pittance of time. Was anything done correctly on this one? The stock traded consistently higher than my mid-month bid. Dominion floated back, so I saved $0.35 a share, which worked out to $350. Would I have been smarter to wait until the $6 or $5.85 level? Absolutely, but unfortunately, my crystal ball was foggy yet again.

"Now, the rationale for the additional purchase of this stock was that the company had just reported nominal earnings in the previous quarter, as compared to a loss in the previous year. While sales were down, cash flow was up by a delightful 50 percent, and the debt-to-equity ratio had fallen from 50 percent to 43 percent. Plus—and here's where instinct comes in—if you've had a stock for a few years and the price has pretty well held its own, this is an excellent indicator that the company will turn around. This is because, and the rationale might sound a touch strange, survival begets survival. Once a company has worked through the initial stages of a comeback, it becomes simpler for the other pieces of the puzzle to fit into place. The question remains: 'When?'"

"How long will you wait, Joan? At my age, long-term is not a viable option."

"It's difficult to say, Mr. McCleary. Hope imagines a fast gain and a quick sale. Now the reality. Mitel, as noted, has been in the stable for over ten years. For some people, that's an inordinately long time, while at the far end of the spectrum, growth investors will hold virtually from cradle to grave."

"Any suggestions for Liam?" asked Tina.

"Well, my most recent purchase was made for the lad. Irwin Toy was the pick-up at $4.70. Look at the numbers for the past ten years, and notice how this one fits a magical annual pattern, making my target price of $7.20 simple to justify. This one has excellent potential to be kicked out by spring next year if history repeats itself."

IRWIN TOY

Year	1	2	3	4	5	6	7	8	9	10
High	$10.00	6.63	7.50	6.88	7.00	8.25	7.25	8.38	9.50	8.75
Low	$5.25	5.00	5.00	4.60	4.05	6.50	4.75	4.95	6.50	4.45

"Do they give owners toys?" squealed Liam.

"Some corporations do give their shareholders small gifts, but that is less and less common. About the best one can expect is a free lunch. Last week at the Cineplex annual general meeting, there were all kinds of fancy sandwiches. But being in gourmet mode, I downed a couple of hot dogs with popcorn and a Coke, while my pockets magically filled with licorice, chocolate bars, and other goodies that were being given away. I probably scarfed twenty bucks worth of food, plus a ton of smiles every time something was digested at their expense. I thought of it as a dividend."

"Our candy drawer always seemed emptier after you departed, Joan."

"Talk to your son-in-law about that, Mr. McCleary. I was simply his accomplice."

Peter pretended to concentrate on the game.

"Professional training," said Phillip.

"A lawyer's selective hearing."

"Now, listen to the sales in the past quarter. The final shake of Great Pacific was dispensed. Bought this long-term holding about seven years ago at $11.30, and the final allotment went out the door at $54.95. Rumours abounded that the majority owner, Jim Pattison, was planning on taking the firm private. But the gossip had been out there for so long that I discounted it. Unfortunately, a few months later, Pattison did pounce at a price in the $80s. I kicked myself a few times on that one.

"The other sale was Sears, and this one had a much shorter time span. Purchased two years ago at $7.13, it was sold at $13.20, a dandy move in less than two years. Later, it topped $20, but that's the nature of the game.

"On the real estate front, Grubb & Ellis finally moved. In the first quarter of the year, it was the number three gainer on the NYSE, up 111 percent. My patience was finally rewarded."

"Real estate was reviving," stated Peter. "The value of our house went sky-high and many popcorn parties were held to celebrate."

"Lots of butter, I hope," laughed Raj.

Bucky's voice was gaining in intensity. "The Blue Jays are bringing in Sprague as a pinch-hitter. He's been on the DL most of the season, nursing a recurring shoulder injury. Where's Brooks Robinson when you need him? Here comes the pitch. Sprague lashes the ball to left-centre field, and Larry Walker…Larry Walker makes a dazzling sliding catch! Larry Walker—former MVP, the first player in the National League since 1948 to record more than 400 total bases, only the third player in major league history to have 200 hits, 40 home runs, and 30 stolen bases in the same season—shines once again with his oft-overlooked defensive magic. What a play! Hard to believe he didn't win the Lou Marsh Trophy as Canada's outstanding athlete that season."

"A great, great ballplayer," agreed Tom. "Too bad the Expos were too cheap to keep him."

"No more time for Expo bashing, Tom, as our sponsors are ready to have their say."

Joan excused herself to use the facilities and grab another glass of wine. When she returned, everyone was studying the first box score she handed out. Phillip had a particularly studious glow on his face as he said, "It's fascinating, Joan, how many stocks have moved in the past year and a half. It's quite dramatic."

Joan smiled. "Keep watching, sports fans. More action ahead."

Rules
- Before buying, test your idea on people you respect
- Always think in percentage terms
- Divide your funds into weighted investment packages
- Before buying, check the order quantities
- Buy when a stock has few friends

Inning 8
The Set-Up Man

*Stocks do not sell for what they are worth,
but for what people think they are worth.*

—Garfield Drew

The Hold

"Tom, with the Mets leading 3-2, Guzman is coming to the mound for the Jays."

"He'll try to keep this one close, Bucky. If Juan has a decent inning and the Jays don't get at least a run in their half, it'll be interesting to see if Henke is thrown in without the lead. Who would have imagined that Tom Henke would come out of retirement and pitch again in the World Series? Here's one of the greatest, most underrated relievers in baseball, and one of the few athletes in any sport who retired at the top of his game, came back, and resumed playing at an all-star calibre."

"Other underrated greats, Tom?"

"For my money, Bucky, Dan Quisenberry. There's a guy who didn't get past the first ballot for the Hall of Fame and should probably be there. The voters don't know how to rate relievers yet. Joe Torre should be there. Dewey Evans—great arm, hit for power. And for my money, Pete Rose. Charlie Hustle played the game all out. If all the gamblers and carousers were eliminated from the Hall, it would be half empty. Baseball's a funny game, Bucky. A funny game."

"And voting for the Hall of Fame even funnier. Hey, Reggie Jackson got in on the first ballot! If that doesn't say something about hype, what does? Too much emphasis is placed on being on a winning team, but that takes twenty-five players. What about the poor schmuck who's a brilliant player in his own right but is surrounded by has-beens and never-wases? And stays in the same city because he's loyal to the fans? No credit is given there. Look at Dave Stieb."

"All good points, Bucky. All right. Ready to roll here. Top of the eighth. Guzman winds...it's a...."

"Now," began Joan, "be prepared to enter the world of mundane patience."

"No!" moaned Steve. "Action! Action!"

"Morocco said, 'In the gate of patience, there is not crowding.' Definitely not your gate, Steven."

"Relaxing isn't my strength," said Steve.

"Nor mine," said Peter.

"Tell us something we don't know," said Tina.

"A prime directive of my system is the not-so-simple act of waiting. The buy was made and here's the rule that comes from it: **...sit...relax...wait....** Remember how the target price was a minimum 50 percent higher than the buy price? And how sometimes the target is 400 to 500 percent or more away?" Almost everyone nodded as Joan continued, "That means that before the stock reaches the selling price, sitting tight is mandatory. Six months or a year is possible, but expecting a wait of years is more realistic. Best to put the stock away and check in periodically."

"What if major changes occur in the fundamentals of the company?" queried Phillip.

"Here's the rule that applies: **Review stocks you own every three months, concentrating on their debt**. As some stock prices are beaten up because of excessive debt, watch to make certain that management has it under control."

"Depending on how many stocks are in your portfolio, this can take a fair bit of time," Tina noted.

"True," agreed Joan. "For me, twenty-five stocks is the most I feel that I can handle well. Plus, this number gives me excellent diversification. Although having only fifteen companies with excellent potential is preferable to owning twenty-five companies of which fifteen are excellent and ten are mediocre."

"How many stocks would you recommend for someone like me?" asked Phillip.

"That's a tough question, and the answer depends on your assets. The more equity you have, the more feasible buying additional stocks becomes. But remember the old rule: greater diversification equals lower returns."

"Five to ten stocks is enough for me," concluded Peter. "I want to go with my best shots. Better quality, easier to watch, more time for each. Besides, Joan, couldn't it get to the point where all twenty-five of your stocks are spinning their wheels?" Peter appeared proud, as if he finally had Joan cornered.

"Possibly, but it's never happened. Certainly, there are a few in the portfolio that sit. But then, when it feels like everyone has forgotten about them, off they trundle. Suddenly, their sell targets get bypassed."

Peter started fidgeting with a paper clip, since Phillip had taken control of the remote. Finally he blurted, "Okay, in the meantime, what do you do?"

Ongoing Research

"Remember the Stock Watch list?" responded Joan. "At a minimum of every three months, I review each of them to get a better feel for what's happening out there, while hoping that a buy pops into focus. Checking on the Net is quite effective, and is especially ideal when the company's been tracked for a number of years and appears to be improving with only a nominal movement in the stock price. Don't confuse this with the three-month look-see where every stock on the TSX and American stock exchanges is checked for their one- and ten-year price ranges."

"That sounds positively boring," said Steve with a yawn.

"Boring can be good. Remember, out-of-favour stocks usually have a volatile past. When the excitement subsides, and the public and institutions ignore the company, that's often the best time for contrarians to move. Then wait for the company to be rediscovered."

"Makes sense to me," said Phillip. "More companies have been reborn in my lifetime than I can think of: Chrysler, Navistar, Apple...."

"Okay, Dad. We get the idea."

"Sounds like the system repeats itself somewhat," said Peter.

"In a sense, it does. You can mark yearly dates for the analytical process, although that rigidity isn't my idea of a good time. I used to do many of my initial scans on airplanes, going line by line through the stock pages to pass a few hours. Now, fast filters via the Internet are the ticket and it is so much quicker. The key is to maintain discipline and stick to the system."

"My, you've changed, Joan. Not the insecure young woman who used to hang her hat here."

"I'll take that as a compliment, Mr. McCleary. Now take a gander at the ongoing results. This data is given to all clients to help them draw their own conclusions about whether the system works for them. Happy viewing."

BOX SCORE INNING 8 — July 13
TORONTO STOCK EXCHANGE

Stock	Purchase Price	Current Price	Initial Target
BUYS			
Bovar	0.95	0.75	4.63
Cinepiex	1.77	2.48	3.85
Denison	0.36	0.36	1.45
DomTex	7.50	8.35	16.63
FCA	2.21	2.62	10.75
Irwin	4.70	5.30	7.20
Noma	5.13	4.70	12.50
Princeton	0.29	0.33	1.05
Roman	1.20	1.40	2.85
HOLDS			
Breakwater	1.93	5.10	6.25
Cambridge*	100.00	24.50	185.00
Gulf	3.95	12.05	13.50
Journey's End	2.01	5.25	7.25
LaidlawA	9.10	23.00	21.63
Mitel	3.00	8.75	10.38
National Sea	5.94	8.00	21.50
Newf. Capital	1.81	5.65	9.25
Stelco	5.88	11.90	23.25
Trizec	17.91	29.75	40.25

NEW YORK STOCK EXCHANGE

Stock	Purchase Price	Current Price	Initial Target
BUYS			
Armco	4.63	4.06	11.63
Bethlehem	8.75	10.63	17.75
General Host	2.38	4.44	13.60
Hartmarx	4.63	7.50	18.38
InterTAN	5.75	3.75	9.63
Kaneb	3.25	3.88	15.63
Mesa	4.50	6.00	12.75
Unisys	6.00	8.50	18.50
SELLS			
Cinc. Milacron*	10.93	26.69	22.50
Grubb & Ellis	2.55	16.94	14.25
HOLDS			
Navistar	9.38	20.38	44.38
NovaCare	6.50	14.31	18.50
Occid. Pete	17.50	25.13	32.50
R.J. Nabisco	31.95	32.25	86.50

*partially sold

Liam turned to Joan and said, "What's next? Even though I've been quiet, with my eyes closed a bit, my ears are open."

"All right," Joan said. "Let's apply my hold strategy to the current portfolio. Notice how stocks are watched in a more relaxed manner after they are purchased. Take a look at Grubb & Ellis. For almost five years, it hardly budged from the purchase price. Some investors certainly got jittery and dumped the company, taking their losses. But I hung in there, resolute to the core. Perhaps one of my advantages was that local newspapers didn't cover the stock because of its low trading volumes. This meant that I only viewed it once a month or so. In a roundabout way, patience was automatically enforced: out of sight, out of mind. Then, strikingly, for the first six months of the year, Grubb was the number one gainer on New York, up 280.6 percent. So 78 percent of my position was sold from $14.39 to $16.00.

"Here's another interesting tidbit. When the final buy in Grubb was recorded, it weighted out to 3.27 percent of the portfolio. The huge price increase meant that the sales worked out to the equivalent of 10 percent of the portfolio holdings. Still, 22 percent of the original position remained as additional gravy, which demonstrates how radically weightings in a portfolio can change in a short time frame, especially when stocks purchased at a low price jump in an updraft.

"Parker Drilling was also sold. That company had also slumbered, and then during the previous six months, it had kick-started and flown past the target. The complete holding sold at $12.50, a long way above the purchase value of $4.75.

"Buy...hold...buy...hold...relax...breathe."

The Fool's Game of Stop Losses

"Is that your mantra, Auntie Joan? My parents have mantras but they won't tell me what they are."

"Maybe, Liam. Many people worry if a stock doesn't move for a couple of years, and they tend to panic, especially if a downturn occurs immediately after they buy it. Many experts suggest that if shares fall 10 percent from the purchase price, the stock should automatically be dumped. Often, a 'stop loss' is recommended. This means that if a stock sinks to a specified value, it's automatically jettisoned at the best available price. The purpose of this is to insure against a further downslide. Label this 'The Fool's Game.'"

"Because the stock dips and is nabbed from the portfolio before it can bungee back?"

"Precisely, Raj."

"But Joan, the momentum and eroding fundamentals that push a stock down often make it slide further. My thought would be to cut losses and run," said Peter.

"That's a good point, but my belief is that dumping stocks works more against investors than for them. I suggest making a 'mental stop loss,' meaning that if a stock is beaten down, consider whether it should be sold.

"There's another prime reason at work here: sophisticated traders pick off stops. On trendless days, these guys often go about knocking out stop losses and momentum buy orders above the market price. They do this by selling stock to drive the price down, triggering the stop losses, and then buying back the shares. Then they continue buying, sending the price up and triggering the buy orders, at which point they unload their shares. An easy way to make money if the market has no direction! The rule: **Never use stop losses**. Leave this one to the pros.

"My method here is definitely contrarian. If the stock price falls below my purchase price, once it stabilizes, my reaction is to see if it should be repurchased. The logic here is simple: If the firm was a good buy at $10, then it should be a better buy at $8."

"Joan, that's the methodology I applied to Bre-X," said Phillip. "The results were obviously not good. This strategy, given my experience, is psychologically dangerous. It prevents the investor from seeing that fundamentals in the company have deteriorated and creates a false confidence that past decisions were correct."

"The voice of bad experience speaks," said Joan. "Do not go in blindly, but carefully re-evaluate the situation. A primary reason I don't buy stocks right after their initial fall is that information is often hidden from the general public, of which I am definitely a part. But if you're patient, the vital information should eventually become more evident. Just keep in mind the adage, 'It can't get any cheaper'—this can be filled with false promise. So **If a stock sinks, consider averaging down**. I used this methodology on Mitel, which was partially spun out this quarter. That hold has been one long story. Quite a different affair than National Education Corporation, which received a takeover offer this past quarter and saw the final portion divested at $21. NEC is going into my Stock Hall of Fame."

Takeovers

"Here's one more thing to remember: When tendering on a takeover, there are no commissions. So when one is announced on one of my positions, I virtually always tender to the offer rather than selling earlier. Selling earlier can be negative in two ways. First, the commission applies, and second, the price is usually slightly below the takeover value. For example, with NEC, it would have been easy to sell at $20.63 in the week before the deal was finalized. But this would have been over 1.75 percent less than the buyout price. Tally in a commission and then figure what this adds up to over a year's time; effectively, the additional returns are at plump rates of interest!"

"That's a rule, then, isn't it?" asked Raj. "**Wait to tender on a takeover**."

"Exactly," responded Joan.

"But the downside is the deal could fall through," Peter uttered. "That would be a major ouch!"

"In my experience, this is almost always a risk worth taking. It's worth observing that *Contra* stocks have had takeovers for sixteen straight years. Given that the number of companies owned at any one time normally varies from fifteen to twenty-five, this percentage is staggering. Takeovers have been a major reason for the excellent financial returns."

"Impressive," said Phillip.

"All right, back to buys. Denison Mines this time. I'd followed this company for years as it underwent major difficulties. They were a huge uranium explorer in Northern Ontario and almost went bankrupt when they lost their major client and had to deal with the mine's cleanup costs. A new uranium play is expected to come on line, and a number of other drilling possibilities are in the works. Finally, it appears that enough positive moves are being made that it's safe to jump in. They seem to be turning the corner."

"Hopefully not the proverbial corner," said Phillip.

"We'll see," said Joan.

"One more question," Peter said, combing his fingers through his few strands of hair yet again, like a Brink's guard protecting the payroll. "The question of re-examining stocks you own. Any positions under a keen microscope?"

"Bovar," said Joan. "It was bought at $0.95 and is now down to $0.75 with a good possibility that it might head lower and be a potential tax loss situation."

"And that ends the inning!" Tom's voice said, chillingly for Blue Jays fans. "The New York Mets are an inning away from being world champions and will send Gesner, Brown, and Silver to the plate in the top of the ninth."

RULES
- ...sit...relax...wait....
- Review stocks you own every three months, concentrating on their debt
- Never use stop losses
- If a stock sinks, consider averaging down
- Wait to tender on a takeover

Inning 9
The Closer

There are two fools in every market; one asks too little, one asks too much.
—Russian proverb

Hunting the Sell Target

"Selling elicits a spectrum of emotions," began Joan. "Sometimes an exceptionally good sale is like hitting a grand slam. Other times, it's less clear and more like a hit-and-run play. Wait on first, get a lead, and run like hell, knowing the batter's swinging away, then slide into second not knowing if you're safe or out. Then, if the stock keeps moving up after the sale, it feels like one runner's safe at second but the batter is out at first."

"Should I laugh or cry or both?" asked Raj.

"That depends," said Joan. "Look at GenRad. I bought it at $4.38 and sold it as high as $21.63. Later, it climbed to almost $35. Laugh? Cry? Move on? But my classic was Geac Computer, which I purchased at $1.35 and sold in the teens. That became a $60 stock. Those gains could have been mine!"

"I know the feeling," said Peter. "Sometimes I'm certain my client's obviously guilty, but there isn't enough evidence for a conviction. So we plead 'not guilty,' win the case, and he gets off scot-free. Part of me feels miserable knowing that a murderer is back on the street, but another part feels like a schoolboy who got kissed by the prettiest girl in the class."

"Here's the rule: **Reanalyze but don't ulcerate over your sales**."

"Is that a word?" Raj wondered. Joan ignored him.

"Can I share a story?" asked Phillip. "It might shed some light on the sell decision. This one harkens back to the market crash in '87. The day after the tumble, I called up a buddy of mine from my Halifax days, and we moseyed for lunch at one of the restaurants the financial people frequent. Sitting at the next table was this woman talking about how she sold out two days before the crash. Part of me was impressed, but another part thought she might be full of cow pucky. Years later, it occurred to me that even if she was telling the truth, the logical next question was, 'When did you buy in?' Because if her purchases were recent, then about 5 percent would have been lost because of commissions in those full-discount broker days. This is one of those stories without a conclusion, but it made me realize how sell decisions relate closely with the timing of buy decisions, especially in a bear market."

Staging the Sell

"Thanks, Phillip, you've given me a good intro to my next point. Remember talking about placing the buy bid, going under the offer, and even the current bid price? On the sell side, the exact same procedure applies. The goal is to scratch every additional cent and percentage point possible from the sale.

"To review, examine the price for the preceding week to see if an extra quarter or half a point can be jimmied. Now remember, simply because a stock hits its target doesn't mean the moment to sell has arrived. Odds are a year or two or five will have passed since the purchase, and during that period the fundamentals of the company, industry, and economy have probably changed. Reanalyze and see if a higher target price might be in order, but remember that when the stock was purchased, you set the target for a good reason. Don't go all mushy and fall in love with the company because it has done well. Remain analytical and don't forget that the further up the stock has moved, the farther it has to fall. My rule, although this one isn't completely steadfast: **Sell at least 50 percent of the stock near the target**. At the same time, outline a second, and preferably a third, target for the price. Then, after the initial sale, keep watching the price. Try not to get sucked into the minutiae of everyday pricing.

"You'll often hear the advice: Let your profits run and cut your losses. This is a good theory, but a difficult practice. Being right is not easy, except in hindsight. Being in the ballpark is the best one can normally expect. That's why people say things like, 'Gee, if only I'd waited to sell my Nortel," and then six months later, it's, 'Gee, if only I'd sold my Nortel.'"

"Joan, this makes sense to me, although at my age, it's a bit like teaching an old dog new tricks. But why not? Better to keep learning and do this as a hobby than curl up and die like the majority of my cronies."

"So what do we do while we're waiting, Joan?" asked Peter.

"First, prepare to rerun the rules and apply them as you would when buying a stock. See how the company has grown or regressed. Re-examine debt levels, price/earnings, and other ratios. Check for insider trading, et cetera, et cetera."

"All right," Steve said. "My stock has moved. It's at the sell target. I re-examine my rationale for the purchase, I double check the fundamentals, and then I decide to sell. Exit stage right."

"Beautiful," said Joan, applauding. "So easy, I'm going to add on a whole other level of signs to watch for when making stock transactions."

Sell Signals

"Be wary of excessive executive compensation—mega-salaries, tons of bonuses, and stock options galore. On the same page, if the CEO is highly dictatorial, you should start asking questions. When Gulf Resources decided to move their head office to Denver, it appeared to me that the move wouldn't benefit anyone but their number one guy, who preferred Colorado to Calgary.

"Also beware of nepotism. When I purchased Noma, the president's daughter was quickly moving her way through the ranks. In fact, during the time this stock was held, she became the head honcho. Does this worry me? Not in this case, as she seems very capable. But it can definitely be dangerous territory.

"Other danger signals include ongoing difficulties with labour and excessive litigation. Many corporations are unnecessarily litigious, and while their lawyers prosper, shareholders suffer. Of course, as I mentioned before, these sell signals are also reasons to avoid buying.

"Hey, lawyers can use the work," moaned Peter.

"As far as I'm concerned," Joan argued, "the corporate population is way too quick to pull the legal chain. It costs Joe and Jane Investor far too much money." Peter nodded begrudgingly. "If possible, it's worthwhile to attend the shareholders' meeting. At the annual general meeting, try to get a better understanding of the key people in the company. Note whether the CEO seems forthright or evasive in his responses to questions. Evasiveness should raise alarm bells in your head.

"Also check the notes to the financial statements. If they seem particularly long or complicated, it can be dangerous. Plus, if the corporate structure seems overly complex and constant tax questions are lurking, beware."

"If we do everything you're suggesting, there won't be any time to invest in the market!" Steve complained.

"Scared? A few more then. Be wary of companies that make deal after deal, or enter all kinds of fields not related to their main focus. Also, be skeptical of firms that promise suspiciously high returns."

Phillip interrupted. "Your suggestions aren't difficult to understand, but there are so many different areas and rules to follow."

"Maybe this will help." Joan dug into her briefcase once more. "Though this is an incomplete list, there's more than enough here to stimulate your thinking."

"Everything in there including the kitchen sink?" said Tina.

"Just about," said Joan.

SAMPLE CHECKLIST — BUYING AND SELLING STOCK

POSITIVE   NEGATIVE   DON'T KNOW

1. Debt Levels
2. Cash Flow
3. Book Value
4. Management
5. Insider Trading
6. Sales Growth
7. Earnings per Share
8. Price/Earnings
9. Demographics
10. Competitors
11. R & D Expenditures
12. Legal Liabilities
13. Complex Finances
14. Numerous Complex Notes
15. Dividends
16. Historical Price
17. Shares Outstanding
18. Stock Volumes
19. Order Quantities
20. Order Ratio
21. Good Relations with Employees

"That's twenty-one things to look for," said Joan. "Blackjack! Enough to keep you all thinking."

Phillip nodded. "What ratio of positives to negatives means buy or don't buy, sell or don't sell?"

"That's a difficult question," Joan responded. "Quite frankly, there's no absolute in my mind. This isn't a precise science. But to get it as precise as possible: **Re-evaluate the stock carefully when considering a sale**.

"One more thing. After the sell trigger is pulled, keep the company in the back of your mind. Glance periodically to see what it does. Don't be disappointed if it keeps going up and moan about what might have been. That will only drive you crazy. But concentrate on whether your sale was the right move or a similar situation should be handled differently next time. So to help keep you on track, here's another portfolio."

BOX SCORE INNING 9 — OCTOBER 12
TORONTO STOCK EXCHANGE

Stock	Purchase Price	Current Price	Initial Target
BUYS			
Bovar	0.95	0.82	4.63
Cinepiex	1.77	2.01	3.85
Denison	0.36	0.39	1.45
FCA	2.21	3.00	10.75
Irwin	4.70	5.55	7.20
Noma	5.13	5.25	12.50
Princeton	0.29	0.33	1.05
Roman	1.20	1.90	2.85
SELLS			
Breakwater*	1.93	7.70	6.25
Journey's End*	2.01	11.00	7.25
Mitel	3.00	11.80	10.38
HOLDS			
Cambridge*	100.00	150.00	185.00
DomTex	7.50	12.00	16.63
Gulf	3.95	12.20	13.50
Laidlaw	9.10	20.80	21.63
National Sea	5.94	7.50	21.50
Newf. Capital	1.81	8.05	9.25
Stelco	5.88	11.00	23.25
Trizec	17.91	36.30	40.25

NEW YORK STOCK EXCHANGE

Stock	Purchase Price	Current Price	Initial Target
BUYS			
Armco	4.63	5.82	11.63
Bethlehem	8.75	10.38	17.75
General Host	2.38	3.31	13.60
Hartmarx	4.63	8.31	18.38
InterTAN	5.75	5.63	9.63
Kaneb	3.25	5.81	15.63
SELLS			
Grubb & Ellis	2.55	15.00	14.25
HOLDS			
Navistar	9.38	28.13	44.38
NovaCare	6.50	17.31	18.50
Occid. Pete	17.50	28.75	32.50
Pioneer **	4.50	42.13	12.75
R.J. Nabisco	31.95	33.50	86.50
Unisys	6.00	15.25	18.50

*partially sold
** previously Mesa Corp.

"Five stocks exited the portfolio—Cincinnati Milacron, Breakwater, Grubb & Ellis, Journey's End, and Mitel—with each one giving a different picture of why stocks are sold. Now, in the last four cases, all were partially kept. This exemplifies the sell strategy of playing both sides of the fence, so to speak: ditching part of a stock when near the target price, while hoping that the value will continue to run. With Cincinnati Milacron, a partial sell had previously been made."

"So this is done all the time?" asked Raj.

"Quite often, but not always. In an up market, forward momentum can give quite the helping hand, regardless of corporate fundamentals. But my major focus remains on the company.

"More Grubb was sold at $16. Remember, 78 percent of the position was sold at $14.38. It was questionable whether the stock had much potential left after the huge burst it had in the early part of the year. Certainly, all the right moves had been made. On an annual basis, revenues were up 19 percent, while net income soared from $2.1 million to $19 million. And here's a beauty: Proceeds from their two stock sales had completely eliminated long-term debt, which we know drastically reduces an investor's risk. Plus, unprofitable offices had been closed and some new initiatives started, including alliances with 11 independent brokers in 14 regions. So, with all this good stuff happening, it was time to take my leave.

"Cincinnati Milacron was also spun out on good news. Sales had increased by 50 percent in three years, and book value had almost tripled from $4.50. This type of performance was well-rewarded in the market, as the stock had moved to $27.50 from $18.13 in less than six months."

"That seems counterproductive to me," said Tina. "Wouldn't this be the ideal time to milk profits? Things get good, you desert the party."

"I admit I sometimes bail out too early. But don't forget, I'm not selling on the initial good news. My purchases were made on positive accomplishments that weren't yet recognized by the majority of the investing public. In the cases of Cincinnati and Grubb, the proof is in the pudding."

"Is that because people read about the positive developments in the newspaper or on the Internet?" asked Tina.

"Absolutely. Remember to be circumspect, though. When news about a corporation seems too good, it probably is. When stock market happiness hits the front pages of major newspapers, smart investors watch for an overbought market. For many smart investors, this signifies the moment to take their money and run."

"Newspapers are funny, Joan," offered Phillip. "The pundits always have a rationale, every single day, for the market's movement. 'Dow up 32 points because of interest rate fears.' 'TSX down 32 because of interest rate fears.' Seems bogus to me."

"Journalists have pages to fill. They quote today's 'facts.' As an investor, watch for the news behind the headlines. Keep a clear head to understand the logic of real cause and real effect.

"Back to where we were. Here are two other examples of partial sells and an excitable public: Breakwater Resources and Journey's End. Neither had done anything for years except slip downward. Now, as people recognized how both companies had cut debt and improved operations significantly, the bandwagon effect took over. Fortunately, I was ahead of it.

"Breakwater was sold between $6.40 and $6.90, a far cry from our purchase price of $1.93 less than a year before. And Journey's End, which had been parked at around $2.25, was partially sold at $7.45. Had these companies improved that much in less than a year? I think not, but people's perceptions of them had."

"Now, surely you weren't selling them at the bid price."

"Definitely not, Phillip" confirmed Joan. "And in one case it cost me big time. Breakwater left the stable in two parts. The first was on the way up where 40 percent of my position went between $6.40 and $6.50. Then the stock careened up to $9.50, and if I had been smarter, I would have sold more, but $12 seemed close at hand. On the fall, I offered 30 percent of my original position at $6.90, but only 3 percent was picked up. Now I wish I had sold the whole mittful at the bid of $6.85. With 57 percent left, the stock is worth less than one-third of the high. But that's the nature of the game."

"Next time out, Joan, I'll buy dinner. We'll cry together in our milk."

"Since you're buying, cognac would be preferable, Peter. But this is precisely the reason to have a diversified portfolio. Though I didn't make as much as I'd hoped to on Breakwater, my total gains for the year were still over 50 percent. Remember, receiving the best price on any transaction is rare. More often than not, stocks continue upward. It's all a part of the game. Don't get too upset. The important measurement is your overall numbers.

"Now, one last note before moving on. From the last quarter to this one, not one stock was purchased. With markets at record levels and the December tax loss selling season not very far away, it seemed best to sit back and practice patience yet again."

Meanwhile, Smith laced a hit. The umpires moved to their respective positions to cover the play. Svabenicky fielded the ball and threw it hard to second. The tag. The ump signalled out. Johnson scooted from the dugout and went jaw-to-jaw with the ump, like two cocks in a ring. After a few minutes, and two commercials, the theatre was played out. Ossea moved from the batting circle to the plate. A pitching change was called. The lefty, Petzall, was brought to the mound. Vercoe, the righty, was still warming up in the bullpen. Both looked ready.

Rules

- Reanalyze but don't ulcerate over your sales
- Sell at least 50 percent of the stock near the target
- Re-evaluate the stock carefully when considering a sale

Inning 10
Any Buddy's Game

The less a man knows about the past and the present,
the more insecure must be his judgment of the future.

—Sigmund Freud

"Tom, this has been one incredible game. You hate to see it end with a loser. Excellent pitching backed by tight defence. Some clutch hitting. And now extra innings. What more could one hope for?" asked Bucky.

"It's all here today. That was one beautiful piece of hitting by Ossea to tie this game. But the only statistic that really matters is the winner. Sports is harsh that way. Remember the 1960 Pirates-Yankees series. Hard to debate who was the better team there. The awesome Yankees blew out the Pirates in three games. But the champions were the team from Pittsburgh on Bill Mazeroski's homer, and he has been a hero ever since. Wouldn't know anyone else in the Series hit a tater."

"Maz sure smacked the snot out of that ball, didn't he?"

"Sure did. All right. Top half of the tenth and the Blue Jays have Henke on the mound. What a magical finish if he's the winner, pitching in his ninth play-off game. Proctor and Olson continue to warm in the pen."

"No reason to save anybody. Lots of time in the off-season to rest," said Bucky.

"Baudriller leads off as a pinch-hitter. Henke is ready. He winds, the pitch...."

"Maybe our concentration should be on the game," said Joan.

"Could take another six innings," said Phillip. "It's important to finish what we started. The ballplayers will finish what they started. We'll cheer. Everyone will go home."

"Yup," said Steve. "And this is from the number one fan here."

Taxing Planning

"Okay, then. There are two measurements to consider when playing the market: before-tax and after-tax returns. The latter is the one that counts and must be considered relative to after-tax returns on other investments. This is ultimately the final score. Here's an example that compares the difference between returns before and after tax. Two people buy stock A on January 1."

"Aren't the markets closed on New Year's Day?" queried Peter. "My hangover is always so bad there's no way I could work."

"Spoken like a true lawyer. On January 2 then. Both people buy the same stock on January 2, 2001. The total outgo after commissions is $10,000. On December 31, both stocks are up 50 percent. Person one, let's call him Impatient Peter, sells stock A and buys stock C. Person two, call him Precocious Liam, holds.

"Year two. Both stocks A and C go up 50 percent. On December 15, Peter sells, needing money for Christmas presents. Liam sells after New Year's to buy some stereo equipment and a TV during the January sales. What are both of their returns?"

"That's easy," said Peter. "If all three stocks returned 50 percent each year, then everyone's even-Steven. Like this baseball game."

"No they're not, dear. Liam's trouncing you. Hats off to you, but at the end of the day, it wasn't even close," Tina smiled.

"Well, you're both right," said Joan, "because this is another of those percentage games to watch for. The before-tax before-commission return of both father and son was 50 percent, but this only tells half the story. In fact, Liam beats Peter hands down. As Tina said, Peter blew some money, because in year three, he'll have to pay tax on the gains for the previous two years, based on his marginal tax rate. Hypothetically, that could be zero, but depending on where he lives, it could be 20 or 30 percent or more."

"This is tricky," said Steve.

Tax Deferral

Joan agreed. "Now, Peter was at least semi-smart the first year. Since he sold the stock December 31, the three-day settlement rule kicked the gain into the following year for tax purposes. But in year two, by selling mid-December instead of waiting a couple more weeks, he triggered the tax payment for the following year. Liam deferred, holding off the tax woman for another year by waiting to sell until January. This move allowed him to not only make interest on the money deferred in the following year but also earn money on this gain ad infinitum. The rule: **Defer taxes where possible**.

"Now, Liam pushed even further ahead because Peter would also have paid commissions on his additional purchase and sale. Assuming the rate is 0.5 percent in and the same out, Peter lost another significant percentage."

"Your son is killing you, old man," Tina laughed.

Peter shrugged. "That's why I wanted children. To support me."

Capital Gains

"How does the tax advantage for capital gains work?" said Phillip. "This has always confused me."

"Good question. It's obvious where Liam acquires his financial wisdom. Geographically, the numbers vary from locale to locale, and often from one year to the next, depending on the government in power. So my best advice is to stay on top of current regulations. But let me give you an example of how this works. Let's say you earned $10,000 when National Education was sold. Now, imagine you're in the 50 percent tax bracket."

"Wishful thinking," interjected Steve.

"If capital gains are taxed on only 75 percent of profits, as they are in certain jurisdictions, then the payment would be on 50 percent of $7,500, which is $3,750, leaving $6,250 in your pocket. If you'd earned this money as interest income, where the tax is 50 percent, then $5,000 would be left in your pocket. Stock earnings leave you better off by $1,250."

"And not only would that additional money be in my bank account," said Peter, "but future earnings would stream from it. Even at only 10 percent a year, that would give me another $125 before taxes, plus the earnings on that, et cetera."

"Great Caesar's ghost, Peter is catching on. Liam might have a little competition," said Raj.

The Importance of Dividends

Joan continued. "So, as capital gains are taxed at a preferential rate, so are dividends. This means that a 5 percent return from bonds and a 5 percent return from a stock dividend are not equal. The latter return is higher because of the lower taxation rate. As a general rule, the relative yield of dividends to interest-bearing alternatives can be grossed up 33 percent in today's taxation climate. This means a dollar earned in dividends is approximately equivalent to

$1.33 in interest income, given the highest marginal tax bracket. So here's the rule: **Buying dividend-paying stocks is a definitive advantage**. Plus, and if you only take one thing with you tonight this should be the one—"

"Again," Peter interrupted.

"—Even if an investment mistake occurs and the stock takes a long time to turn around, the dividend stream usually still arrives on a quarterly basis. Some advisors even argue that the investment value of a common stock equals the value of all its future dividends. This leads into the concept of present worth versus future worth."

"Now I'm lost again. Present worth?" asked Steve.

"This is important during inflationary periods. Say a $10 stock pays a $1 dividend. The dividend yield is therefore 10 percent. A year later, the stock and dividend are exactly the same, but inflation has been 10 percent. In effect, the buying power of the money received has shrunk 10 percent. That buck will only get you nine-tenths of the soft drink it would have bought last year. Therefore, the present worth of the dollar is greater than the future worth of the dollar."

"Doesn't that future dividend idea also take into account the growth in the stock price?" asked Peter.

"Indeed it does. I'm impressed. In fact, for purposes of this equation, adding dividends and the stock growth together makes good sense. From this, you can extrapolate the perceived future value of the stock and guesstimate where it might be in five years."

"That seems impossible," said Phillip.

"It is difficult," agreed Joan. "But another thought for you to consider."

"My brain is going to explode," Steve complained.

"All this knowledge, and if the Mets lose the Series...."

"Go on, Joan, and quickly," Raj grinned. "I don't want to miss that."

IRAs and RRSPs

"One of the best ways to save money is with IRAs in the States and RRSPs in Canada. Although the governments are constantly toying with the maximum percentages and totals to invest here, the principle remains the same: Money in some IRAs and RRSPs can accumulate tax free, which means the full proceeds of money earned on these investments can accrue and be reinvested without any of it leaving your hands. This is why many people prefer to keep their stocks in this arena.

"Depending on the investment plan you choose, the money might be taxed when it's withdrawn. Still, the tax advantages here are dramatic. First, income is earned on money that would otherwise have disappeared into government coffers. Second, your tax bracket is likely to be reduced during the retirement years, so the money pulled from the plan is taxed at a lower rate."

"The money I placed in RRSPs was always at a guaranteed rate of interest," said Phillip. "I didn't want to risk blowing my retirement savings."

"That's the flip side," replied Joan. "As I mentioned before, higher returns are virtually always associated with higher risk. Personally, I also use my RRSP for fixed-term investments, which guarantee a set interest rate. I could have accumulated way more money if I had invested my stock money in the market. But, as we discussed, when you're older you need to exercise more caution with investments."

"Wait a second," said Raj. "The government giving a free lunch? I don't get it."

"There are still taxes, Raj. But they are deferred. So it's not exactly a free lunch but definitely worth an appetizer or two, with some toxic beverages to boot."

Tax Loss Selling

"Now, I've already brought this up, but it's important to be perfectly clear on it. Hopefully, lots of profits have come your way because of your magnificent stock picking. Still, some losers are in the portfolio, and they don't appear to be going anywhere. Sell them and subtract the losses from your gains. What it comes down to is paying less tax."

"I've done that a few times," said Peter. "Last year I made about $18,000 on three stocks. One loss totalled $14,000, so I sold the stock, writing it off for a slimmer capital gain of $4,000."

Income Splitting

"Exactly," said Joan, "The next tax technique is income splitting. This method works when there is a disparity in earnings between spouses. The object is to have the lower-earning partner record as many of the gains as possible in cases where income can be applied to either partner. This means the total gains will be taxed at a lower rate, which leaves the team with more money in their collective pocket."

"Maybe all this will make 'Tax Freedom Day' fall earlier in the year," Tina mused.

"Tax Freedom Day?" asked Steve. "For me, every day has been Tax Freedom Day."

Tina explained. "The idea is that until a certain date of the year, usually sometime in May or June, all of the average person's income goes to the government. After that, the rest stays in your pocket."

"May or June? Yikes! You're saying that almost half my year is spent working for the government?"

"You got it, Raj," responded Tina. "Think about Liam's situation. Because of the huge debt load governments rang up, he was born in debt to the tune of about $20,000. Effectively that's money our generation, and our parents' generation, stole from him—the modern version of indentureship."

"Ugly. Another reason for Raj and me not to have kids."

"Well, by learning a bit more and following the obvious rule—**do tax planning**—maybe you'll make enough money for the restaurant to sponsor a kids' baseball team.

"Now, when you're scanning over the next portfolio update, cast your glance back to some old ones to see how the numbers have changed. This is like a game. Rooting for the Blue Jays, I know it's not my game to win or lose. With stocks, my own record's at stake."

BOX SCORE INNING 10 — JANUARY 18
TORONTO STOCK EXCHANGE

Stock	Purchase Price	Current Price	Initial Target
BUYS			
Bovar	0.95	0.63	4.63
Cinepiex	1.77	1.95	3.85
Denison	0.36	0.34	1.45
FCA	2.21	3.00	10.75
Noma	5.13	5.15	12.50
Princeton	0.29	0.18	1.05
Semi-Tech	1.24	0.90	9.35
Spar Aero	8.35	9.75	16.15
SELLS			
Mitel*	3.00	11.10	10.38
UniHost*	2.01	9.25	7.25
HOLDS			
Breakwater*	1.93	2.95	6.25
Cambridge*	100.00	140.00	185.00
Gulf	3.95	8.65	13.50
Irwin	4.70	5.40	7.20
Laidlaw	9.10	20.55	21.63
National Sea	5.94	8.00	21.50
Newf. Capital	1.81	9.05	9.25
Roman	1.20	2.05	2.85
Stelco	5.88	10.10	23.25
Trizec	17.91	34.00	40.25

NEW YORK STOCK EXCHANGE

Stock	Purchase Price	Current Price	Initial Target
BUYS			
Armco	4.63	4.88	11.63
Bethlehem	8.75	8.75	17.75
Farah	5.06	5.25	8.75
Fleming	15.11	15.63	32.75
Hartmarx	4.63	7.31	18.38
Hecla	4.81	4.94	11.75
InterTAN	5.75	5.38	9.63
Kaneb	3.25	5.06	15.63
HOLDS			
Navistar	9.38	25.19	44.38
NovaCare	6.50	13.19	18.50
Occid. Pete	17.50	27.31	32.50
Pioneer	31.68	24.00	84.50
R.J. Nabisco	31.95	36.38	86.50
Unisys	6.00	15.88	18.50

*partially sold

"Looking at this portfolio, how about addressing some of the tax considerations? I do hate paying the tax man."

"All right. Obviously, the *Contra* guys and I are not playing the preferred stock game at all. This is more relevant to Phillip's situation than Steve's. As one ages, preferred stocks certainly have more of a position in a portfolio, since they diminish risk. These investments would be mostly in blue chip enterprises that pay dividends. While stocks that pay dividends attract me, most of my turnaround plays can't afford to pay shareholders. Some exceptions in my portfolio are: RJR Nabisco, Cambridge, Fleming, Laidlaw, Occidental Pete, Newfoundland Capital, Roman, Stelco, and Trizec. Certainly the quarterly cheques are desirable, and more would be appreciated.

"In this year, no tax loss selling took place. Some portfolio managers would have ejected Bovar and Princeton, but I believe both will move rapidly forward."

"Did you do anything at all for tax?" Raj wondered. "In the restaurant business, half of my so-called profit comes from government avoidance. Otherwise, I couldn't possibly live in the manner to which I want to become accustomed."

"Recall that inaction can be the optimal form of action. In one fall, I made seven sales for tax reasons."

Phillip's face lit up. "And then you repurchased five of the stocks, right?"

"Exactly," said Joan. "It was a clearing of the house, so to speak, only most of the furniture was kept. Many pieces were refurbished and repaired with the tax loss."

"That isn't the way I'd look at it," said Peter. "As long as the gist of it is clear. Another clean-up campaign is possible this fall, although few candidates exist right now."

"That's ideal, though, isn't it?" Tina queried.

"Definitely. I'd certainly prefer writing a cheque to government over losing money.

"The primary tax advantage technique in this quarter was buying other people's losers. Take a look at the additions to the portfolio. There were five: Farah, Fleming, Hartmarx, Semitech, and SPAR Aerospace. All were trading near the bottom end of their 52-week range and appeared to be bargains. Investors were selling at reduced prices to lock in tax losses, and those shaved percentages became my gravy. As you'll recall, I dispense with carcasses before most other people begin any tax loss activity. Then, when other investors dump, the share supply increases, and the stock price gets trashed, my bids are ready and waiting. Of course, this plan is easier in theory than in practice."

"Like the sacrifice bunt," said Steve. "The goal is to advance the runner, but sometimes he gets thrown out in the process."

"Basically," Joan agreed. "And you'll recall that my December buying ritual carries with it the bonus that the last two trading days of the year and the first four of the new one regularly show an upside. I repeat the Joan Beliveau double play because it is an important edge: buy a bit cheaper and receive an honourary New Year's boost."

"Buys? What did you buy?" Peter asked.

"Forget the buys for now, Mr. Impatient. In the meantime, here are a few sells I should mention.

"All were partial positions: Mitel at $12.55, UniHost at $11.00, and Newfoundland Capital at $9.40. Each of these companies had made stellar gains, but I felt the time had arrived to take more money from the market, so I targeted these gainers. Still, some shares were held, since ongoing growth was indicated. Mitel had recently acquired Gandalf Technologies, a recent flyer in the high-tech patch. This firm, which excels in remote-access products, had seen its share price increase dramatically before crashing and burning. Mitel might have achieved a major bargain here.

"UniHost, the former Journey's End, had recently purchased franchisees' interests. They were also receiving ongoing benefits from their acquisition of Commonwealth Hospitality, and they seemed poised to continue on an upswing, particularly if the Canadian dollar remained low relative to the U.S. currency. This would encourage Canadians to travel in their own country and attract Americans across the border, keeping room occupancy rates high.

"I heard titters and jokes galore when I bought Newfoundland Capital at $1.81. No longer. The company boasts one of the lowest P/E multiples on the TSX at 2.6, which under many circumstances, would be a reason for buying rather than selling. But, with the share price appreciation, my stake in this firm had grown handsomely, and it seemed appropriate to let some ride while pulling back on a percentage."

Bucky's voice screamed from the TV, "...and there's the pitch. Geris lashes the ball down the first-base line. Smith will score! Smith will score! The Blue Jays have won the World Series! The Blue Jays have won the World Series! The Blue Jays have won the World Series!" The announcers uncharacteristically pushed themselves to silence, allowing viewers to appreciate the revelry of ecstatic boys at play.

And except for Steve, who was inconsolable, the crowd at Peter and Tina's was as excited as the announcers.

"Okay, back to the *Contra* portfolio," Peter insisted. "Another year has ended, so we can get some year-end results."

"Enjoy the Blue Jays victory, Peter. You've waited all year for this."

"But this can make us money, Tina. Money!"

"Oh, Peter. Sometimes money costs too much. Let's celebrate with Liam."

"The Blue Jays won! The Blue Jays won!" Liam cried. "Hooray! Hooray! Put me on your shoulders, Dad!"

Peter looked dubious for the briefest moment, but his son's smiling face won him over. "All right, Liam. Up on my shoulders."

Giving Something Back

Hoisting his son onto his shoulders, Peter turned to Tina and admitted, "You're right, honey. Some things money simply can't buy."

Phillip smiled heartily. "How about another rule: **Don't always focus on money; make dinner with your honey**."

"I'll buy that," agreed Tina.

RULES
- Defer taxes where possible
- Buying dividend paying stocks is a definitive advantage
- Do tax planning
- Don't always focus on money; make dinner with your honey

The Post-Game Show
Calculating Returns

We make a living by what we get; we make a life by what we give.
—Winston Churchill

The champagne was being uncorked and splashed in the dressing-room. Gales of laughter and hooting and hollering were everywhere. Everyone was living in the moment, casting their glance neither a moment ahead, nor a moment behind.

"That's the thing about baseball, Tom," Bucky declared. "The champion Blue Jays will be remembered for years to come, and the opposition Mets will be merely a footnote in history."

Everyone was quiet for a moment, soaking in the win, until Phillip said, "Joan, I've been thinking about this all evening and I'd better ask before you leave. Baseball analogies seem to be your forte. Is this simply because it's the seventh game of the World Series, or is it something you ordinarily feel is a valid comparison?"

"When Greg Maddux posts an ERA amongst the best in the league season after season, every general manager knows he'd look good in their uniform. In contract negotiations, there's no way a .220 poker with three home runs can brand himself as an offensive threat on a par with Mark McGwire. In baseball, as in stocks, numbers speak for themselves. At the end of the day, a gain of 20 percent is better than one of 10 percent, which is better than a loss of 15 percent."

"Isn't that stating the obvious?" queried Peter.

"If only it were so," returned Joan. "People often have no idea what their financial returns are."

"Doing those tallies fills me with trepidation. Yecch! Ugly! My worst nightmare."

"Oh, Steven. Don't be such a baby. Instead of your nightmares, how about one of my dreams?

"One of my childhood goals was to be the general manager of a sports franchise. Now, as a teenager I didn't notice that female executives were absent in the NBA, the NFL, the NHL, and major-league baseball—there were zero, nada, zip. Perhaps if I'd been older and more astute, I would have given up entirely. Instead, I did a comparison and determined that the easiest sport to manage a team in would be baseball. In the other leagues, many more intangibles come into play. For example, Dennis Rodman was not a gifted scorer, but his rebounding was unparalleled. That's worth a whole slew of points every game. Todd Gill didn't get the most points of any NHL defenceman, but his astute play and toughness made him a very solid rearguard.

"But baseball is easily measured in statistics. Over the 162-game season, averages will almost always balance out. But going all the way in the playoffs to win the World Series is more of a crapshoot. The results of four games out of seven defy statistical variance more than the regular season. The better team will win more often than not, but the shorter the time frame, the better chance the weaker team has. It's the same deal with stocks."

Annualized Returns

"This is the home stretch. In every portfolio, some stocks will be losers. If eight out of ten stocks are losers but gains offset losses with a nice percentage left over, the portfolio is successful. If eight out of ten are winners, but the two losers went bankrupt, leading to a negative overall return, it's a failure. The problem here is that most people don't bother or don't know how to calculate their returns. And this is not very complex. It can be done with a calculator, a spreadsheet program, or the help of websites that provide this information. My calculations work right to the day, but for most of you, it isn't necessary to be that precise.

"Here's one way to calculate it using the stocks in the Canadian 'Buys' section as of January 1 and their finish as of December 31. Numerous other methods to calculate this do exist."

	JAN. 1		DEC. 31		NUMBER	GAIN/
	PRICE	VALUE	PRICE	VALUE	OF SHARES	LOSS
Bovar	0.85	3,400	0.75	3,000	4,000	(400)
Cineplex	1.95	9,750	1.87	9,350	5,000	(400)
Dom. Tex	7.00	3,500	14.50	7,250	500	3,750
F.C.A.	2.15	5,375	2.91	7,275	2,500	1,900
Noma	3.40	8,840	4.95	12,870	2,600	4,030
Princeton	0.32	960	0.20	600	3,000	(360)
Roman	1.20	4,800	2.15	8,600	4,000	3,800
Total Value		36,625		48,945		12,320
+ Dividends						100
- commissions						0
Grand Total						12,420

Percentage Return 12,420 / 36,625 = 33.9%

"Take a look at this handout for my methodology."

Step 1: Calculate "Total Value" as of January 1 by multiplying "Price" by the number of shares for each stock and then adding the results together.
Step 2: Do the same thing for December 31.
Step 3: Subtract December 31 stock values from January 1 and enter this in "Gain/Loss."
Step 4: Add up "Gain/Loss" column to obtain the total for the year.
Step 5: Add dividends received during the year onto this total and subtract the commissions paid to obtain the "Grand Total."
Step 6: Calculate the "Percentage Return" by dividing the "Gain/Loss" by the value on January 1.

"Now, this is the scenario if no transactions occurred during the year. For me, that's never the case. Therefore, let's say a stock is sold on January 15. I would add the gain or loss from this transaction to my total at the end of the year and subtract my commissions. At the same time, I would calculate a weighted average for the amount I'd invested. For example, say all the Bovar was sold for $1 per share. The total added to my gain at the end of the year would be the gain of $0.25 x 4,000 shares = $1,000. The commission of $35 would be subtracted from this, leaving me $965 to the good.

"At the same time, my average amount invested would be recalculated. My original total was $36,625. From this I subtract the $2,250 that Bovar was worth at the beginning of the year to arrive at my new total of $34,375. Now the real tricky part comes the next time I buy or sell a stock. Let's say this happens on the last day of the month, and I purchase 1,000 shares of Dominion Textile at $6.35. This increases my average investment for the year by $6,350. That amount is added to the weighted average of my original portfolio. The equation is:

(36,625 x 15 days) + (34,375 x 16 days)) / 31 days = $35,290

"The 15 is because I sold Bovar fifteen days into the year, and the 16 is the number of days between the sale of Bovar and the purchase of Dominion. If there are no other transactions during the year, my final equation to arrive at my financial return calculation is:

((35,290 x 31) + (34,375 + 6,350) x 334)/365 = $40,263

"The $6,350 is the amount invested in Dominion, and the 334 is days remaining in the year after the thirty-one days that have passed are subtracted.

"The total gain or loss is then divided into the $40,263. So, for example, picking a number out of the air, if $9,853 was earned, the financial return for the year would be:

9,853/40,263 = 24.47%

"Simple? Not really. But try this yourself on paper tomorrow when your heads are clearer. Or, better yet, use a spreadsheet program or download these calculations from the Net."

Phillip appeared pensive. "Joan, I can almost touch the logic here. Essentially, a weighted average is created with January 1 as day one. Then with every transaction, you add and subtract to the prior total. The day of the trade is important because this is when your average amount invested changes. At the end of the year, dividends are added to the gains or losses. Next, commissions are subtracted. This total is then compared as a percentage against the weighted average."

"Good work, Phillip. It really sounds much more complex than it is. When I taught this kind of process at night school, people were always baffled the first time, but after duplicating my numbers themselves and then doing another exercise or two, the method became quite clear."

"Maybe I'll even try it," said Steve. "But late at night is when my head is clearest, so that's when I'll give it a whirl."

Currency Translation

"An additional twist. My only concern has been Canadian stocks. As U.S. corporations are also in the portfolio, there is a currency translation, which should be considered. To do this, I multiply my U.S. holdings by the exchange rate on January 1. Then, if a stock is bought or sold, I tally my gain or loss using the exchange rate on the day the transaction settles. This becomes more important if rates are fluctuating quite a bit.

"Finally, for stocks in the portfolio at the end of the year, the closing exchange rate on December 31 is used. But for you guys, this might be taking calculations to an extreme. If money is not being converted back and forth from one currency to another, you can simply say, 'A dollar is a dollar is a dollar.'

"But an investment edge can be gained here. If the perception is that the American dollar will drop dramatically, then it's wise to avoid converting Canadian funds to buy U.S. stocks. Conversely, if the feeling is that the American dollar will increase in value relative to the Canadian, then it can be beneficial to convert to buy U.S. Don't think for a moment that I am suggesting you guys become currency speculators, but when investing in another country, the exchange rate is an important consideration.

"Let me add one other point here. I don't convert funds back and forth. When I was younger, I changed some Canadian for American, which has remained my American nest egg. My feeling is that by leaving these funds in U.S. dollars, I am diversifying my portfolio by having two different currencies. Still, at the end of each year, I calculate my financial returns as though my American money were converted back to Canadian dollars."

Joan paused momentarily, as the group looked a bit baffled. "This isn't simple, but with an honest effort, you'll get it. Hey, I could have pulled something from my hat like the 'Modified Dietz Method.' This is the method a number of North American investment advisors and chartered accountants recommend. Here's the calculation from the *AIMR Performance Presentation Standards Handbook,* and I wouldn't worry about it unless you feel like being driven crazy. Normally, I don't bother with this at all, so there's just the one copy here for everyone to share."

MODIFIED DIETZ METHOD

$$\text{RDIETZ} = \frac{(\text{MVE} - \text{MVB} - \text{F})}{(\text{MVB} - \text{FW})}$$

MVE = Market value of the portfolio at the end of the period
MVB = Market value of the portfolio at the beginning of the period, where the market value for the beginning of the period is the market value at the end of the immediately preceding period
F = The sum of the cash flow within the period
FW = The sum of each cash flow, Fi, multiplied by its weight WI
WI = The proportion of the total number of days in the period that cash flow FI has been in (or out of) the portfolio WI = (CD - DI) / CD
CD = The total number of days in the period
DI = The number of days since the beginning of the period in which cash flow Fi occurred

"This calculation is completed on a monthly basis, and the monthly returns are linked together to determine the three-month, one-, three-, five- and ten-year rate of returns. The three-, five-, and ten-year returns are annualized."

"Like that's supposed to make sense to me," whined Raj.

"What makes sense to me," said Steve, "is that if I'm going to play the market, returns must be calculated. Otherwise, there's no way to know how well or poorly I've done. It's like a batter who doesn't have a clue what his batting average is. And once calculations are done, a re-evaluation should take place to decide if the methodology works or needs changing or, perhaps, to admit that someone else should be managing the finances."

Phillip nodded sadly. "Over forty years of investing and not once did I sit down to calculate my returns. Starting tomorrow, I'll retrace my footsteps as far back as possible and see what the numbers say."

Incisive Investing

"Excellent," said Joan. "One other thing. Many calculations of returns do not take into account the dollar value of the investments. For example, imagine you've invested $100,000 in the market on January 1, 2001. Your return was

$50,000, or 50 percent. Convinced that the market will go down, you pull $100,000 off the table on December 31 and invest in a treasury bill. And guess what? The market takes a shit-kicking, and your portfolio, which started the year at $50,000, has been sliced in half. As the math indicates, 50 percent of your investment has been lost. But lo and behold, because you had the foresight to switch your funds to another investment, your stock market return over the two-year period is really still superb. Many systems that calculate percentages don't take this into consideration, and it is exceedingly important to truly understand returns and portfolio management."

"Interesting," was Peter's simple response. "Of course, if this money was pulled off the table and the market turned upward, then the move wouldn't have been so smart."

"Precisely, Peter," agreed Joan. "Now, let's run the final portfolio and then call it a night."

FINAL BOX SCORE — APRIL 19
TORONTO STOCK EXCHANGE

Stock	Purchase Price	Current Price	Initial Target
BUYS			
Bovar	0.95	0.88	4.63
Denison	0.36	0.33	1.45
Spar Aero	8.35	10.00	16.15
SELLS			
Mitel*	3.00	19.70	10.38
UniHost*	2.01	9.80	7.25
HOLDS			
Breakwater*	1.93	2.89	6.25
Cambridge*	100.00	145.00	185.00
FCA	2.21	9.50	10.75
Gulf	3.95	8.05	13.50
Irwin	4.70	4.90	7.20
Laidlaw	9.10	20.45	21.63
National Sea	5.94	9.20	21.50
Noma	5.13	7.65	12.50
Princeton	0.29	0.10	1.05
Roman	1.20	2.35	2.85
Semi-Tech	1.24	0.30	9.35
Stelco	5.88	12.85	23.25
Trizec	17.91	33.85	40.25

NEW YORK STOCK EXCHANGE

Stock	Purchase Price	Current Price	Initial Target
BUYS			
Armco	4.63	6.44	11.63
Fleming	15.11	18.88	32.75
Hecla	4.81	6.56	11.75
InterTAN	5.75	5.50	9.63
Kaneb	3.25	5.56	15.63
Utah Medical	6.63	7.81	12.25
SELLS			
Unisys*	6.00	21.31	18.50
HOLDS			
Bethlehem	8.75	16.56	17.75
Farah	5.06	6.18	8.75
Hartmarx	4.63	8.31	18.38
Navistar	9.38	32.19	44.38
NovaCare	6.50	14.00	18.50
Occid. Pete	17.50	29.56	32.50
Pioneer	31.68	24.38	84.50
R.J. Nabisco	31.95	28.94	86.50

*partially sold

"What a game!" Peter said excitedly.

"Maybe the most exciting in Series history," agreed Steve. "Although the wrong team won."

"And the television stations must be happy," cooed Raj. "The biggest darn market in the States and Canada contesting seven games of great baseball. Maybe media stocks should be purchased?"

"Maybe," said Joan. "Although that would be mighty short-term thinking."

"I wasn't referring to the baseball game," an irritable Peter said. "Doesn't anyone understand me? The portfolio game. It's zoomed ahead with these April results. Look at the way FCA has moved since January. From $3.00 to $9.50. Wow! There must have been a few happy campers there, Joan."

"There were. A takeover was happening. Stocks like that should come around more often."

"And Mitel from $11.10 to $19.70! Another takeover?"

"Wishful thinking. A stock finding its stride. In fact, I sold some, first at $15.20 and then at $19.20. Not bad at all."

"Peter, pessimistic lout you are, I'm surprised you didn't mention how Semitech tanked? What's the story there, Joan?" asked Raj.

"Well, their debt was downgraded by Moody's, and Standard and Poor's had them under review. Asian flu wasn't helping either, as these guys are tied big time into that region, especially Hong Kong. Two mistakes there. The first was when the company announced major layoffs at their subsidiary Singer. The stock shot up and I bought in at $1.41, afraid to miss the boat. My second error was reinvesting again a week later at $0.97. Should have followed my own advice and been more patient. Now I'm reaching for a life jacket on that fiasco. Still, my feeling is they'll turn around, but a number of pundits predict bankruptcy. We'll see."

"Any buys? It's funny, but when stocks are purchased, it feels like they're auditioning."

"No, Steve. The audition is before the buy. Then, like FCA, they can be a big success, or a flop like Semitech. Although FCA looked like a failure for a year-and-a-half before skyrocketing. Back to the question. Two buys. One was a repurchase of Denison at $0.30. The other was Utah Medical."

"Anything on the sell side, Joan?" asked Peter.

"A bunch. Newfoundland Capital, which was sold initially in January at $9.40, was dispensed with at $12.20. Now, some people might consider it a bit of a failure since the stock could have been sold at about 33 percent higher a mere few months later, but, again, the crystal ball isn't a perfect instrument, so taking a large profit like this suits me to a tee."

"So, once again, you missed the high," Peter stated cynically.

"Once again," agreed Joan. "And the same thing happened with Mitel. In February, a piece was sold at $15.25. In April, more went at $19.20. Waiting again would have proven beneficial, but with an average purchase price of $3.00, both were lovely profits. And, quite frankly, record-setting markets make me nervous, so cashing in seems particularly fortuitous."

"Unisys did roughly the same thing—50 percent of the position went out the door at $18.63, and the stock climbed further. Cineplex was booted out at $2.59, as the upcoming share consolidation scared me. Decided to take my profits and run. Think of it as having a lead in the late innings of a baseball game and throwing in your best defensive players. The stock then scurried up another 5 percent or so. I should check where it is today after the merger with Loews."

"Did everything go up after you sold it, Joan?" asked Peter.

"There was one which didn't. NCO Group put in an offer to buy FCA at $9.60 a share. That deal has now almost closed."

Tina was checking the numbers. "But your target was $10.75. That does not quite cut it."

"I bought the stock in August for $2.21. Less than two years later, it will be sold at $9.60 without commission. That I can live with. Imagine a ball game that's rained out in the seventh inning with your team ahead. The entry is in the win column, and the time has arrived to wash down a cold one."

"I get you," said Tina.

"That covers the final portfolio. But the story will unfold further with the passage of time."

Ethics

"Joan, during all of these reviews, not once has RJR Nabisco been mentioned. This stock has been in your index a long time, and tobacco is in the news every other week. What gives?"

"Quite frankly, my feelings are mixed, as something about investing in tobacco seems inherently unethical to me. But lots of people enjoy a cigarette, whether for the buzz or to be cool. People choose whether or not to smoke, and I'm all for that. And don't forget that RJR is also a huge food concern, making all kinds of different snacks and products. Today, if I was making the decision again, I probably wouldn't buy it. But ethical choices aren't always clear ones."

"Ethics are tricky," Raj agreed. "For the restaurant, I sometimes consider buying cheaper ingredients that aren't quite as good, because 99.9 percent of my customers would never notice a difference. Still, that's not my way."

"I've faced a multitude of ethical dilemmas when investing," Joan said. "Besides tobacco, nuclear power is a concern. Forestry and mining firms that pollute and destroy the environment or businesses that exploit labour and overlook humanitarian practices are avoided. Corporations that support corrupt political regimes are also on my no-list."

"Seems like an awfully long list, Joan," said Peter. "Even in my demonstration days, there weren't that many enemies. My feeling is that purchasing shares in vile corporations that exist anyway does not actually contribute to the problem. Since evil is neither created nor destroyed, no harm is done."

Phillip spoke up. "My feeling, Peter, is that people who own shares in a major polluter are profiting from the corporation's dangerous practices. The sole exception is if the individual buys into the company to go to shareholders' meetings and take an active stance against those reprehensible practices. Funny how many CEOs of corporations want the best for their children and grandchildren but still act in an irresponsible short-sighted manner and justify it in the name of competition and profits."

"Well," Joan offered, "it might help if I pose the following three questions, which I often suggest for my clients' consideration: What do I want to make this money for? Now that I'm making it, what will I actually do with it? What will I give back? For some reason, the last question is often overlooked."

"Joan," Tina began, "do you ever advise against making money? And suggest when it is time to give back?"

"Those are tough questions. I've never advised against making money, but I have suggested that people share with those less fortunate. And certainly one should be willing to accept lower financial returns for worthwhile causes. There's a rule here: **Ask yourself: When is enough, enough?** Which relates to the previous question: **What will I give back?**"

Peter had a strange look on his face. "Hey, I know not everyone always thinks I'm ethical, but there are realities out there. Some people say money doesn't buy happiness, but it does. Without it, our annual ski holiday would be impossible. Money doesn't buy freedom? Of course it does. When the mortgage disappears, and bucks are in the bank, the next bill won't cause any stress. Money can't buy love? Of course it can. Tina almost completely ignored me, and then I bought two tickets to see the so-called concert of the year. Suddenly, Tina found a day for me, which became two, and then three, and then now."

"People get confused," Phillip suggested. "They forget that money has no conscience. It can be used for good or evil purposes. Undoubtedly, the Bible's partially correct when it says, 'The love of money is the root of all evil.' But to my mind, money was the best invention ever, the one that did more to stimulate the development of humankind than anything else, because it facilitates trade. The problems come when people become greedy pigs and forget about those less fortunate."

"Strange," said Tina. "My generation was supposed to make the big difference. We're rapidly gaining control of politics and money but still not realizing our vision. In the parlance of a slightly earlier day, 'We're copping out.' What the hell is happening? Are we merely adopting the values of our parents? How's this for a motto: **Do well, while doing good**."

"Sounds like words to live by," said Phillip.

"Peter, Raj, you remember me as a card-carrying member of our tiny communist club in university. Our belief was that everyone should barter and profits are unethical. My economics teacher always said, 'We wouldn't have the devil of communism if there wasn't the devil of capitalism.' Took me a long time to understand that," Joan offered.

"My concern," said Tina, "is that everything is becoming completely monetized and material wealth is the sole measurement of personal worth. Subjects in school are all becoming math and business and computers. A hike in the woods has as much value as sitting at a computer terminal all day. It reminds me of something Russell Baker said: 'It seems to be a law of American life that whatever enriches us anywhere except in the wallet inevitably becomes uneconomic.'"

Joan nodded thoughtfully. "Perhaps another system for deriving financial returns should be calculated, something with both an ethical and moral base." Phillip was smiling, "Work on it, Joan. That's something I'd love to see in my lifetime."

The Evolving System

Joan noticed how tired everyone looked. "It has been a very full evening. We witnessed perhaps the most exciting World Series in history, while covering a tremendous amount of information. The key now is to synthesize it all and deal with the questions that arise. Here's my last rule: **Re-evaluate your system periodically, allowing it to evolve**. Methodology changes with knowledge and time. It undergoes enhancements as inherent flaws are recognized and new information on investing comes to the forefront.

Essentially, my technique is a recipe that sometimes needs an additional dash of this or that. Hope my little investment seminar has been helpful. Here are a few other readings to put you to sleep tonight."

"Most helpful, Joan," Phillip assured her. "It's hard to believe that the young woman I knew is now giving me and my family advice."

"Feeling old, Phillip? Seems to me there's long-term planning in your stride," responded Joan.

"I don't feel young. Don't want to. But your system will put me through the paces of spring training, and as my learning continues and my grandchildren grow, I'll relish another lifetime or two."

"If you or anyone has any questions, please give me a call. My number is 1-900...just kidding. Peter has the number."

Everyone thanked her before goodnights were said all around. Phillip was staying over and put Liam to bed with a story. Tina crawled under the covers and fell asleep to an infomercial. Peter sat up until the wee hours, reading the *Contra* commentaries.

At 8:58 the next morning, he phoned Joan with a number of questions. She answered them patiently, professionally, and then added, "Remember, this is just about money. Don't forget that."

Rules
- Ask yourself: When is enough, enough?
- What will I give back?
- Do well, while doing good
- Re-evaluate your system periodically, allowing it to evolve

Glossary

arbitrage — simultaneous purchase and sale of two different but closely related securities to take advantage of a price differential

asset — something that is owned

balance sheet — the financial statement that shows what the business owns and owes

bears — people who believe that the stock market will go down; this can also be applied to their view of individual stocks

bear market — a market that has been moving downwards

beta — how the value of a fund or stock fluctuates relative to changes in an index like the TSX; an average stock has a beta of 1.0; the lower the number, the lower the risk

bid price — the price at which someone will buy a stock at a given moment

blue chip — a quality company that usually has a solid track record

bond — a loan to a corporation or government agency, repayable with interest

book value per share — the assets of a company, minus the liabilities, divided by the number of shares outstanding; this is one method of gauging the true value of shares

bulls — investors who believe that the stock market will go up

bull market — a market that has been moving upwards

business cycle — the variations of the business economy as it expands and contracts, leading to prosperity, recession, or depression

capital appreciation — the growth of the initial investment amount

capital gain or loss — the profit or loss on the sale of a stock

common shares — an ownership position in a company; normally common shares give voting rights

day order — a stock order that is good for one day

demographics — a breakdown of the population into various groups; tied in with market segmentation

derivatives — securities, usually in the form of a contract between two parties, whose price depends upon the price of an underlying asset such as a stock or currency

dividend — money paid to investors by a corporation; sometimes instead of cash the payment is in stock

dollar cost averaging — buying a set amount of stock at regular intervals regardless of price

earnings per share — a corporation with a million shares outstanding that earns a million dollars would have an earnings per share of $1 per share; this is an indicator of the financial health of the corporation

economies of scale — the larger the organization, the lower the cost per unit to reach the marketplace; at a certain size, diseconomies of scale can set in

guaranteed investment certificate (GIC) — a certificate that pays a set interest rate; the most common vary in duration from thirty days to five years

income statement — the financial statement showing profit and loss

initial public offering (IPO) — the first time a company seeks to raise funds from the general public

inventory — the assets a business has for sale

leverage — the principle of making dollars work harder; this increases the percentage of gains but also the percentage of losses

liability — something owed

limit order — the maximum price at which you are willing to buy a stock, or the minimum at which you're willing to make a sale

liquidity — the degree to which it is easy to buy or sell a stock in the market

margin account — a line of credit with a bank, broker, or trust company where money is borrowed for investing while using investments as collateral

market order — (at the market) an order to buy or sell a stock at the best price obtainable at that moment in time

market niche — a specialized portion of a market

market timing — a technique whereby an attempt is made to buy and sell stocks in conjunction with the ups and downs of the market

mutual fund — a pool of money to which thousands of people contribute, which is then invested in various financial arenas

net profit — profit after all charges are deducted

odd lot — a stock purchase outside of the standard trading unit of 100 shares

offer price — the price at which someone is currently willing to sell a stock

open order — an order for a specified period of time; watch you don't book it so far in advance that you forget about it

penny stock — highly speculative stocks that generally sell for under $2

preferred shares — shares that usually have a dividend associated with them but normally no voting rights

price/earnings ratio (P/E) — the earnings per share of a stock as compared to the price; e.g. if the price the stock trades at is $10 and the earnings per share is $1, the P/E is 10:1

product life cycle — the time in which a product is introduced into a marketplace and experiences a growth in sales, before sales mature and begin to decline, possibly leading to the demise of the product

ratio analysis — a method of analyzing a business by looking at its balance sheet and income statement

right — a benefit given to stockholders to buy additional stock in a company in proportion to existing holdings for a specified period of time

risk/reward ratio (a favourite of mine) — the greater the risk, the greater the reward; less risk, more reward

settlement date — the three-day deadline after a trade by which the buyer must pay for the security

short sale — a security borrowed from a broker and sold with the intention of making a profit by buying the security back at a lower value

spread — the difference between the bid and offer price of a security

stop-loss order — an order to sell a stock if it drops to a particular price

thin market — a stock that normally has few buyers or sellers

time value of money — the idea that a dollar today is worth more than a dollar tomorrow; this is particularly important during inflationary times

treasury bill (T-bill) — a government note with a specific interest rate

underwriter — a firm, normally a brokerage, that agrees to buy the new issue of a company at a fixed discounted price, which they will then sell to the public at retail value

value investing — buying shares that sell for less than the company's actual worth per share

warrant — an opportunity to buy shares of a stock at a fixed price, usually within a specific time frame; often attached to the sale of shares to make them more attractive

working capital — money to be used in the daily operation of the business; calculated by subtracting current liabilities from current assets on the balance sheet

yield — the rate of return on a security paid in the form of dividends

Appendix I
The *Contra* Philosophies
(As They Appear in Every January Issue)

Philosophy is not a body of doctrine but an activity.
　　　　　　　　　　　　　　　—Ludwig Wittgenstein

- Concentrate on turnaround situations and stocks that are currently unpopular but are likely to regain their lustre in the near future.
- Focus on stocks that have the ability to increase in value by a minimum of 50 percent.
- Carefully analyze corporations' financial statements, concentrating on debt ratios and book values.
- Analyze management's ability to achieve stated goals.
- Invest only in organizations that have been publicly traded for at least ten years.
- Often pick takeover candidates well before takeovers occur, for near-optimal returns.
- Normally sell a minimum of 50 percent of a stock upon achievement of our target price, while "market timing" the remainder.
- Practice patient long-term investing while ignoring the daily pulse of the market.
- Advocate diversification.
- Remain independent of any broker, corporation, or financial institution.
- Put our money where our mouth is by informing our readers about stocks that we actually buy and sell.
- Strictly limit our readership to 1,000 subscribers.
- Appreciate stocks that pay regular dividends.
- Give 10 percent of profits to charity.

Appendix II
Financial Returns

Money is like a sixth sense without which you cannot make use of the other five.
—W. Somerset Maugham

ANNUALIZED FINANCIAL RETURNS

5-YEAR	10-YEAR	15-YEAR
15.4%	16.2%	21.8%

These are the financial returns for the *Contra the Heard* investment letter for the past fifteen years, finishing in 2007.

www.contratheheard.com

Appendix III
The *Contra* Commentaries

What experience and history teach is ... that people and governments have never learned anything from history.
—G. W. F. Hegel

Reading these commentaries should give added insight into the methodology used at *Contra*. It will also give a historical perspective on views held within the time frames they were recorded, so one can easily see where we hit the nail on the head, and where we scarred our thumbs.

Contra Commentaries—January 1996

The Quebec referendum was a nail-biter, with the "No"s forestalling a "Yes" victory by less than 1 percent. While a larger margin would have been appreciated on both sides, markets were calmed by the outcome and statements from the separatist camp that there will not be another referendum forthcoming in the immediate future. But their current position is that 1997 could be the next call to vote. That is the immediate future, unless one is under twelve years of age! Unfortunately, this uncertainty will continue to burden Canadian markets, and become weightier as the next referendum approaches.

The U.S. continues to work on a budget accommodation to eliminate the deficit by the early 2000s. We'll believe that when it happens. To give it a shot, here are a few suggestions. First, many economists in North America now define full employment as a 5 percent jobless rate. Many advocate this high level of unemployment in order to reduce the possibility of a high rate of inflation. Hogwash! The benefits of full employment far outweigh the overall costs of this short-sighted policy. While 2 percent unemployment would certainly lead to more demand for goods and services, the impact on inflation would easily be offset by a reduction in the government's need to borrow to fund social services. Certainly, a shorter work week and restrictions on overtime would allow more people to gainfully participate in the economy without adding significantly to inflationary pressures.

Government has been overly worried about inflation at the expense of the deficit. The basic philosophy to control inflation has been to slow the money supply growth and raise interest rates. Unfortunately, this often leads to many viable businesses becoming insolvent, as organizations that make reasonable decisions to borrow money at lower rates cannot function when rates increase. While this is simple economics, governments cannot seem to grasp that their efforts to ward off inflation often drive viable businesses into bankruptcy. Unemployment and government dependency are the result, leading to a higher deficit, choking both government and citizens in the long term. It is time that North American governments make a clear policy decision to keep interest rates below 7 percent at the high end, creating enough stability for business owners to make decisions.

Another suggestion: raise the minimum wage. By keeping the bottom salaries low, the government discourages people from working. Currently, the difference between working at low wages and collecting social assistance is marginal. A reasonable salary is necessary to create the motivation for people to work.

Contrary to current conventional wisdom, a strong economy consists of high wages, a strong currency, and a manufacturing sector at near capacity. Countries selling their goods, particularly non-renewable resources, at low currency values are like organizations that are always having sales. This ultimately lowers a nation's standard of living.

Want to balance the budget more quickly? Raise corporate taxes. Those big businesses are laughing in the back rooms at the pittance they are paying. Will they squawk when the government hints at raising rates? Of course they will. They are supposed to. Protecting the firm's interest is their job. But enlightened organizations also recognize the benefits of contributing to a stable functional society. This will not be possible if the percentage of tax revenue coming from corporations continues to erode as it has for the past generation.

April 1996

The Internet. Tons of media coverage. Lots of heat. Very little light. Soon the graveyard for companies as obsolete as VisiCalc and WordStar. Undoubtedly, the long-term impact of this new medium will be far-reaching, but for the time being, all of the hype is providing few hints of where this technology is really going.

Today's Net is constrained chaos ruled by cooperative anarchism. If one can wade through the dross, one can find the definitive answer to the burning question: Are Twinkies sentient? or view compelling personal relationships, such as "Me and my gerbil"; or learn how to build bombs; or, even more important, how to change your boring Doom bad guys into super donut-spitting Homer Simpsons; or any of a plethora of other must-have lessons.

And what input do we have from the corporate sector? Mostly pathetic attempts to get wired...with all the excitement of a framed copy of a weekend flyer. What a heap! People are so excited by the revolution that they have forgotten that part of "publishing" is having something to say.

Meanwhile, while the Internet birthing process continues, established Internet hacks are already composing ballads to the good old days on the Net, while rolling their eyes at the legions of "newbies." Like frontier scouts bemoaning the feckless homesteaders, they cry to their buddies on IRC. (That's "Internet Relay Chat" for you newbies.)

Welcome to evolution...where the only sure constant is change. In a computer industry used to a compressed life cycle, many Internet products live about as long as a fruit fly. Even heavyweights such as Rupert Murdoch, who took a licking when he chopped staff at his Delphi Internet service by 50 percent, can easily be ambushed. It's a minefield! The myriad standards; the rapidly shifting alliances between the big players; the competition between phone, cable, and wireless technologies for the method of delivery; the difficulty of converting people who are happy to use shareware into consumers willing to spend real money—it all leads to a world of unknowns. Under such conditions, many companies that currently dominate parts of the market will be barely remembered in five years, while the giants of tomorrow are probably still little more than a twinkle in the eye of ambitious and talented entrepreneurs.

So what can we know?

In the mad scramble to commercially exploit the Net, it is easy to overlook the fact that a key impact will be in the political and social sphere. No, this doesn't have to do with the spread of porn, although that is an instructive example in the difficulties in controlling cyberspace content. The Internet is poised to cement the dominance of "Western culture" on the planet.

While English was already well established as the international language of academics, international business, and science, the medium now exists to accelerate the growth of this language everywhere. As people search further afield for more, a common language is a necessity. Feeble attempts, such as Quebec's newly published *Vocabulaire d'Internet* for surfing "Le Web," are doomed to be swept aside. English will be the Esperanto for the new millennium.

With the Net also comes a spirit based on Western values of political pluralism and individual freedom. This is a direct threat to authoritarian regimes who continue to preach their values of stability and social conformity. Even in the U.S., where freedom of speech is a hallowed right, the wide open nature of the Net is alarming. In the same way that photocopiers and video cassettes undermined the Eastern Bloc, and fax machines promoted Tiananmen Square, the Internet is a tool of subversion. Although countries from China to Singapore are locked in a hopeless struggle to filter, censor, and muzzle incompatible "Net-thought," they still wish to capitalize on the technology for their own ends. The social changes that wrenched North America and Western Europe in the '60s are percolating into cultures that, until recently, had been able to avoid "Western moral decay."

Whether or not this is cultural imperialism is a moot point. The combination of technology, affluence, and education is a force of change that no country or government can control or avoid if it wishes to be part of the international community.

Although heroes such Netscape's Marc Andreessen are most likely to get on the cover of *Time* magazine, there are other individuals who have not commercially exploited their contributions but have still had an enormous effect on the Net. Take New Zealander David McCleary, whose Pegasus Mail is on a par with products from giants such as Netscape and Symantec. With 4.5 million Pegasus users, McCleary himself is a giant, yet his attitude remains one of unbridled idealism: "I believe communication is a basic human right, as basic as freedom of speech, and that e-mail is just an expression of that. It seems immoral to me that people should have to pay for that right."

Then there's Philip Zimmermann, who released his controversial freeware program, Pretty Good Privacy (PGP), a brilliant scheme to allow users to exchange information in complete privacy—privacy so tight that Zimmermann is now being hounded by the U.S. government, which fears that millions of people could (gasp!) actually communicate without the threat of government snooping. It is the capacity to capture the hearts and minds of geniuses that is perhaps the most significant aspect of the Net, which assures its creative explosive power.

The future of the Internet? A hodgepodge. Popular hits, critical successes, and the equivalent of tone-deaf yokels strumming in the garage. But, like rock 'n' roll, the Net is definitely here to stay.

October 1996
A few choice questions are being presented as an introduction of sorts to this issue. Are you ready?

1. Is the ultimate goal of society to buy cheaper toilet paper from Wal-Mart?
2. Is one of today's main measures of progress truly to be able to receive 500 television stations? And is the investment of $200 million by the Canadian government to make better shows and therefore glue more people to their televisions worthwhile? Will this lead to mass craziness as people deliberate, "TV No. Participaction. No. TV. No. Partici...." Perhaps there is something to this "docile population" idea....
3. Do moral imperatives really exist? If so, how many are there?
4. If all 80 million people in the United States who tried illicit drugs were arrested and thrown in jail (irrespective of whether or not they had inhaled), would this dramatically boost the North American economy? Would there be additional inflationary pressures? What impact would there be on the deficit? What will happen as people's sentences expire and they are released back into society?
5. A final warm-up. If a corporation's sole goal is only the bottom line, as many insist it should be, what does this say about civilization? Think about it.

January 1998
Well, we always did love all the new supposedly fail-safe mechanisms built into the new safer stock market. Our favourite is the stoppage of trading at 50, 350, and 550 points—a surefire method many pundits pointed out to soothe sellers' fractured souls. But, alas, as happened in Hong Kong ten years ago, when the index there dropped 33 percent after a four-day closure, it was the buyers' ardour that waned. Time added perspective to what appeared cheap as even cheaper appeared on the horizon, encouraging bidders to pull their orders, accelerating the free fall. So while everyone talks about creating conditions for cooler heads to prevail, buyers became downright frigid. What will be the next fail-safe mechanism?

Here's one fail-safe that worked but doesn't receive any positive press. As the dross hit the proverbial fan, investors could not get a hold of their traders. This meant that a barrage of sell orders, which would have exponentially increased the decline, couldn't reach the market. While brokerage firms boast about their ability to handle a huge number of transactions (hey, that's marketing), perhaps the stock exchanges should surreptitiously encourage them to lessen their capabilities. A return to the three-martini lunch, perhaps? Nasty, we know, and not something expected to happen. But fodder for the merit of system "failure."

A fascinating aspect of Gray Monday's aftermath was the "analyst-speak" that took place. The vast majority of analysts, politicians, and financial advisors offering soothing advice and refraining, "Stick it out for the long term," was mind numbing. Nary a voice was heard to suggest that panicking early, before the crowd, might indeed be a wise choice. Instead, they rhapsodized about leaving money on the table, and many experts insisted upon leaving it there until eternity strikes. This is foolhardy, like a roulette player in Vegas who wins and always presses the bet. At some point, there will be big-time losses. Plus, the philosophy of letting money ride into perpetuity precludes utilization. Gains from the market are not merely to be hoarded for hoarding's sake. Enjoy the fruits before spoilage occurs.

Market mavens who take the Asian crisis seriously are fond of talking about "dominoes" to describe the relentless march of currency devaluations and economic chaos. This metaphor misses the mark, as it exemplifies a knockdown situation. Instead, the condition is like a complex machine of interlocking gears, where the loss of one tooth sends shockwaves through the system. As these accumulate, the entire system goes haywire. That bearish grinding noise you hear is cogs losing teeth and throwing the whole mechanism out of whack.

Lastly, we've been doing a read on the IMF-Asian situation with our focus on Indonesia, looking for the incisive investor's edge. We think the answer is now clear.

It's obvious to us that the IMF guys, with their squirts of WD-40, have vastly underestimated the amount of money needed to help the masses there. Currently, the powers that be are allocating $40 billion to the region. But common knowledge states that this country might be the most corrupt in the world. So take 10 percent off the top for the benevolent rulers to open their country to receive IMF aid, another 10 percent for their relatives and friends, a further 10 percent to grease the wheels to change the normal lines of communication and distribution, plus a further 20 percent for "normal" shrinkage. Thus, 50 percent reaches the people at the bottom of the ladder. Unfortunately, due to the currency stimulus, the price of the goods most important to these people doubles, leaving them 25 percent worse off than before.

But, of course, the story doesn't end here. Those at the top of the totem pole—who took the top 30 percent of the IMF money—send the funds to Switzerland for safe keeping. This increases the demand for Swiss francs, sending the currency ever higher. Moral of the story: Go long on the franc and stock up quickly on Toblerones.

April 1998
If you read through the typical company prospectus or annual filings, somewhere you will read a bunch of stuff about risk. The kind of risk factors that will be mentioned are things like the impact of competition on the company's new and existing products, management, access to marketing channels, efforts to reduce costs, availability of capital, reliance on key personnel, and so on. All nitty-gritty issues, and as anyone who has participated in a business can attest, points that must be taken seriously.

A very interesting thing happens when people look at mutual fund portfolios to evaluate their risk. All such "meat and potato" questions are pushed aside and the evaluation of risk is concentrated on a single attribute: the fund's volatility.

Volatility is measured by calculating a fund's standard deviation, i.e. the variance of its monthly or weekly returns over a longer period of time is quantified. This is often expressed as a fund's "Sharpe ratio." Named for Nobel laureate William Sharpe, this measure compares a fund's return in excess of a guaranteed investment (the 90-day T-bill) with its standard deviation. When analysts talk about "risk adjusted" returns, they are usually talking about yields that take the Sharpe ratio into account. But how useful is volatility in measuring overall risk?

Let's look at a baseball analogy, with two hitters who have similar stats for batting average, home runs, and RBIs over the course of a season. One is a consistent .325 hitter, the other a "streaky" hitter, but who also has a .325 average for the year. If we looked at each batter's "returns" for every week of the season, the streaky hitter would have a much higher standard deviation than the consistent hitter.

As a manager, which player do I prefer? Well, all things being equal, I'd probably take the consistent guy. He sounds a lot like a Paul Molitor or Robbie Alomar, dependable players who will get you runs week in and week out. But if Paul and Robbie are spoken for, I'd be quite happy to take the inconsistent player (.325 hitters are pretty scarce!), as long as I knew I had him for a *whole* season.

The key point here is that the usefulness of volatility as a worthwhile measure of risk is entirely dependent on your time horizon. If you are saving for retirement or to put your kids through college, volatility really doesn't matter; it's the long-term batting average that counts. But, if next summer's vacation fund is your concern, it's an entirely different story. In this case, volatility could really hurt and minimizing risk over the shorter term becomes far more important. So if I'm a manager at the trading deadline, looking for a player to help out with the stretch drive, a batter prone to slumps *will* scare me. But if I can have him for long enough, I know the swings will even out—what the statistical types call "regression towards the mean."

Ah, but the experts will show you data that show how it's mathematically possible to have a high standard deviation of returns while exhibiting no downside risk, in the real world, the larger the swings in a fund's return, the more likely it is to dip into negative territory. How come?

For starters, when individual stocks fall, they rarely do so in a slow, graceful manner. The more common pattern is: a company suddenly goes out of favour, investors head for the exits, and the stock drops like a stone. We don't have any data to back this up, but our hunch is that with all of the nimble funds around these days, this is even more likely than in the days when the majority of stock was held by sleepy institutional investors. So if your fund had a big bet on Oracle, the standard deviation numbers are bound to be high. It turns out to be a bit of a tautology really, stocks that dip into negative territory will almost always have high standard deviations.

The other big issue is compounding. The crux of this concept is that old bugaboo, the difference between average annual returns and annualized returns. (The Beardstown Ladies' returns are another story altogether.) A bad year will hit your annualized return hard because it means you need to have a superb year to make up the difference on the cumulative return. This is where the baseball analogy breaks down. In investing, the effect of compounding is optimized when returns are consistent.

But if a portfolio *can* achieve the good annualized long-term returns, it means that the growth spurts are strong enough to outweigh the periods of poorer performance. For these portfolios, high volatility, standard deviation, and Sharpe ratios are all pretty much a moot point. The proof is in the pudding, and whether the track is a straight line or has a few hills like the Boston Marathon is irrelevant to the long-term investor.

Tools which an astute investor would consider in assessing risk for a company, such as competition, government regulation, technical obsolescence, currency fluctuations, et cetera, are difficult to calculate. The Sharpe ratio is a preferred measure because it's objective and quantitative, which greatly pleases academics and analysts alike. Sharpe ratios are cut and dried. They can be graphed. Hey, you could even do a standard deviation analysis of...Sharpe ratios! This material keeps the statistically inclined busy and happy, but how much it really has to say about risk...well, we have our doubts.

Is the Sharpe ratio high for the *Contra* portfolio? We haven't bothered to actually calculate it, but it's guaranteed to be up there. So what? When FCA jumped to $6, you can be sure that we weren't worrying about what volatility was doing to our Sharpe ratio.

Conclusion: A straight line is simpler to draw, and apparently more efficient, but any long-term path, with the same end points, is ultimately equivalent.

Investor's Digest named the April 1998 issue of *Contra the Heard* the "Letter of the Week."

October 2000

When Benj worked in Nepal last year, one of the most common expressions was, "Ke garne? Ke garne?" Translated literally, it means, "What to do? What to do?"

This is a question we've been faced with lately as our financial returns have dwindled over the past couple of years from their stratospheric heights of the previous eight. Should we shed our contrarian spirit and adopt another philosophy? Is it time to become momentum players and hop on the Nortel bandwagon? Run to the Internet and high-tech stocks? What's the best solution when it appears the crowd is starting to run ahead and your feet are mushing around in quicksand?

One of the initial steps is to re-evaluate your system. Has it been working well for one year? Five? Twenty? The longer one is successful with any given methodology, the more likely it is that failures are simply a temporary aberration. Everyone knows of moments in their lives when the fat ball of bad luck rolls off the hill and won't be swayed. Even Wayne Gretzky had periods where plays backfired and goals and assists dried up. In investing, difficult times occasionally rear their head and one has to be patient and roll through them.

What is bad luck in a *Contra* sense? Let's take a straightforward example: Suppose you're a bottom fisher and you choose five stocks where there is a 10 percent chance of bankruptcy but a 50 percent chance of tripling your money. This will work out well in the long run, but in the short run, three or four busts in a row are possible. To be sure, it is difficult to perfectly define the odds. We are not actuaries. Sometimes even insurance companies end up making huge payments for multiple hurricanes, even though their weather actuaries had accurately assessed the odds.

Of course, sheer bad luck is often a simplistic excuse. That may wash with the denizens of Vegas who take deep bows for their crafty strategy when they win and blame bad luck when they lose. Citing bad luck in this case is a pathetic rationalization to soothe wounded pride. Certainly, this same rhetoric undermines many who gamble on the stock market.

But stupidity is just another in a list of reasons for failure. Sometimes cycles are the beguiling devils that impact returns negatively. An investment methodology that works during one period may be suspect at best in another.

When analyzing the *Contra* technique, it was obvious that, over the past couple of years, money has not been thrown in our value direction. Warren Buffett and David Dremen, two leaders in this field, have suffered along with us. For a few months, there was a deluge of articles about Warren losing his touch. Well, if anyone in the world can afford to have a dry spell, Warren is the man, but his humbling streak was plainly a product of the times. Investors were lapping up technology stocks and IPOs, hoping to ride a meteoric wave in areas in which Mr. Buffett chooses not to dabble.

The nature of money is that, at any given point in time, it is finite. Therefore, it can only move in so many directions. If major funds are being invested in the technology sector, then less money is left for the value arena. This was a key reason why investors like us were recently left out in the cold, dreaming of warmer climes.

Waiting can be confused with indecision, but patience is often the best solution when stock market returns are substandard. But even when plain ol' bad luck might be the cause, this should not be an excuse for laziness. We carefully re-evaluated the *Contra* system and perused it for holes. As usual, we found a few minor flaws, leading to tinkering to augment the investment results.

We also did another key thing. We didn't panic, going off half-cocked, making all kinds of trades that would have meant forking over commissions and enriching brokers at our expense. In practicing patience, we slowed down. Since May, we have only made tax loss sales, exiting positions that should leave more money in our pockets when the reckoning is done.

In their fascinating book, *Why Smart People Make Big Money Mistakes and How to Correct Them,* Gary Belsky and Thomas Gilovich present a number of startling facts regarding investor behaviour. One states that from 1984 through 1995, the average stock mutual fund posted a yearly return of 12.3 percent, yet the average investor in these funds earned 8 percent. The authors suggest that this makes about as much sense as being told that the average commercial jetliner flies at an altitude of 35,000 feet, while the average passenger in a commercial jetliner flies at 15,000 feet.

Why the shortfall? Many investors frequently switch from fund to fund, chasing higher returns. As part of their yearly review process, they'll often chuck the underachievers and switch to whomever holds the hot hand of the day. However, the authors say the data shows that "by investing with the herd, many investors take their money out of poor performing funds just before they begin to rebound and put their dough into zooming funds just before they stall. Then they repeat the cycle over again."

Sticking to your guns and waiting for the trend to turn in your favour should not be confused with another failing strategy, in which investor overconfidence is combined with paralysis. It is a psychological fact that people tend to overvalue investments in which they have taken a position. As a result, they tend to hold on to losing investments, believing themselves to be correct, even when the overwhelming weight of information indicates otherwise.

This overconfidence is difficult to overcome, but the best bet is to confront this belief by re-evaluating the losing stock as though you didn't own it, as though it were sitting out there on your watch list. Would you buy it? If the answer is, "Interesting, but no," then you should seriously consider replacing it with something else that appears to be a better purchase. The bottom line is that while being patient can be a blessing, paralysis is a curse.

We are great believers that one makes one's own luck. The more we study, the harder we work at something, and the better our luck seems to be. But we should recognize when the investing winds are blowing badly, calling for a retreat. Taking a vacation from the market can be the pause that refreshes, helping to restore clarity and insight to the investment vision.

Ke garne? Ke garne? At *Contra,* we've been lying lower. Don't forget to put this very viable, but low-key, option in your strategic repertoire.

April 2002
Many of our readers have asked us just how to interpret the "Ratings" that are part of every "Buy" e-mail. Others have asked why we seem to issue so few "Buy" e-mails, but more on that later. Suffice it to say that, after a placid quarter in which not a single position was added to the stable, it seems as good a time as any to explain this element of our methodology.

Think of the stock-buying process as a two-step procedure. First, of course, is the decision of whether or not to purchase a stock. Then, once you determine that a buy makes sense, the next logical question is how much of your hard-earned savings you should plop down on the position.

That's where the Rating comes in. It's an indicator, based on a scale of one to four, of how large a position we've taken in a stock. A Rating of 1 represents the minimum amount of money needed to open a position, while a 4 corresponds to the maximum amount. Logically enough, we plow four times as much cash into a firm with a 4 rating as we would if it garnered only a 1. To express it another way:

1. Light
2. Moderate
3. Heavy
4. Ceiling

So far, so good. So how do you apply this to your own situation? We would be remiss if we didn't point out that it's up to you. Remember, the purpose of the Rating is to give you a guide to match our confidence in a stock with your purchases—that is if you choose to follow our system, which is a mighty big assumption.

Let us be crystal clear when we say that we do not advocate that you adhere mechanically to the *Contra* methodology. The farthest thing from our minds is to create another "herd" of investors who blindly parrot a system.

As independent investors, you need to assess the risk/reward profile differently to suit your own unique financial circumstances (stage of life, temperament, etc.), which are huge factors affecting the size of your bets. We've had a good run lately, but long-time subscribers know perfectly well our capacity to make the odd bonehead error.

With this in mind, if you wish to match the *Contra* performance—for richer and for poorer, in sickness and in health, for better or for worse—then you'll want to make use of our Ratings.

Let's run through an example to show you how it works. Suppose you have $40,000 to invest and you would like to spread it over eight stocks. If you were to distribute the funds evenly, you'd plunk down $5,000 each. Assign this amount to the midpoint on the Rating scale, which is 2.5. It's a linear scale, so we simply divide $5,000 by 2.5 to find that a stock with a Rating of 1 is worthy of the minimum investment: $2,000. Moving up the line, a "2" stock gets $4,000, a "3" is worth $6,000, and $8,000 should be thrown at a stock rated at 4.

Let's apply this to the purchase of a stock. Say you want to buy the beaten-down three-legged dog that we just acquired on the NYSE. It's trading at $3.20. The first thing to bear in mind is that this stock trades in USD. Now look up the Rating—we'll say it's 3.07. Multiplying your minimum investment ($2,000) by 3.07 yields a product of $6,140 CDN. Assuming an exchange rate of $1.58, we have $3,886 USD to invest in this stock. Divide by the stock price, and you'll find you can buy 1,214 shares.

There is just one more thing to remember: odd lots are a pain. It is worthwhile to round off your purchase to a board lot. In this example, cast your gaze on acquiring 1,200 shares.

The beauty of this system is that the scale can easily be adjusted to suit any portfolio size. Over time (we hope!), you'll need to recalibrate the scale to reflect the growth in your holdings. Say your $40,000 portfolio doubles to $80,000 and you wish to stick with eight positions. The minimum punt would now be $4,000, while the maximum would be $16,000.

A further adjustment would be in order if you change your mind about the number of stocks in your stable. For instance, if you decide to go from eight to ten positions in an $80,000 portfolio, the new range would be $3,200 to $12,800.

All well and good, you say, but how do we come up with our Ratings in the first place? That's a complex matter. It's not as simple as "better potential, more money." In fact, stocks with huge upsides sometimes get a fairly light weighting.

For instance, Kelman Technologies had a low Rating of 1.07, though we reckon it could be a four-bagger. That lukewarm Rating reflects the stock's speculative nature and the firm's near-death experience a few years ago. Plus, at $0.40, you can buy a heck of a lot of shares, meaning that they can be spun out more easily in stages as the price treks upward.

Stride Rite, on the other hand, garnered a more solid Rating of 2.22, even though its target price of $14.69 represents a more modest expected gain of 153 percent. That's because this firm offers a high margin of safety, so we are comfortable with a higher capital exposure.

The combination of a heavy Rating with a monster target, as are the cases with Sodisco-Howden and OfficeMax, indicates companies that have superb prospects and will likely be in the portfolio for many years. Fortunately, pleasant surprises sometimes kick in and stocks rush out of the portfolio more quickly than even our fertile imaginations can envisage.

Finally, sector concentration also needs to be taken into account. Claude Resources was a better prospect than a Rating of 1.43 would suggest, but with Richmont Mines already in the portfolio, it didn't make sense to go hog wild on gold. Yes, Ollie, remaining adequately diversified is a consideration.

You should take care when interpreting the Ratings on stocks that have been kicking around on our Buy list for a while. Would we purchase exactly the same amount if we were pulling the trigger today? Perhaps, but any number of factors might subtly influence the mix and produce a different assessment as to the optimal number of shares to be procured.

That doesn't mean the company isn't still a good buy—in some cases it may even be a little better. Just bear in mind that a historical number reflects a reality from the past, which may not jibe with today's circumstances.

We've tried to come up with a better name for the Rating concept, but have so far run dry. We're aware that the presence of a list of "Rating Adjustments" (now simply "Adjustments") at the end of past editions of *Contra* might have muddied the waters for some. Perhaps our readers have the answer. Any ideas? The lines are open.

October 2002

Stocks are dead! Stocks are dead!! They have had their day, but it has passed, and investors are so turned off that they will stop buying stocks altogether. Please remember that you read it here first, on the *Contra* website, before *Time, Newsweek, The Economist,* or even *MAD*.

By using a complex blend of both fundamental and technical analysis, combined with the synergies of five psychologists locked in a closet together with only one chamber pot, the *Contra* Guys are not only willing to make the above statement conclusively, but we have also ascertained that trading will gradually subside until November 31, when investors will be so disgusted that no one will even place a buy order! At that time, a best-selling book will appear on bookstore shelves: *Dow 36,000...If Trading Ever Resumes*.

Having so concluded, we contemplated selling all our positions in a massive flurry, but since the media watches us so closely, we deemed this a losing proposition; everyone would also be aware of what was about to happen, and because markets are perfectly efficient, a stampede for the exit would ensue. So, except for you, dear readers, no one knows what we know: yesterday, at exactly 2:22 a.m. (a time chosen based on the lunar alignment, which pointed to the old TV show *Room 222*), we shorted every single stock on every market in the world. With this windfall, we plan to buy first-class, 'round-the-world bus tickets. The *Contra* Guys—always thinking about fine travel.

However, before we embark on this magnificent voyage and lose touch with you completely, we felt it best to share a few additional thoughts. The public has lost its taste for the markets, optimism has dissipated, the bubble has been pricked and gone *pffft,* and the dire search is now on for "The Bottom." New paradigms be damned; the established norms of human psychology and business cycles once again rule the day. Who'd 'a thunk it? Same old, same old. Again. Déjà new = old-style pessimism.

The question is, can future booms and busts be prevented? Dream on. Human psychology suggests that the way we react is too deeply ingrained. Our best hope is for a semblance of moderation, with lower crests and shallower troughs. How this might be achieved, short of reprogramming people's brains? (Something that isn't necessarily against our personal belief systems, but which others might find abhorrent—hey, those are my stem cells!)

What is the primary means of regulating the economy today? Interest rates. Things getting too hot? Raise rates. The economy's cooling? Lower them. While this is definitely a powerful lever, an overemphasis on interest rates is simplistic. Here are a few other ideas, offered in no particular order.

Speculation must be curtailed. One way to achieve this is to force people to fork over more money for their purchases, increasing the margin requirements when people buy stocks. Perhaps during periods of "irrational exuberance," no margin should be allowed.

Alan Greenspan, one of the more powerful voices in the world, recently said in a speech at Jackson Hole (no, that's not a pun on the state of the economy), that it was impossible to stop the bubble and that raising the margin requirement would not have made a difference. However, back in 1996, Mr. Greenspan said, "I recognize that there is a stock market bubble problem at this point...We do have the possibility of raising major concerns by increasing margin requirements. I guarantee that if you want to get rid of the bubble, whatever it is, that will do it. My concern is that I'm not sure what else it will do."

Stricter margin requirements do dampen demand; they also reduce margin calls when stocks are weak, thereby creating less likelihood of an ensuing downward spiral. Unfortunately, the best time to do that passed with the mania, but graduated steps can be implemented now to phase this in before the next episode of what Warren Buffett calls a "mass hallucination."

We wonder, but don't have an answer, how much of the bubble can be blamed on efforts to contain nascent bears way back in the halcyon days: the Asian Contagion of 1997; the Russian default and LTC meltdown of 1998; or the crazy flush of liquidity that was let loose to pre-empt Y2K problems.

These events all figure in what we are experiencing today. The dramatic increases in the money supply to contain these episodes surely had a major impact on priming the bubble. Government must remain vigilant when using this mechanism, acting judiciously in the short term while maintaining a balanced focus on the long term when the economy is on an expansionary or contractionary kick.

Back on the subject of jerking knees, bankers tend to do this far too often. When do they adopt loosey-goosey policies and lend money like Niagara Falls? When times are good. When are they misers? When the twinkling is dire—precisely when leniency is imperative. Somehow this mindset should be inverted, but it obviously is not easy to do. Maybe a course in "contrarian banking" should be made a mandatory part of MBA curricula.

Derivatives, as we have cautioned before, are a disaster in waiting. They have already taken their pound of flesh, but this is nothing compared to the major munch that is yet to come. While these instruments supposedly smooth the waters, they are too often abused by little boys in suspenders who have only a limited understanding of their dynamics. Many who trade in this field are not doing so to create stability but solely to increase profits, often at tremendous risk. Some banks and major corporations face the peril of being wiped out as these bets are flung back in their face. Get ready to count the job losses, along with the associated economic straitjacket.

Next? A June column in the *Globe and Mail*'s *Focus* section said, "Twenty years ago, senior executives earned about 45 times as much as an ordinary employee. By 1997, the factor was 305 times as much. And between 1997 and 2000, when profits grew little, the multiple reached a jaw-dropping 458." Heck, 305 times seems jaw-dropping enough for us, but what do we know?

We are aware of the trickle-down effect, whereby money works its way through the system from the top down. But this is far from an optimal method of distribution. We propose the "spread-the-wealth-around effect." We bristle when guys like John Roth receive payouts of $145 million or so. It's not that we don't like Mr. Roth, or Mr. Stronach, or their ilk; we just think that a wider range of snouts should be allowed to nuzzle their way into the trough.

Think of it this way: An individual such as Roth can only spend so much money on his own. There's a limit to how much he can fire the economy with his $145 million. But spread that same money amongst 10,000 people, giving each a cheque for $14,500, and a lot of cars and dishwashers and brooms and other neato stuff will be purchased. But, you say, Big Bad John got the $145 mil as an incentive/performance bonus. When you look at his already fat salary, how much extra performance could Nortel really hope to induce? Now, if you dangle a $14,500 carrot in front of 10,000 souls, we'll bet that the aggregate performance boost is a heck of a lot higher.

Let's do some math. An executive who makes about 100 times the minimum wage, or $700 per hour, will—based on an 80-hour work week 52 weeks a year—earn about $3 million a year. Let's be even more generous and ratchet that up to 200 times—that works out to a cool $6 million. That's enough for anyone to earn in one year, isn't it? Let's cap the compensation there and either return the excess to the corporation or tax it away.

Let's face it, the business cycle, with its ebbs and flows, is a staple of life. This is unlikely ever to change. However, we can deal with it better than in the past, thereby creating a more stable economy that will function more smoothly and allow a recalibration of the highs and lows.

Our guiding philosophies appear elsewhere on our website and are published every January in the print edition of *Contra*. Here are a few other simple rules and concepts that guide the day.

A question that we are regularly asked is: Given the sell-off in some stocks and their penny status, how low can they go? The answer remains the same as ever: zero. It is important to remember that $10,000 invested in a stock at $124 a share is the same as $10,000 invested at $0.82, if the firm goes under. A stock trading at a low price is not necessarily cheap. There is no point in making an investment based on a stock price that seems low if the fundamentals do not suggest that a turnaround is realistically in the cards. We know that stocks in general are better buys with the Dow at 7,500 than at 12,000. This also applies to the TSE—er, TSX.

We know that if we are choosing a fantasy baseball team of no fewer than three batters, and the goal is to assemble a team of hitters who average the most home runs per player, we would not put the entire league on our roster. We would likely pick A-Rod, Bonds, and Sosa. The same rationale applies to cherry-picking individual stocks instead of backing indexes.

We know that telecom and high-tech stocks are more likely to perform well over the next five years than oil and gas. We also know that, at this particular time, more people will invest in the latter than the former. We know that real estate remains hot at the same time that tons of economic thermometers are chilling, and that this is normally a harbinger of worse things to come in this sector.

We know that a $28 billion court judgement is ludicrous and makes a mockery of both the judicial system and money.

We know that the Kyoto Protocol cannot be all bad; it will certainly cost jobs, but new ones will be created too.

Before departing this quarter's commentary, we should mention to those who have some free time that there are still some seats available on the bus reserved for our subscribers. The vehicle happens to be one of Laidlaw's finest, although in the interests of full disclosure, we must reveal that it doesn't have a toilet; we lent that to the psychologists. However, it does have a big "11" on the side for easy identification. Please come and join us on this magical excursion. It should be a hoot.

January 2006

Income trusts should be a major story in 2006. And notwithstanding a little RCMP investigation, there is so much in this sector to feel good about. Take, for instance, the stock brokerage firms and investment bankers who implored the government to maintain these financial instruments, lest the defenseless senior citizens who own them have to consider cat food a delicacy. It's a good thing, too, because seniors across this great land of ours have seemingly become as ecstatically addicted to trusts as felines to catnip.

Ottawa, after much fretting and protesting about the endangered flow of dollars to federal coffers, committed The Big Waffle, allowing the existing regulations to stand for now. And just to keep things "fair," the Goodale Gang lowered the tax rate on dividends, further stanching the flow of funds to government coffers. How illogical is that?

The upshot is that trust IPOs have been breeding like rabbits gone amok, while an insatiable public can't get enough.

How quickly things change. Around the new millennium, as technology stock valuations grew by leaps and bounds, dividend-paying stocks were written off as relics of the Stone Age. Around that time, Benj was coining one of our favourite lines: "Dividends help me to be stupid longer."

How true it remains. If a stock price does not reach the target price for years and years (if at all), at least one can take solace in the annual payout. Of the stocks currently in our portfolio, more than a third pay dividends. In our point tally assessment system, a point is awarded to companies that tip their hats to shareholders in this way.

When tech was pummelled to the canvas, investment bankers recognized that it was necessary to find another golden goose to pay for the Lamborghinis, and investment trusts, with their high dividends—er, distributions—fit the bill. "Hurray!" responded the public, faced with barren returns on their GICs and like-minded investments. "Sounds mighty attractive to us!"

The history of these investments in Canada would fit a slim volume. It begins in 1985, with Enerplus, through which Marcel Tremblay and John Brussa pursued a strategy of selling aging oil wells to retail investors.

In 1995, when Labrador Iron Ore Royalty Trust was spun off from Norcen Energy Resources, the first mining trust was born; two months later, there was the first corporate conversion: Enermark Income Fund, which was devised to avoid the company being gobbled in a hostile takeover. Today, there are about 250 business trusts, with many more in the pipeline.

Why are they so popular? Well, for those in the finance industry pushing the IPOs, the rich fees cannot be overlooked. Owners of enterprises love them because of the jackpots they receive, which are much higher than the prices professional buyers would pay.

Lawyers and accountants also reap revenues from them. Once you get past all that (easy, eh?), tax advantages are at the core—and, all things being equal, these accrue both to the operating entity and to investors.

The names themselves—"income trust," "real estate investment trust"—seduce many investors into thinking that they offer very limited risk. If only it were so.

Income trusts have become so à la mode that they are now included in the S&P/TSX Composite Index. Some investors might instinctively be reassured by this. Unfortunately, while the index does have extensive rules and methodologies, not enough attention is paid to an astute analysis of balance sheets, financial ratios, and the potential for ongoing success.

This is not to put the kibosh on the whole trust sector, because there is no question that there are some that make perfect sense. The best have stable dependable cash flow and income, as well as reasonable payouts, far below cash flow.

Debt loads should be nominal, and assets must be plentiful enough that the rate of depletion is not a significant danger. Ideally, the underlying business will not be cyclical, and economic conditions will not have a major impact.

Changing interest rates will not quash them. Capital-spending requirements should not be onerous.

Many of the newly minted issues are not of this ilk, and to add insult to injury, they are bundled up and sold when the enterprises are near their peaks, garnering the greatest riches for the salespeople.

Want an example? The first trust to go bankrupt was Heating Oil Partners Income Fund, three years after the initial offering. When this turd was foisted on an unsuspecting public, it had lost money for three straight years.

After the IPO, it lost money for three more. A year before the grand finale, $30.2 million worth of additional units were sold. What were those who made the offering thinking after so many years of losses?

Perhaps, like a hometown announcer commenting on a batter in a major slump, their attitude was, "Hey, he's due." Or maybe, all they could see were the banking fees of $9.3 million.

Now that the sector is in a veritable frenzy, even Air Canada is getting in on the act. This IPO is the farthest thing possible from what a trust should be. It's hard to imagine who might sell this piece of bird splat with a straight face, but CIBC World Markets and RBC Dominion Securities will step up to the plate.

The current distribution, in the range of 9.5 to 10.5 percent, won't last—we're as certain that it will be vastly reduced, if not all the way to zero, as we were when we pronounced Air Canada an excellent short on ROBtv.

To prevent the further bastardization of this sector, and thereby protect investors, we thought it would be useful if there were certain preconditions that must be met before an income trust can be formed:

1. The organization must have existed as a stand-alone entity for at least five years. Rationale: Without a track record, it is difficult to anticipate future performance.
2. Neither the trust nor its parent can have gone bankrupt for at least ten years. Rationale: If this has happened, one can assume that the enterprise is not stable.
3. It must have been profitable for a minimum of four of the past five years. Rationale: We'll allow one bad annum, but any more than that and it should still be a corporation—but, heck, it can still pay dividends.
4. In four of the past five years, the enterprise must have had a net profit before tax equal to or greater than the proposed level of distributions. Rationale: Inability to sustain distributions is the bane of these organizations.
5. If a trust eliminates payouts within five years, those involved in issuing the trust must use fees earned to cover half the distributions that would have been paid (based on the initial distribution), to a maximum of those fees. Rationale: This will help to insure that the issuing organizations truly do their due diligence before selling these offerings.

Will our recommendations be followed? We hear the guffaws from the peanut gallery. However, if major investor grieving in 2007 follows the record number of IPOs in 2006, the popularity of trusts will sink like a stone. That would ultimately spur some new regulations to protect clients, but it's a pity that regulators will only be moved to action after the wreckage has occurred and the movers and shakers have moved on to the next big thing.

October 2006

Fifteen months ago, we wrote about the "Darkness of 2006," our forecast of the impact of a pronounced economic downturn in the United States, caused by trade imbalances, government deficits, and rising consumer debt, as well as high oil prices and an expected slump in the real estate market.

Were we wrong, or just early? That's open for debate, as housing prices have started to decline in some parts of the U.S. and economic weakness did encourage the Federal Reserve to stop raising interest rates.

But overall, the U.S. economy has chugged along merrily: unemployment remains very low, foreign lenders continue to happily lend to cover the deficits, and the stock market has forged ahead, taking the Dow Jones Industrial Average to a new all-time high.

One prediction that we did get right (darn it!) was that our own portfolio would likely suffer. Back in January 2005, it contained twenty-five stocks, every single one of which was up in value. Of the current eighteen companies, twelve are up, or 66 percent.

The response to this state of affairs, as gleaned from our mailbag, has been interesting. Some of our newer subscribers are feeling somewhat shell-shocked as they survey their results.

But many who have been with us for a while are apparently blithely unconcerned, as they have harvested some nice gains along with us this year with the sales of such oldies as Claude Resources, Hudson's Bay, Stride Rite, and Xanser.

So, are the pessimists a bunch of nervous Nellies who are unable to put a short-term gyration into perspective? Or are the optimists a crew of Pollyannas who just don't get that line on the front page that says, "Past returns are not necessarily indicative of future returns"?

When we consider our historical record, the examination always starts with our ten-year annualized return, which best encapsulates whether the *Contra* methodology is working or not. When people complain that the portfolio has not performed well since January or April, we are unperturbed, though we do acknowledge that it is always better to be up than down in any time frame.

Many of our readers ask questions about more specific details on our performance, so the archive was opened and loaded into the mother of all Excel spreadsheets to try to come up with some answers.

We examined all stock sales since January 1996. For many companies, there were multiple sale points; in these cases, we considered only the initial sale—with the exception of firms sold and then bought back after the mandatory 30-day waiting period for taking capital losses. In these cases, each holding period was counted distinctly.

For the record, this approach increased the number of losing transactions, and included companies that were eventually nicely profitable the second time around; we think this policy provides a more balanced picture of our success rate.

The screening process left ninety-three sales for us to study. Without further ado, then, here are some of your questions and the results:

What percentage of your picks are winners?
Forgive us if we seem Clintonian, but that depends on how you define a "win-

ner." By the broadest measure—simply those we made at least some money on—71 percent qualify.

More meaningful, however, is the percentage of stocks sold after appreciating by at least 50 percent—a key element of the *Contra* methodology; 59 percent cleared that hurdle, and 42 percent at least doubled in price.

What percentage are sold for a loss?
Twenty-nine percent went out the door on the negative side of the ledger—a higher ratio than we expected to find.

What percentage reaches the initial sell target?
At 41 percent, this was lower than we anticipated. Paradoxically, one factor that knocked this ratio down was our success in acquiring stocks that later became takeover targets.

Buyouts have been highly profitable for us: Dominion Textile, Noma, Royal LePage, Minolta QMS, CompUSA, OfficeMax, Leitch, Sodisco-Howden, FCA, Gulf Canada, General Host, and Hudson's Bay were all lovely plays that offered up capital gains of between 75 and 334 percent.

Yet all of the bids came before we had held the stocks long enough for them to get within striking distance of our targets. If we add these gobbled-up stocks into the mix, the success rate increases to 57 percent.

What percentage are wipeouts?
Overall, 9 percent have this nefarious distinction. Losing most of our deployed capital on an investment is something we strive to avoid, and progress has been made in this area: All cases in which we lost more than 90 percent of our investment occurred in the period from 1996 to 2001.

In the last few years, the only really big loser has been Stelco, cast off in 2003 after a loss of 67 percent. However, Fonar is looking mighty ugly right now, to be sure.

What percentage gain does the average sell target represent?
Our initial sell targets vary widely, depending on our assessment of the potential appreciation. On average, targets were 245 percent higher than our buy point; the lowest was Dynex in 2001, at 48 percent, while the highest was Markborough in 1996, at 1,700 percent.

Neither made it while we owned them, but Dynex has done outstandingly well since our sale. More patience would have helped on that one.

Are lower initial sell targets achieved more frequently?
To determine this, we divided all of the companies into quartiles, from those with the most modest targets to the loftiest. The results were surprising and somewhat mysterious.

The first quartile, ranging from a hoped-for gain of between 48 and 112 percent, had a success rate of 46 percent. One would expect that these targets, being the lowest, would be easiest to achieve, and though the rate was better than the overall average, it was still less than a coin flip.

The second group, ranging from 113 to 186 percent, had a much poorer achievement rate of only 31 percent.

But it was the third quartile that really shone: With optimistic targets ranging from 187 to 298 percent, the success rate was 57 percent.

For the fourth bunch, in which we were shooting for between 310 and 1,700 percent, only 30 percent cleared the bar.

Perhaps this is just a statistical fluke; if not, it is difficult to reckon what this says about the methodology. There seems to be a sweet spot of expectations in the triple-to-quadruple range that, for some reason, the methodology is most efficient at identifying.

What is the average holding period for a Contra *stock?*
This is a little trickier to ascertain, as some stocks are bought multiple times, as well as sold off in chunks.

To simplify the calculations, we used only the time of the first purchases and first sales. The average holding period for the ninety-three positions was 3.5 years. For stocks that achieved the initial sell target, the holding period was longer, but not by much at 3.9 years.

Some were with us seemingly forever—Mitel was in the stable from 1987 to 2000, while High Liner, a holding since 1993, is the current "iron man."

What's the longest period a stock spent as a loser before eventually hitting the target?
Looking over the data, it's quite startling how many companies spent long periods as dogs before becoming swans. The most noteworthy transformation was probably InterTAN. Purchased in December 1996 at $5.75, it sat forlorn on the *Contra* Buy list for the next eight issues, at $4.12, $3.88, $3.75, $5.63,

$5.38, $5.50, $5.25, and $3.56. In 1999, it not only hit its target of $9.63, but blew through it, resulting in sales at $11.25, $16.19, and finally $21.19.

What's the biggest percentage of losers that the portfolio has had?
The worst point for the portfolio was reached in October 2001, when nineteen of twenty-six stocks, or 63 percent, were lower than what we had paid for them. However, in *Contra* fashion, while that sounds gruesome, the portfolio had actually done very well, with numerous stocks popping in value and being sold.

By July 2002, only 17 percent of our stocks were below their purchase points. In terms of our overall returns, the period from January 1, 1998, through December 31, 2000, was downright ugly, as the portfolio dwelled in negative territory. That was three long years of crud, folks!

The techies had a good laugh at our expense during much of that time. It was also a period when our subscriber base declined.

During the dark days of January 2001, we wrote that our portfolio was better than it had been in years. And it was: The next three years saw spectacular returns. And when we later wrote that our portfolio was not nearly as good anymore, people continued to sign on and have been surprised that returns were not so stellar.

The key to all of this is not to simply assemble the data, but to analyze it. During this "information age," time, effort, and money are wasted on conducting research and compiling reports, which are filed neatly away and forgotten. And then the cycle repeats. Even individuals are now so overloaded with information that it becomes too overwhelming to synthesize and make use of it.

The question is, what can we do with the information that came out of this exercise? One move is to pay additional attention to that third quartile, which isn't to say that other levels of returns will be ignored.

A second resolution is to try to choose our buys more effectively. The 29 percent that depart the portfolio at a loss seems too high and makes us question whether we might be even choosier than we are. And, given that several of the losers we did not repurchase went on to do very well after our sale, we may need to be even more rigorous about deciding when to give up on a company.

It should be noted that while the ins and outs and ups and downs and variations on themes are interesting to contemplate, at the end of the day, the numbers that still speak the loudest and clearest are the overall financial returns.

Fortunately, over the long term, our returns stack up with the best in North America. That makes us proud. However, years such as this one make it clear that we cannot afford to spend too much time polishing our trophies; instead, we would do well to ensure that our thinking caps are well fastened.

January 2007

The brilliant writer C. S. Lewis stated, "The future is something which everyone reaches at the rate of sixty minutes an hour, whatever he does, whoever he is." Extrapolating from this, one would assume that sixty minutes 200 years ago would measure the same as today.

On one level, that is correct; however, given technological change, the possibility of completing a task today dwarfs that of two centuries ago, to the point where, in some respects, an hour today is not the equal of an hour of yore.

Consider, for instance, that as recently as two decades ago, it could easily take ten days to get a letter to Europe—and that doesn't even take into account the writing. Now that e-mail has superseded airmail, we can write to a colleague on the continent in mere seconds (though it may sometimes be a good plan to wait just a moment before hitting that Send button—the better to let one's emotions cool).

Not so long ago, calling long-distance to many locales was an ordeal; today, we can connect effortlessly with all but a few points, and at a fraction of the cost. And it's apparently not enough for people to take calls at home or the office; with cell phones and voice mail, it's very nearly impossible to be unreachable (much as one might enjoy being left with nothing but their own thoughts to occupy them). Although, judging by the number of people chattering as they drive or walk down the street, few feel they can afford to be unavailable.

The trick is to use and control technological advances like these rather than be enslaved by them. For instance, a friend recently commented that she and some friends were venting about the ways in which today's time- and labour-saving gadgets seemed to be complicating and constraining their lives.

Of course, technology has had a comprehensive impact on investing. Curious about a corporation? No need to phone or write the company for material; just send an e-mail request—and in most cases, you can download annual reports and financial data directly from the firm's website. Even more information, from a variety of perspectives, is just a Google search away. (It kinda makes us wonder whatever happened to Ken Olsen, whose company brought out the minicomputer. In a 1977 address to the World Future Society, he said, "There is no reason for any individual to have a computer in his home.")

But while the gathering of information is easier than ever, synthesizing it is not. The sheer volume of the data can in itself be overwhelming, and much of it generates more noise than harmony. Separating the wheat from the chaff can be a challenge and a task that, ironically, takes more time than it used to.

Where once there were incisive, substantial, in-depth articles, today there is "content" designed to attract your attention quickly and direct your gaze to the vicinity of the accompanying advertising. *Shorter* and *faster* are the watchwords, because longer articles take time to read and, as a certain wise Benjamin Franklin said, "Time is money."

Our attempts to work within this New World have not always proven successful. Sometimes it has indeed felt as though we were moving too quickly. Just as it is possible in this "information age" to drown in data, it is also easier than ever before to pull the trigger rashly, without due diligence, on a purchase or sale—just go to the broker's website and click, and the deal is done in a New York second.

Once the stock is purchased, many people use the Internet to track the price like a lemming in heat. This compresses time, catching one in the random noise surrounding the investment position and/or making it seem as though the market valuation is not moving quickly enough in a positive direction.

This overzealous focus tends to make one antsy to trade, when the optimum approach is the opposite: relax and ignore it for a while. It also makes it tougher to understand the nature of "real" investing, which does not depend on results after a week, month, or even a year, but three, five, and even ten years.

We cannot count the number of stocks in the portfolio that have done little of a positive nature for years, only to suddenly double or triple. Remember, a stock that takes seven years to double in value is generating an annual return of 10 percent; if it doubles in five years, that's 14 percent per year. Either would beat the pants off of historical norms of both the market and other investments.

As this is a time for resolutions, our task in the days ahead will be to remember that while the times are changing, the job of critically assessing, evaluating, and coming to conclusions should not. We want more synthesis of thought before we pursue the deal.

We know that research must be done, that haste can be waste, that there is a time value of money where having it sooner is better than later given present value. But the key, in our minds, is to not be sucked into the eddies of time and to try to avoid the noise of explanation that accompanies every trading day.

Related to this, and fully relevant to investing, is that human psychology at its core level is unchanging. People still swat the pendulum too far in one direction when the going is good and push it too far in the other when the outlook takes on a bleakish hue. This allows for greater profits.

We also know that in the interrelationship of quality of life and time, time is more than money and it is better enjoyed in increments. As Theodor Seuss Geisel writes,

> How did it get so late so soon?
> It's night before it's afternoon.
> December is here before it's June.
> My goodness, how the time has flewn.
> How did it get so late so soon?

Within this elongated train of possibility, the manner of exploitation rests in the incisive words of Napoleon: "Take time to deliberate; but when the time for action arrives, stop thinking and go in."

January 2008

The last five years have been a particularly busy period for us. With a maxed-out subscription base until last year, there were times when our daily e-mail inbox filled up faster than a Michigan landfill. So we thought it was a good idea to review the reader-mail archive.

One observation was that the predominant line of enquiry has changed from "What should I plow my profits into now?" to "How do I avoid losing my shirt?" Wholly expected, as a string of boffo years was followed by more moderate results and then an abysmal 2007.

Another finding was that a diverse and dynamic group of subscribers brings with it an equally varied degree of understanding of numerous issues—indeed, even some seasoned subscribers were fuzzy about the procedures, policies, and philosophies unique to *Contra the Heard*. So we'd like to take this opportunity to make ourselves crystal clear.

One matter of prime importance is that of independence. We consider you, as an individual investor, to be a self-reliant free agent. We have no knowledge of your wants and needs. You may or may not have a financial planner, advisor, accountant, wealthy barber or set of pushy in-laws who assist you in considering possible investments. There are myriad factors that you should take into account and evaluate critically, using the resources you deem useful, before you come to a decision you can live with.

As writers of an investment newsletter, we tell people what we do and use our experiences to attempt to educate others about investing. We addressed the idea of starting some sort of mutual fund in our January 2004 commentary. In short, it ain't gonna happen. Instead, subscribers get to look over our shoulders as we manage our portfolio.

The design of the portfolio is predicated on our personal risk tolerance, lifestyles, and financial conditions. The likelihood that these circumstances mirror yours is about the same as bumping into Barbara Amiel in the clothing department at Wal-Mart.

The point is that we expect subscribers to act on their own in order to achieve their personal goals. Many have become confident enough to use *Contra* as a complement to other investing ideas and styles within their total portfolio. Others say they emulate us but allow themselves flexibility—they may wait to purchase a stock until it falls further or buy on the way up, even after it has appreciated substantially.

Setting higher or lower sell targets is something we've heard quite a bit about. Subscribers can, and do, beat our own returns. How do we know? Because some of you have been renewing at the rate applicable for people earning 12.5 percent on the *Contra* selections. In the past year, that's an accomplishment. Perhaps we should be peeking over your shoulders!

Independence has another meaning that is applicable to us. We act alone and are not beholden to any broker, corporation, or financial institution. It truly is our cash, sitting in various accounts, that is being used to buy these equities.

As far as what brokers to use, we consider the analyses written by columnist Rob Carrick of the *Globe and Mail*'s *Report on Business* to be the gold standard when it comes to answering that question.

We put our money where our mouths are by informing readers about stocks we actually buy. This includes those in the April issue that one or both of us like but didn't make it into the *Contra* portfolio. Perhaps even more important is that we inform readers via e-mail of our decisions to sell. This isn't standard operating practice in this industry. Normally, we unload some or all of a position at our initial sell target, which is set when the purchase is made.

When we say that *Contra the Heard* is not for everyone, we mean it. The contrarian investing style leads us towards companies with scary problems that are often described in gory detail in the newspapers or to firms so completely ignored that it is hard to imagine them ever being popular again. Under these conditions, the cheap often get cheaper, and the stock price can stay stubbornly low even after the emergence of tangible evidence of fundamental improvement. This can be tough on a person's constitution—a patient, almost stoic, attitude is essential.

Oh, how people love to ask about holding periods, i.e., "How long will it take for a stock to hit the target?" We never know, even with all the tea leaves, crystal balls, and astrological charts that clutter our office. Financial rewards sometimes arrive quickly, but there are many untimely duds that stay down for years.

While such delayed gratification may be frustrating, the targets are far enough above the purchase price that, once they are finally hit, the results remain excellent. The ones that spiral into oblivion are the ones that really hurt, and, last year notwithstanding, their numbers have been cut back in recent years. Such spectacular failures must be accepted, for to give up on all the losers would mean missing out on some multi-baggers that counterbalance those blowouts.

Some investors are looking for more action than we offer; there are plenty of other services that cater to that need. Our focus is on our investment results, and careful stock selection is therefore imperative; trading for its own sake isn't on the menu.

As indicated on our website, we send emails when we buy or sell something, or if a takeover offer occurs. Normally, that results in fifteen to twenty-five e-mails per year, but, unlike other newsletter services, we don't distribute these evenly throughout the year. Why such an unpredictable schedule? No two years are ever alike, for one thing. Second, our contrarian methodology favours buying towards the end of the year and early in the New Year, partly to take advantage of tax-loss selling. Expect to hear from us quite often at these times.

In some years, bargains are hard to find and stocks are not hitting our bid or offer targets, so there will be extended periods when we have nothing to say. The bottom line is that we won't send you an e-mail just so we can tack up a number.

Some subscribers feel they have to match *Contra* purchases at the time they are made, but as we have written in past issues, stocks often drop below our purchase price. Note also that every quarterly issue lists the stocks already in the portfolio that we would buy for ourselves today if we didn't already have a stake.

Sometimes, subscribers write that they have not heard from us for a long time. As noted above, this could be because of the seasonal and unpredictable nature of the releases. Or it may be because our e-mail addresses, contra@email.com and contra@3web.net, are not on the recipient's safe list, so our words are shuttled into a spam bucket. If this happens, we have no way of knowing about it.

One measure we have taken is to issue a quarterly e-mail on the 10th of January, April, July, and October. If you don't hear from us on one of those dates, please check with your Internet service provider. If spam filtering does not appear to be the problem, then contact us. Also, on our website at http://www.contratheheard.com/cth/subscribe/commstatus.html, the dates of our releases are listed, so you can easily find out whether you have missed anything.

Nowhere in any of our material, or on our website, do we offer any guarantees—or promises of refunds for renewals or freebie extensions after a bad period. Our belief is that people who have renewed know what they got into by subscribing. Still, we are not completely hard-hearted and will give refunds to new subscribers within their first three months under certain circumstances. We understand how they might have subscribed to a service that is not what they expected, and if they do not want to be with us, then we can accept that.

While we don't know anything about your personal situation, it certainly hasn't stopped some of you from asking if there is something wrong in our private lives to account for the proliferation of poor picks over the past couple of years.

Nice of you to be concerned, but really, there's nothing to report. We're neither on the bottle, nor on the wagon, and mid-life crises have been limited to a few delusions of grandeur at *Grand Lizard* and *Guitar Hero* (can you dig it?). Our spouses and kids continue to put up with us, and there is no truth to the rumours that we have started a chinchilla farm in Red Deer.

It's important to own up to mistakes of judgement, and we've made some doozies, but that doesn't change the fact that this job isn't always easy.

Though most investors recognize that no methodology will work all of the time, it's one thing to accept that fact on an abstract intellectual level and quite another to work out just how many hurdles will have to be cleared on a practical level. All the companies we buy have problems, but the character and intensity of those difficulties changes with the bull/bear market cycle.

After a long bull market in which the market caps of most companies have increased, those who pursue bargains are faced with a diminished pool of prospects. Not surprisingly, hot money chases even enterprises in trouble, or, in the parlance of The Street, "Even the turkeys fly." At these times, we buy gingerly, but we still do buy.

By contrast, after a bear market, our "Stock Watch List" swells, as even well-run firms with excellent long-term prospects lose their lustre. The probability of doing well on stocks that just need the economy to pick up rises sharply, and it is an optimal time to deploy cash reserves into the market.

As indicated in the "Year in Review," in terms of opportunity, we are currently somewhere in between the scenarios of feast and famine. Many value stocks have been royally hammered, but it doesn't mean they won't fall further. If the economy slides into recession, higher-quality companies will get trashed, and the attraction to put more cash to work will grow.

For those who want a better understanding of just what we do, be they older or newer subscribers, this website is an excellent resource. The commentaries over the last ten years or so cover a lot of material. Benj's last book, *The Contrarian Investor's 13,* examines our modus operandi in depth.

All in all, we do enjoy feedback, be it good or bad, so if you have something to say, or ask, contra@email.com is listening.

Appendix IV
Recent Purchases

If everyone was a value investor, then value would be acutely limited.
—Jaromir Novak

Given that I wrote about the companies in the box scores of this book from 1995 to 1998, it is fascinating to see what has happened to them since. This helps one reflect on the nature of the buy-and-hold strategy while looking at what occurred with a live portfolio.

Canadian Stocks

Agnico Eagle became an $80 stock. It could almost convert us to the buy-and-hold philosophy. Almost.

Bovar made a special payment to shareholders of $0.50 a share in 1999. This allowed a recoup of about half of the original investment. The rest was sold for $0.30 later in the year for a small tax loss. The company that was bought for the *Contra* portfolio as a leading-edge environmental company had its short day with waste management before selling their Swan Lakes plant to the Alberta government. The company is no longer listed.

Breakwater Resources, after the quick sale of 43 percent of the position for a lovely gain and a continued flight upwards from there, later plummeted. The rest was sold for a tax loss at $0.92. Since then the stock has remained for the most part in penny range with the odd spurt upwards, including passing the $3.50 level. As is natural, this one moves in harmony with the zinc price.

Cineplex ended up filing for bankruptcy and being resurrected for a monetary song under the mantle of the Onex Group. Currently it appears to be thriving like hot buttered popcorn.

Denison Mines, after languishing for years, became a huge gainer for those who held their position. This was due to the renewed popularity of uranium. The price later lagged, but it remains far above where it was. Unfortunately, we exited for a loss in 1999 and did not realize the gains.

Dominion Textile had a lovely run. Then it went bankrupt, as North America was no longer the place to be for producing textiles, given the cheap competition from Asia. This is a sector that got hit as ugly as ugly can be.

FCA was taken over by NCO at $9.60 a share, about four and a half times the *Contra* purchase price. The bid came out of the blue while the stock was trading within the range of $2 and change. Crazy things like that sometimes happen and make the stock game seem easy! If only it would happen more often.

Great Pacific, under the auspices of Canadian billionaire Jim Pattison is a thriving enterprise. We follow Jim. Apparently, he also follows us.

Gulf was sold after a triple. It did lots of dancing on the way, as most companies do. Avoiding daily noise certainly helped on this one. That sale was pretty much the finish of oil and gas in the portfolio, except for Kelman Technologies, a small seismic and archiving firm. And though we did extremely well in this sector, if we had waited, more riches would have been the result. Same as with our positions in commodities. The pendulum swings....

International Aqua was ahead of its time as aquaculture has since taken off. However, as far as I know, this outfit currently swims under the ocean.

Irwin Toys was sold for a tax loss and soon afterwards it moved up smartly on a takeover. Later, it went bankrupt. Evidently, the people who bought it probably were not feeling supremely intelligent as they filed the "end-of-the-line as a public entity" papers.

Laidlaw gave us a number of chances to depart with a lovely gain. However, it was held to long and we got wasted—nevertheless, not as badly as some others as this one sank into bankruptcy. There are always questions about operations in this sector, as it seems to attract many unsavoury players. Yes, it smells.

Markborough Properties is one of Canada's largest shopping centre developers. It also operates in the U.S. and U.K. They have become a part of the Brookfield Properties kingdom.

Mitel doubled almost immediately after we sold it during the culmination of the tech boom. It was subsequently taken over.

National Sea (now High Liner Foods) is still in the portfolio, the longest hold in our history. It trades little; the stock price moves little and is like a cantankerous uncle who hangs around beyond his time. It did hit the Initial Sell Target but unfortunately was not ejected. It recently swallowed FPI, another player in the seafood field, which makes it a much larger company. Maybe this will boost the stock price?

Newfoundland Capital continues to trade slowly and help keep the province listed on the stock sheets.

Noma was purchased by General Chemical at $9.25 in 1999, another lovely deal for us. It's pretty impressive how many of our companies get taken over, eh?

Princeton Mining was split into two companies, Imperial Mining and Madison Properties. Both were minor players in the *Contra* portfolio, with Madison quickly ejected. The stock price went up about five times since the sale.

Roman Corporation was a funny sort of play. As we got to know management, our feeling turned to one of disdain and doubt. Still, we managed to sell for better than a double, but from there it quadrupled. Later, it went bankrupt, management fulfilling our conviction. It's pretty sad how many of our companies go bankrupt, eh? Fortunately, the vast majority have already been sold. The number of corporations that do disappear is not just part and parcel of the *Contra* portfolio—it's definitely a larger issue for investors.

Sears Canada was sold for an excellent gain. Then it went up and up to the $44 level, but has since tumbled. This one is as cyclical as unemployment figures.

Semitech went into receivership and was sold for pennies. This story that looked so promising when acquired was actually rife with corruption. The principal ended up going to prison. Sometimes, one can be bamboozled, plain and simple. Perhaps the complexity of the annual reports should have alerted us to avoid it. When something is very difficult to comprehend, avoid it and leave it to someone else. This is something that I do now with other investments in all fields, and I find that this rationale has proven beneficial.

SPAR Aerospace was sold for better than a triple. This was the second *Contra* play on this stock. Naturally, when one buys a stock for a second time, it is better known. That should aid results. SPAR was subsequently taken over.

TrizecHahn was sold towards the end of 1998 for a 56.3 percent gain. Now it is another cog in the Brookfield Properties empire.

UniHost was bought lock, stock, and barrel by W-Westmount Corporation at $7.00, down from our previously sale at $11.00, but up substantially from the purchase price of $2.01 four years prior.

American Stocks

Anacomp is struggling along today, trading the odd time. It has basically gone from rags when sold, to other rags.

Armco transitioned into AK Steel, and we missed a sell on a jump. It fell to earth, pushed upwards, and went out the door. As steel regained popularity, it then quadrupled. While we were correct about the recovery of this sector, our timing was all screwed up. Buying late into momentum can be as negatively fateful as buying early.

Bethlehem Steel was sold when it entered Chapter 11. This was an ignoble fate for this long-lived company. However, if one scans backyards, it's amazing the number of former blue-chippers that end up in the graveyard. Time moves on and companies—"living" entities that they are legally—die.

Cincinnati Milacron was a big gainer for the *Contra* Guys, but is now listed on the NYSE as Milacron and is fighting to survive. It is one of those enterprises, though, that always looks good when one reads the CEO's letter, yet somehow the results are not a fulfillment of the words.

Fedders had quite a ride after it was sold during this book. Ultimately, this company with the squeaky clean balance sheet soiled it by taking on onerous debt, and then it ended up filing Chapter 11 and shareholders were SOL. This is a perfect example of why I love companies with clean balance sheets: The bank(s) won't come a-calling, demanding payment.

Fleming was sold at $9.75 for a tax loss even though we still liked the company. In fact, we thought enough of it to repurchase it, and it did better than a quadruple before our sale at $31.46. How sweet! Far more delightful than when it slipped into Chapter 11. Fortunately, we were long gone by that point.

General Host was another company that filed for Chapter 11, but, again, after we sold it for an excellent gain. This occurred in 2002, but then the firm recovered. Not for long, though. In 2004, the enterprise filed again and this time was put out of its misery via liquidation.

GenRad was bought by Teradyne with a stock exchange in 2001. At *Contra,* we always prefer cash. What does that say about us?

Grubb & Ellis soared after our sale, and then almost died and ended up on the over-the-counter market. I bought more in this Wild West show market at $1.11 and sold nine months later in November 2004 for $3.85. It's too bad because in an event that I cannot ever remember happening with a stock under my purvey, it relisted on the NYSE and shot up over $13.00. I would have sold for less, but still. Given this situation and others of its ilk that have occurred, it is rare that I will sell a gainer towards the end of the year, always attempting to defer taxes and take advantage of the September–May timeline when stocks seem to do well overall. Not every year, of course.

Hartmarx was sold for a tax loss. Then, sadly for us, the stock quadrupled.

Then, sadly for those who did not sell, the price dropped back to the level of our tax loss. Roller coaster city!

Hecla was sold for about 20 percent of our purchase price for a brutal loss during the era when commodities were way out of favour. Since then, it has gone up by about fifteen times and broached our initial sell target which was about twelve times above our sale. Since then the price has retreated.

InterTAN was RadioShack when it was purchased, and after doing not much more than lose ground, we thought of disposing of it. The name began to bother us more and more. Radios seemed to become more and more like *Flintstones* technology, and what thinking person would buy into a "shack"? Lots of people, apparently, as the company turned around operations, the stock price caught a tsunami, and we sold in a number of tranches, the last on a takeover offer.

Kaneb was sold after a triple, and the company also spun off Xanser to us, which also proved to be very lucrative as it developed into a quadruple. It has been rare in the *Contra* history to receive a spinoff, and naturally once received, it must be assessed for a sell target. This is not always easy and requires a good deal of guestimating, given the lack of trading history. It is definitely not within the realm of pure science.

Navistar was sold for a 375 percent gain. Currently, almost ten years later, it trades slightly higher than where we sold it. However, at one point, it was significantly higher, showing how market timing can be a handy tool. Nevertheless, it's easier said than done.

NovaCare was going oh so delightfully. It then caught a bug and things turned. We should have jumped but didn't, and the bug was more serious than we thought. Before we knew it, NovaCare was bankrupt and we had scraped a few distasteful crumbs off the hospital room floor.

Occidental Petroleum was sold for about a 50 percent gain but about 25 percent below the target price. We justified that because our feeling was that management was overly greedy. Our belief never changed. However, after our sale, oil began its long trajectory upwards and the stock tripled. Yowzer!

Parker Drilling was a delight, and more so for those who held after we sold. Commodities and the related companies are fascinating, and if one could only accurately foresee and know when to ride the various waves before jumping, this game would be so much simpler. The company constantly survives with a huge debt load, but perhaps once this will trip it up.

The RJR part of RJR Nabisco was sold for a slight loss. At the same time, we decided to no longer invest in cigarette companies. Ethics can change over time.

Tesoro Pete is the kind of corporation that can make investors who sell early cry into their beer caps. We're still crying, even though the stock price has come back.

Unisys turned out well and was another that climbed and climbed afterwards. Now it is once again in the dumps. The problem with tech stuff is they constantly have to keep reinventing themselves and stay on top of markets. It ain't easy.

Utah Medical, in what seems to be an ongoing explanation, did well for us and kept on going. It then plopped but is now doing better than ever. They have the same CEO at the helm all these years later.

Zapata never gained a lot of traction. Today it exists, sitting with a lot of cash on the books while trying to figure out how to reinvent itself, as it no longer deals with either fish or autos, except perhaps for the top brass who drive to their favourite fishing holes.

Appendix V
Bibliography and Further Readings

If you only keep adding little by little, it will soon become a big heap.
—Hesiod

Charles H. Brandes, *Value Investing Today* (New York: McGraw-Hill, 1998)
This book has quite an extensive section on global investing, which most books hardly bother with. For someone looking for an overview of this area, this is one of the better books to examine.

R. A. Brealey, *An Introduction to Risk and Return from Common Stocks* (Cambridge, Mass.: M.I.T. Press, 1983)
A book that takes risk/reward parameters to another level. Certainly not the book a neophyte should commence with, but perhaps it's one for later reading.

Wesley D. Camp, *What a Piece of Work Is Man!* (Paramus, N.J., Prentice Hall Inc., 1990)
All kinds of quotations about all kinds of things.

Frank Cappiello, *Frank Cappiello's New Guide to Finding the Next Superstock* (Philadelphia: Liberty House, 1988)
I like Frank, having watched him off and on for over twenty years on *Wall $treet Week*. His book is decent, but a better effort was expected.

David Chilton, *The Wealthy Barber* (Toronto: Stoddart, 1989)
An entertaining book, which has almost a full page of investment advice! Okay, half a page. Still, it's worthwhile as an investment primer. Call it the *Celestine Prophecy* of investing.

David Dreman, *The New Contrarian Investment Strategy* (New York: Random House, 1982)

This guy has got one big following these days, which in itself can make him worth a read.

Phillip Fisher, *Conservative Investors Sleep Well* (New York: Harper & Row, 1989)
A solid book packed with lots of insights.

David Foot, *Boom, Bust and Echo* (Toronto: Macfarlane, Walter & Ross, 1996)
A refreshing look at trends and demographics. It's wonderful to see that such a thought-provoking book can stay on the best-seller list for such a long time.

Benj Gallander, *The Canadian Small Business Survival Guide* (Toronto: Hounslow Press, 1995)
Hey, I'm biased here. What would you expect? The book was first published in 1988, became a best-seller that is still out there, has sold in over a dozen countries, and has been used at colleges and universities. It's currently in its twelfth printing. That must say something.

Benj Gallander, *The Contrarian Investor's 13: How to Earn Superior Returns in the Stock Market* (Toronto: Penguin Group, 2002)
Take away the baseball of *The Uncommon Investor* and add somewhat more investing depth and you have this book that was published in both hardcover and paperback. I still have copies for sale if you want one or two. (gall@pathcom.com)

Benjamin Graham & David Dodd, *Security Analysis* (New York: McGraw-Hill Book Company, 1934)
This book is a behemoth and a veritable bible in content. At 700 pages plus, it is not a mere jaunt for a Sunday afternoon. I've gone through it twice in twenty years. The second time was far simpler, as an accountant had left yellow highlighted notes in the work. They were good ones. That copy is somewhere in the library system of the City of Toronto.

Douglas Hofstadter, *Godel, Escher, Bach: An Eternal Golden Braid* (New York, Basil Books, 1979)
Gee, I wish that this whole darned book was clear to me, but unfortunately

it wasn't. Good challenging reading, which is sometimes accessible and sometimes makes ya wish you were a mite more intelligent.

Charles MacKay, *Extraordinary Popular Delusions and the Madness of Crowds* (New York, Farrar, Straus & Giroux, 1841)
   It drones on a bit too long, but it's still a classic work that gives an excellent historical and psychological look at people turning into lemmings.

Burton G. Malkiel, *A Random Walk Down Wall Street* (New York, W. W. Norton & Company, 1996)
   On the cover of my edition, it reads, "The Best Investment Advice Money Can Buy." Don't buy it. Borrow it from the library. Expense the cost of the borrowing card. Worth a look, as it is a well-constructed work.

Reginald McKnight, *Wisdom of the African World* (New York, New World Library, 1990)
   This is chock full of good insights from Africa. It's difficult to find differences from North American philosophies, although the phrasing is often dissimilar.

Mohnish Pabrai, *The Dhando Investor*, (New Jersey, John Wiley & Sons, Inc., 2007)
   "Heads, I win; tails, I don't lose much." That is the essence of this work. It's an enjoyable read that focuses well on reducing risk. A tad redundant at times.

Mordecai Richler, *The Apprenticeship of Duddy Kravitz* (Toronto, McClelland & Stewart, 1959)
   A great read. Loved it in high school and should read it again. You too can become a mogul.

Peter Lynch, *One Up on Wall Street* (New York, Simon and Schuster, 1989)
   I read it nearly twenty years ago, when Lynch was the man of the day. Good book. It's not as analytical as I'd like to see, but it's an easy read.

Seymour Schulich, *Get Smarter Life and Business Lessons* (Toronto: Key Porter Books, 2007)

This is a simple book on the surface but with lots of interesting thoughts, lessons, and confirmations. It's worth a read.

Madelon DeVoe Talley, *The Passionate Investors* (New York: Crown Publishers, Inc., 1987)

This book is chock full of the philosophies of known and lesser greats of the investing world. Both the repetition and differentiated techniques of these people provide a good forum for study.

Henry David Thoreau, *Walden and Civil Disobedience* (Philadelphia: Running Press, 1987)

This is a classic read. It teaches about money and living and spirituality and....

Index

accounts payable, 131, 137
accounts receivable, 130, 137
acid test ratio, 136
after-tax returns, 174
"all or nothing" orders, 147
analyzing mistakes, 98-99
annual reports, 119, 122-123, 228
annualized returns, 185
arbitrage, 75
asset growth ratio, 139-140
averaging down, 47, 68, 162, 163
averaging up, 68

back-end loads, 56
balance sheets, 130-132
bandwagon effect, 23-24, 78
Beardstown Ladies, 98, 210
beta, 33
bids, 146-150
book value, 132-134
brokers, 90-93
business cycles, 102-103
buying on margin, 71
buying on weakness and strength, 68
buys, 44

capital gains, 175
cash flow, 133
chartists, 85
churning, 92
compound interest, 29-31, 42
Contra the Heard
    Contra commentaries, 203-234
    Contra philosophies, 201

contrarian, 21-23, 24-28
corporate stock buybacks, 110
corporations as information sources, 119, 124
currency translation, 188-189
current equity, 71
current ratio, 135
cycles, 99-105

debit balance, 71
debt growth ratio, 140
debt to equity ratio, 136
derivatives, 58
discount brokers, 88-89, 91
diversification, 36-37
dividends, 53, 95-96, 175-176
dollar cost averaging, 69-70
due diligence, 125

earnings per share, 110
efficient market theory, 65-66
emotional health, 79
excess margin, 71

fallen angels, 114
financial goals, 30, 31
financial statements, 127-140
front-end loads, 56
full-service brokers, 90-92
fundamental analysis, 84-85

goodwill, 133-134
Greater Fool Method, 68
gross profit to sales ratio, 138

growth ratios, 139

head and shoulders formation, 85
holds, 44-47

inflation, 40, 176, 203-204
income
    splitting, 177
    statements, 127-129
insider information, 66
insider trading, 125-126
interest
    compound, 29-30
    rates, 30, 38, 40
Internet, 122-124, 204-206
inventory, 128-130, 136-137
investing
    bottom-up, 87
    during December, 100-101, 174
    early, 40
    ethical, 194-196
    growth, 87
    methods, 22
    sectoral, 87
    top-down, 87
investment
    alternative, 37, 88
    bases, 31
    clubs, 114
    future worth of, 176
    goals, 33-36
    present worth of, 176
    quadrangle, 32
    theories, 65-67
    trusts, 54, 221
IRAs, 176

laziness, 83-84
leverage, 71, 136
liquidity ratios, 135

management
    talking to, 124-125
margin accounts, 72
market
    price, 161
    timing, 85-86
    tops, 70, 76
    turns, 118
Modified Dietz Method, 188-189
momentum theory, 85
mortgaging to invest, 39
mutual funds
    advantages of, 54-55
    defined, 51
    disadvantages of, 56-59
    types of,
        balanced funds, 53
        bond funds, 52-53
        dividend funds, 53
        equity funds, 53
        ethical funds, 53
        fixed-income funds, 52
        investment trusts, 54
        money market funds, 52-53
        mortgage funds, 52-53
        no-load funds, 56-57
        venture capital funds, 54

net profit to sales ratio, 138
newspapers, 122, 171

offer price, 146
order quantities, 149-150
order ratios, 149

partial fills, 147
paying down debt, 38
portfolio dressing, 58
price/earnings ratio, 116
pro forma statements, 132
product life cycle, 103-105

profit growth ratio, 139
profitability ratios, 138

qualitative analysis, 126
quantitative analysis, 126, 211

random walk theory, 67
ratio analysis, 132-140
reading stock tables, 114-119
research, 63, 69, 84, 99, 125, 158, 227
research and development spending, 63
resistance levels, 85-86
returns
    calculating, 184-186
    on investment, 138-139
reverse splits, 49, 143
risk tolerance, 31
risk/reward ratio, 32-33
RRSPs, 176-177
"Rule of 72", 30

sales growth ratio, 139
sell signals, 166
sell targets, 76-77, 82, 121, 164-166
sells, 44
shareholders' meeting, 166
Sharpe ratio, 209, 211
short selling, 70
stock
    alternatives to, 39
    buying, 146-150
    consolidations, 49 *see also* reverse splits
    holding, 156-163
    market
        investment methods, 84-88
        theories, 65-72
    ownership by management, 83
    penny, 108
    reviewing, 157
    selling, 164-168

Stock Watch List, 121-125
stop losses, 161-163

takeovers, 75, 162-163
tax
    avoiding, 111
    deferral, 174
    loss selling, 177
    planning, 174-178
technical analysis, 84-85
three-day settlement rule, 174
tickeritis, 92
trading volume, 86

Value Line, 84, 122-123

websites, 119, 123
working capital, 135

zero serial correlation, 67

Do you know someone who could use a copy of this book? Or a sample or subscription to the investment letter? It could make a worthwhile gift for a family member or friend.

Name:_____
Address:_____
City:_____ Province:_____
Postal Code:_____
Telephone #:_____
Email:_____

Send me or the person(s) whose name is enclosed _____ autographed copies of *The Uncommon Investor III* at $25 (CDN and U.S.) each. Prices include tax, postage, and handling charges.

I have enclosed a cheque payable to Benj Gallander for _____, or

Send me or the person(s) whose name is enclosed Contra the Heard:
        a sample _____ (check here)
        an annual subscription_____ (check here)

I have enclosed a cheque payable to Gal-Stad Investments for _____.

A sample copy is $50 (CDN and U.S.). An annual subscription is $500 (CDN and U.S.) plus tax. For each annual subscription ordered, a free copy of the book will also be included.

My address is:
Contra the Heard
34 Stonegate Rd.
Toronto, ON
M8Y 1V5
Telephone: (416) 410-4431

Please allow four weeks for delivery.
If there are questions or comments, please e-mail me at gall@pathcom.com.